TIME

FOR KIDS

ALMANAC

2010

Calmar Elementary School

TIME FOR KIDS

ALMANAC 2010

PRODUCED BY

DOWNTOWN BOOKWORKS INC.

PRESIDENT: Julie Merberg
EDITOR AND PHOTO RESEARCHER: Sarah Parvis
ASSISTANT PHOTO RESEARCHER: LeeAnn Pemberton
SENIOR CONTRIBUTORS: Kerry Acker, Marge Kennedy, Jeanette Leardi, Mickey Steiner
SPECIAL THANKS: Patty Brown, Pam Abrams, Steve Levine, Brian Michael Thomas, Morris Katz, Nathanael Katz

DESIGNED BY
Georgia Rucker Design

TIME FOR KIDS
MANAGING EDITOR, TIME FOR KIDS MAGAZINE: Martha Pickerill
EDITOR-IN-CHIEF, TIME LEARNING VENTURES: Jonathan Rosenbloom
SENIOR EDITOR, TIME LEARNING VENTURES: Lorin Driggs

Time Inc. HOME ENTERTAINMENT

PUBLISHER: Richard Fraiman
GENERAL MANAGER: Steven Sandonato
EXECUTIVE DIRECTOR, MARKETING SERVICES: Carol Pittard
DIRECTOR, RETAIL & SPECIAL SALES: Tom Mifsud
DIRECTOR, NEW PRODUCT DEVELOPMENT: Peter Harper
DIRECTOR, TRADE MARKETING: Sydney Webber
ASSISTANT DIRECTOR, BOOKAZINE MARKETING: Laura Adam
ASSISTANT DIRECTOR, BRAND MARKETING: Joy Butts
ASSOCIATE COUNSEL: Helen Wan
DESIGN & PREPRESS MANAGER: Anne-Michelle Gallero
BOOK PRODUCTION MANAGER: Susan Chodakiewicz
BRAND MANAGER: Shelley Rescober

SPECIAL THANKS
Alexandra Bliss, Glenn Buonocore, Lauren Hall, Margaret Hess, Jennifer Jacobs, Suzanne Janso, Brynn Joyce, Robert Marasco, Amy Migliaccio, Brooke Reger, Ilene Schreider, Adriana Tierno, Alex Voznesenskiy, Jonathan White

Special thanks to imaging: Patrick Dugan, Neal Clayton, Joseph Agnoli

PUBLISHED BY TIME FOR KIDS BOOKS
Time Inc.
1271 Avenue of the Americas
New York, New York 10020

ISSN: 1534-5718
ISBN 13: 978-1-60320-808-6
ISBN 10: 1-60320-808-9

TIME For Kids is a trademark of Time Inc.

For more information on TIME For Kids magazine for the classroom or home, go to www.TFKCLASSROOM.com or call 1-800-777-8600.

We welcome your comments and suggestions about TIME For Kids Books. Please write to us at:

TIME FOR KIDS BOOKS
ATTENTION: BOOK EDITORS
PO BOX 11016
DES MOINES, IA 50336-1016

If you would like to order any of our hardcover Collector's Edition books, please call us at 1-800-327-6388.
(Monday through Friday, 7:00 a.m.–8:00 p.m. or Saturday, 7:00 a.m.–6:00 p.m. Central Time).

Contents

Contents

Contents

Year in Review
AROUND THE WORLD

ISRAEL-PALESTINE CONFLICT

The Gaza Strip is a disputed region along the Mediterranean Sea between Israel and Egypt with a population of 1.5 million people. In the last days of 2008, Israel and Hamas–the controversial Palestinian group that controls the Gaza Strip–ended a six-month truce, or period of peace. The two groups resumed their deadly attacks on each other. After Hamas launched rockets across the border into Israel, Israel responded, bombarding Gaza with massive airstrikes, intensifying the long-term conflict between the Israelis and Palestinians.

The Taj Mahal hotel is attacked.

SOMALI PIRATES

Gar! Pirates became big news in 2008 and 2009, though not as characters in a movie or a musical. In the waters off East Africa, groups of young men from Somalia attacked oil tankers and freighters. They took over the boats and forced companies and people to pay large sums of money to get them back. The situation got so dangerous that some shipping firms changed their routes. Some ships now take a much longer and more expensive route around Africa rather than risk a pirate attack.

Several Somali pirates are arrested.

MUMBAI, INDIA, IS ATTACKED

The morning of November 26, 2008, began like any other for the residents of the Indian city Mumbai and for the many businesspeople and tourists visiting the dynamic city. But that changed when 10 armed men simultaneously terrorized several sites across the city.

The first round of attacks began at the Victoria Terminus train station, when gunmen began firing weapons. They continued onto the streets, shooting spectators and journalists gathered outside a nearby movie theater. Meanwhile, other groups of armed men targeted other Mumbai landmarks, including the Oberoi and Taj Mahal luxury hotels and the Leopold Café, which are all popular with Western tourists. Still another terrorist assaulted a Jewish community center. The attack lasted for three days and resulted in the deaths of nearly 200 people. Evidence has since been uncovered linking several of the attackers to the Pakistan-based terrorist group Lashkar-e-Tayyiba, heightening the tensions between the two neighboring countries.

RUSSIA-GEORGIA WAR

In August 2008, just as the Olympic Games in China were getting under way, war erupted between the country of Georgia and the region of South Ossetia, which are both located to the east of Turkey and just below Russia in the South Caucasus. Officially, South Ossetia is part of Georgia, but it considers itself a separate nation. Georgia, an ally of the Untied States, began shelling the capital of South Ossetia, which is supported by Russia, in an effort to regain control of the breakaway region. Russia responded aggressively to the attack on its ally by launching airstrikes and sending troops to occupy the Georgian cities of Tbilisi and Gori.

Although French president Nicolas Sarkozy brokered a peace agreement, Georgia and Russia severed all diplomatic ties, and Russia recognized the independence of South Ossetia, resulting in strained relations between Russia and some Western countries.

Olympic fans

CASTRO RESIGNS

In February 2008, after leading Cuba as president for nearly 50 years, an ill 81-year-old Fidel Castro announced his resignation in a letter posted in an online newspaper. Castro, who seized power in 1959, ran Cuba as a Communist country, promising his people that there would no longer be rich Cubans and poor Cubans. Under Castro, there were no more free elections, and people who disagreed with Castro were put into prison. Because of Cuba's Communist ideals and its alliance with the Soviet Union, the United States stopped trading with the small Latin American nation. Tensions between the two countries ran so high, the world even came close to nuclear war in 1962.

Raul Castro, Fidel's brother, is now the head of Cuba, and the world is watching to see how Barack Obama's administration will handle relations with America's once bitter enemy.

Raul Castro

WHAT'S UP IN CHINA?

- In May 2008, tens of thousands of people (some reports estimate as many as 90,000 people) died when a 7.9 magnitude earthquake struck the Sichuan province of western China. A month later, southern China experienced the worst flooding in half a century.
- In September 2008, the Chinese found out that a popular brand of baby formula made in their country contained the dangerous chemical melamine. The tainted formula killed six children and made nearly 300,000 babies sick.
- In August 2008, China had something positive to celebrate: the Olympics. Beijing hosted more than 10,000 athletes in the XXIX Summer Olympic Games. The Olympics began at 8:08 p.m. on the 8th day of the 8th month of 2008. China poured huge amounts of money ($40 billion) into the sports and events, seeing them as an opportunity to show the world how prosperous and modern the country had become. China's time in the spotlight also made it the focus of criticism—for its pollution, its oppression of the people of Tibet and its history of human rights abuses.

A HISTORIC ELECTION

The 2008 presidential election will go down in history, as Barack Obama became the first African American to be elected President of the United States. The 47-year-old candidate made effective use of the Internet to build a large base of supporters.

Obama fought a hard race in the primaries, and his toughest opponent was New York senator Hillary Clinton. Both candidates talked of the importance of education and health care, and both were good debaters. In the end, Obama was chosen as the Democratic presidential nominee. He and vice presidential candidate Joe Biden of Delaware ran against the Republican ticket of Arizona senator John McCain and Alaska governor Sarah Palin.

On November 4, 2008, Barack Obama won the election. He received 53% of the popular vote and 365 of a possible 538 electoral votes.

PRESIDENT OBAMA'S FIRST DAYS IN OFFICE

On Tuesday, January 20, 2009, more than a million people gathered at the National Mall in Washington, D.C., to see Barack Obama's inauguration as the 44th President of the United States. The event was watched by millions more, both across the country and around the world, on TV and over the Internet.

The next day President Obama got right to work. Some of the biggest issues facing the new President included the economic crisis, the war in Iraq and the worsening problems in the Middle East.

Two days after the inauguration, President Obama issued two executive orders. One would close the controversial detention camp at Guantanamo Bay within a year. The other was a ban on the torturing of detainees at the camp. Moving to health care, he signed a new bill in February to expand the State Children's Health Insurance Program (SCHIP). In 2008, SCHIP helped more than 7 million kids. The new bill aims to cover an additional 4 million. During his first days in office, the President also made important additions to his cabinet, including former rival Hillary Clinton, who was appointed secretary of state.

guess what? *Can you believe that Barack Obama will be the first U.S. President to use e-mail while in office? It's true. While campaigning, Obama used his BlackBerry to stay in touch with friends and supporters, but when he was elected, the Secret Service worried that this would be dangerous. What if the President's e-mail was hacked? They came to a solution by agreeing on certain restrictions and getting him an extra-secure BlackBerry. To stay up to date with all things presidential, go online and visit whitehouse.gov.*

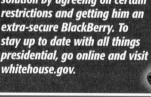

ECONOMIC CRISIS

By 2009, the U.S. economy was suffering greatly. Unemployment was on the rise, and the country was officially in a recession. Understanding what happened is difficult, but one of the main problems involved housing loans. Homes are expensive, and when people want to buy one, they generally take out a mortgage, or home loan, from a bank. The bank lends the home buyer money to purchase the house, and the buyer then pays back the amount over a long period of time. The bank charges interest, which means that it makes money on the loan transaction.

In the recent past, however, bank lenders began offering mortgages to people who weren't able to make their payments. The banks that held these subprime mortgages then sold them to investment banks. The investment banks then traded them with other banks and funds. The investment banks didn't actually have the money to cover the cost of the loans, they had only the promise that a home buyer would repay the loan some day. Because so many people couldn't repay their loans, the banks found themselves in big trouble.

As a result of the financial crisis, many people lost their homes, people slowed their spending, houses became less valuable, banks stopped lending money, businesses suffered and laid off employees, and investment banks fell apart. Because so many individuals, banks and funds were involved, the entire economy suffered. If you find this information difficult to understand, you are not alone. Even the smartest economists and businesspeople have a hard time making sense of it all.

In early February, President Obama signed a massive economic recovery stimulus package, including more than $780 billion to help kick-start the economy.

HOW MUCH?

The price of gasoline went sky high in 2008 and introduced a new word into people's everyday vocabulary: *staycation*. Travelers opted to spend time at home on staycations instead of driving or flying long distances for their vacations.

MIRACLE ON THE HUDSON

U.S. Air Force veteran Chesley "Sully" Sullenberger became famous overnight in January 2009 after performing an emergency landing right on the surface of the Hudson River in New York City. Shortly after his U.S. Airways jet took off, a flock of geese flew into both engines, disabling them. Knowing he didn't have enough power to make it to a nearby airport, Sully safely brought the plane down on the ice-cold waters of the Hudson—avoiding boats and bridges on the way—and saved the lives of all 155 passengers on board.

PEANUT BUTTER SCARE!

In January 2009, American health officials linked a countrywide outbreak of salmonella, a bacterial infection that made almost 500 people very ill, to several products containing peanut butter. The government demanded that more than 100 items containing peanut butter—including crackers, cookies, ice cream and energy bars—be removed from store shelves and school cafeterias. The source of the poisoned peanut butter was found to be a peanut plant in Georgia.

Year in Review
SCIENCE AND TECHNOLOGY

A GIANT LEAP FOR CHINA

In September 2008, Chinese astronaut Zhai Zhigang maneuvered out of the *Shenzhou VII* space capsule to wave his nation's flag. His 18-minute jaunt outside the spacecraft officially made China the third country, after the United States and Russia, to successfully execute a space walk.

TOP THIS SCIENCE PROJECT!

The Large Hadron Collider (LHC), publicized as the biggest science experiment of all time, was certainly the most expensive, costing about $9 billion. The LHC, the most powerful particle collider ever, was built near Geneva, Switzerland, by a group of more than 10,000 scientists and support staff from 111 nations. Activated for the first time in September 2008, the LHC will be used to help physicists understand complex issues such as dark matter and other mysteries of the universe. Mechanical problems caused the LHC to shut down until around the summer of 2009.

guess what? *Many people actually feared that the Large Hadron Collider would be so strong that it would create a black hole and swallow the universe. The good news is it didn't.*

MORE GLOBAL WARMING NEWS

- Scientists in Antarctica examined ancient pockets of air trapped in the ice and determined that our atmosphere has 28% more carbon dioxide now than at any other time in the past 800,000 years.
- NASA recorded that the Arctic Ocean experienced its second-lowest ice coverage since scientists started keeping track.
- The U.S. secretary of the interior officially declared the polar bear a threatened species and therefore protected by the Endangered Species Act. Because so much ice has melted, many polar bears have lost their habitat. There were about 20,000 wild polar bears left in 2008.

ENSURING PLANT DIVERSITY

The Svalbard Global Seed Vault, an enormous chamber buried deep in a mountain between the North Pole and Norway, opened in February 2008. The vault, which was designed to store and protect up to 4.5 million varieties of plants from around the globe, was built in permafrost to withstand such events as war, earthquakes and climate change.

RENEWABLE ENERGY

Scientists researching ways to harness the power of the sun have made some significant breakthroughs. For example, researchers at the U.S. National Renewable Energy Laboratory have come up with a device that converts 40.8% of the light it's exposed to into electricity—that's twice as much as average solar cells can achieve today.

Another important milestone for solar energy: Nanosolar has found a way to make solar power more affordable. The new California-based company manufactures thin-film solar panels, which are lighter and much cheaper than the hefty panels used before.

APPS-O-LUTELY!

One of coolest things about the iPhone—classic, 3G or even iPod Touch—is the App Store. (*App* is short for *application*, another name for a computer program.) With the store, you can download a wide variety of applications made specifically for the iPhone, including games, radio stations, voice recorders, maps and services that provide local restaurant reviews. Users can even create and share their own apps! Here are some of the most popular ones from 2008.

- **TAP TAP REVENGE** A lot like *Guitar Hero* or *Rock Band*, this popular app allows you to play a game by tapping along to the music on your iPhone's touch screen.

- **ROLANDO** The iPhone's version of the super-popular Mario series, Rolando uses both the touch screen and motion sensor for game play.

- **SHAZAM** Ever hear a song and wonder who sings it or what it's called? Put your iPhone up to the speaker, and this free app tells you what song is playing!

- **LABYRINTH** Based on the classic maze game, use the iPhone's motion sensors to tilt the surface of a virtual labyrinth to strategically guide a ball through the maze without letting it fall in the holes.

- **DOODLE KIDS** Make all sorts of cool digital paintings on your iPhone with this innovative app, created by 9-year-old programmer Lim Ding Wen.

SOCIAL-NETWORKING SITES

Even though such sites as Facebook, MySpace, Twitter and YouTube have been around for a while, in the past year or so they have transformed the way we get our news, transmit and receive information, and relate to one another. On-location Twitterers became vital sources of news during events like the Mumbai terror attacks, wars and hurricanes. Social-networking sites also played a significant role in Barack Obama's bid for the presidency.

THREE CHEERS FOR 3G

In July 2008, Apple released an update to the already incredibly popular iPhone, called the iPhone 3G. While it looks basically the same as the original, the new version uses 3G network technology for better quality phone calls, faster transfer of data and more. Like the classic iPhone, the 3G also features a touch screen, has GPS capability, stores MP3s and has motion sensing technology built in. And you can make phone calls with it too!

MARTIAN REFRESHMENTS

Over the summer, NASA's Phoenix Mars Lander spacecraft took soil samples from the surface of Mars that turned out to contain H_2O—good old water, just like on Earth. While the Mars Odyssey Orbiter had already found evidence of water in the form of ice, the Phoenix event was the first time a NASA probe had actually "touched and tasted" water in a sample. This was exciting for the scientists because water—particularly if it gets warm enough to thaw from ice into liquid—is one indicator of the possibility of life on the Red Planet.

Year in Review

TEEN SENSATIONS

- Miley Cyrus, the 16-year-old singer and star of the immensely popular *Hannah Montana,* became even more famous in 2008 and 2009. Her song "See You Again" climbed the pop charts early in 2008, and in the summer she released her second album, *Breakout.* This was followed by the highly successful Hannah Montana/Miley Cyrus: Best of Both Worlds Tour, which was filmed and made into a 3-D movie. Then *Hannah Montana: The Movie* came out in 2009.

- Joe, Nick and Kevin Jonas—otherwise known as the Jonas Brothers—also had an amazing 2008 and 2009. They toured with Miley Cyrus, won an American Music Award for Breakthrough Artist and were nominated for a Best New Artist Grammy. Their much anticipated movie, *Jonas Brothers: The 3D Concert Experience*, came out in February 2009.

Twilight

THE *TWILIGHT* PHENOMENON

Stephenie Meyer's best-selling series of vampire books became a teen literary sensation, and fans turned out in droves when the movie, starring Robert Pattinson and Kristen Stewart, opened in November 2008. The second film, *New Moon*, is scheduled to be released in the fall of 2009.

SUPERSTARS OF THE BEIJING SUMMER OLYMPICS

- U.S. swimmer Michael Phelps captivated audiences around the world when he won an astonishing eight gold medals in eight individual and team events, breaking American swimmer Mark Spitz's record of seven gold medals.

- Twenty-one-year-old Jamaican sprinter Usain Bolt took home three gold medals and shattered three world records in relay events, electrifying audiences with his dazzling and joyous performance on the track.

Miley Cyrus and the Jonas Brothers

BILL GATES'S NEW JOB

On June 27, Bill Gates, who founded Microsoft—the world's largest computer software company—retired from the computer business. The richest man in the world, Gates has decided to spend his time on the Bill & Melinda Gates Foundation, a charity organization that is working to help people in developing countries and to find vaccines for diseases such as malaria.

Bill and Melinda Gates

THE FIRST FAMILY

The 2008 election put more than just Barack Obama into the White House! The President brings with him his wife, Michelle, and two daughters, 10-year-old Malia and 7-year-old Sasha. Many Americans are excited to have young children back in the White House. And the Obama girls are super-excited about the dog their parents promised them during the campaign!

SPORTS HIGHLIGHTS

Pittsburg's Santonio Holmes

- In October 2008, the Philadelphia Phillies won the World Series for the second time ever, beating the Tampa Bay Rays in five games.

- In January 2009, the Pittsburgh Steelers bested the Arizona Cardinals to win Super Bowl XLIII with a score of 27–23. It was a close game that marked the Steelers' sixth Super Bowl win—the record for Super Bowl wins.

- In June 2008, Tiger Woods played through chronic knee pain to win his third U.S Open. Soon after, he announced that he needed surgery and would miss the rest of the PGA season.

GOODBYES

The years 2008 and 2009 saw the loss of several talented and accomplished people. Some of the creative folks mourned by the world include the musicians Bo Diddley and Isaac Hayes (also known as the voice of Chef on *South Park*); the mountain climber Sir Edmund Hillary (who, along with Tenzing Norgay, was the first to reach the summit of Mount Everest, in 1953); comedians George Carlin and Bernie Mac; dancer Cyd Charisse; actors Charlton Heston and Paul Newman (also known for his philanthropic work and his food business, Newman's Own); fashion designer Yves Saint-Laurent; director Sydney Pollack; and writers John Updike, David Foster Wallace, Arthur Clarke and Aleksandr Solzhenitsyn.

Heath Ledger in *The Dark Knight*

Heath Ledger

On January 22, 2008, 28-year-old Australian-born heartthrob Heath Ledger died of an accidental overdose of prescription drugs. His portrayal of the comic book villain the Joker in 2008's *The Dark Knight* won raves from audiences and critics alike, and even won best supporting actor honors at the Golden Globes and the Academy Awards.

SPEED DEMON

When Danica Patrick placed fourth at the Indianapolis 500 in 2005, she became the top-finishing woman ever at the event and was named rookie of the year. Probably because of her youth, her good looks and the rarity of female race car drivers, she quickly became popular with fans. In April of 2008, at the IndyCar 300 competition, Patrick proved that she was more than just a media sensation, steering her Dallara-Honda vehicle to victory, finishing 5.86 seconds ahead of Brazilian Helio Castroneves. Her achievement in this race made Patrick the first woman to ever to win an IndyCar championship event.

Danica Patrick

Animals

FROM TFK MAGAZINE

Good News for Gorillas

SCIENTISTS DISCOVER 125,000 ENDANGERED GORILLAS IN CENTRAL AFRICA

By Vickie An

In August 2008, researchers announced a remarkable find that has wildlife enthusiasts going absolutely ape. A recent census, conducted by the Wildlife Conservation Society (WCS), reported the discovery of 125,000 **western lowland gorillas** living deep in the forests and swamps of the Republic of the Congo, in Africa. If confirmed, the tally would more than double the current estimated population of the critically endangered primate.

A NEW HOPE

The WCS, based at the Bronx Zoo in New York City, worked with the government of the Republic of the Congo to carry out the survey. The project covered 18,000 square miles (46,620 sq km) in two areas of the northern part of the country. In the 1980s, estimates placed the western lowland gorilla's numbers at fewer than 100,000. Since then, scientists believe that the spread of disease and illegal hunting of the animal for food has likely cut the population in half. The new census figures raise the total estimated population of western lowland gorillas surviving in the wild to between 175,000 and 225,000.

OUT FOR THE COUNT

The gorillas are very shy and cautious of people. That makes it harder to count them one by one. To tally the number of gorillas in the region, researchers counted the animals' sleeping "nests." Each night, the gorillas build short-term beds. The nests are put together with leaves and branches.

Western lowland gorillas are found in the tropical forests and swamps of seven central African nations. In addition to the Republic of the Congo, the gorillas also live in Congo, Cameroon, Angola, the Central African Republic, Equatorial Guinea and Gabon. The western lowland gorillas are one of four gorilla subspecies. The others include mountain gorillas, eastern lowland gorillas and Cross River gorillas. The International Union for Conservation of Nature (IUCN) has listed all of them as endangered or critically endangered.

While the new census is important, scientists have made it clear that the gorilla populations in the wild are far from being safe. "The gorillas are still under threat from Ebola and hunting," said Emma Stokes, a lead researcher with WCS. Ebola, a deadly disease, "can wipe out thousands in a short period of time."

A PLEA FOR PRIMATES

The WCS released these census results at a conference on primates in Scotland. The scientists at the conference warned that nearly half of the 634 types of primates in the world—from the mighty mountain gorillas to the tiny mouse lemurs—are in danger of becoming extinct as a result of the actions of humans.

ANIMAL KINGDOM

To keep track of the diverse types of animals found all over the world, scientists classify them according to the following subdivisions:

PHYLUM
CLASS
ORDER
FAMILY
GENUS
SPECIES

Each subdivision is smaller than the one preceding it. In this way, scientists are able to assign a name to every creature on the planet, based on its characteristics. This categorization is called **taxonomy**. Here is the taxonomy for two very different animals: the American bullfrog and the horse.

guess what? Some people use a mnemonic device, or memory aid, to keep track of the order of taxonomy. A mnemonic is often a silly phrase. To help remember the order of the sub-divisions in taxonomy, just think:

King
Phillip
Came
Over
For
Good
Spaghetti.

AMERICAN BULLFROG

KINGDOM **Animalia:** All animals share this kingdom.

PHYLUM **Chordata:** These animals have backbones.

CLASS **Amphibia:** Amphibians live on both land and water. *Examples:* frogs, toads, salamanders

ORDER **Anura:** This order includes amphibians that don't have tails–frogs and toads.

FAMILY **Ranidae:** These are "true frogs." They usually have smooth, moist skin and webbed feet. Most live close to water.

GENUS **Rana:** These true frogs are usually large. They often have wrinkly skin, thin ridges on their backs and long, slim legs. *Examples:* northern leopard frog, Columbia spotted frog, carpenter frog, European frog

SPECIES **Catesbeiana:** This species distinguishes the bullfrog from other common frogs. Bullfrogs are the largest frogs in North America.

HORSE

KINGDOM **Animalia:** All animals share this kingdom.

PHYLUM **Chordata**: These animals have backbones.

CLASS **Mammalia**: Female mammals breast-feed their young. Almost all mammals give birth to live young.

ORDER **Perissodactyla:** These mammals have an odd number of toes. *Examples:* tapirs, rhinoceroses

FAMILY **Equidae:** These perissodactyls have long legs that help them run fast and a single stomach that allows them to digest food quickly. *Examples:* zebras, donkeys

GENUS **Equus:** This is the only genus in the Equidae family to have survived to modern times.

SPECIES **Caballus:** This species distinguishes the horse from zebras (*Equus burchellii*) and donkeys (*Equus asinus*).

17

TOP 5 Pets

Fish are by far the most popular pets in the United States. Americans own more fish than any other animal. Here are the most plentiful pets.

1.	FISH	149 million owned
2.	CATS	91 million
3.	DOGS	74 million
4.	SMALL ANIMALS*	18 million
5.	BIRDS	17 million

*rabbits, hamsters, guinea pigs, etc.

TOP 10 Dog Breeds

BREED	RANK IN 2008	RANK IN 1998
Labrador retriever	1	1
Yorkshire terrier	2	9
German shepherd	3	3
Golden retriever	4	2
Beagle	5	6
Boxer	6	12
Dachshund	7	5
Bulldog	8	23
Poodle	9	7
Shih Tzu	10	11

Source: American Kennel Club

TOP 10 Cat Breeds

1. Persian
2. Maine coon
3. Exotic
4. Abyssinian
5. Siamese
6. Ragdoll
7. Sphynx
8. Birman
9. American shorthair
10. Oriental

guess what? *Cats have more than 100 vocal sounds, and dogs have only about 10.*

Source: Cat Fancier's Association

FIVE FANTASTIC PET FISH

guess what? Being kept in a tiny bowl can keep goldfish from growing.

Goldfish There are more than 100 kinds of goldfish. Goldfish are omnivorous, which means these common household pets eat both plants and animals.

BETTA FISH

Betta fish These gorgeous freshwater fish are also called Japanese or Siamese fighting fish because the males of this species will fight to the death if placed together in a tank. Bettas can be found in many colors, including red, blue, green and even white.

Most **mollies** are black, green, silver or gold. This popular type of fish can have short or long fins. They need some plant matter in their tank to remain healthy and happy.

Tetras are tiny fish from South America that make a pleasant addition to many fish tanks, as they live peacefully with other fish. Bigger fish will sometimes eat them, though. One popular variety of tetra has a bright, neon tail.

TETRAS

Catfish are bottom-feeders. They will park themselves at the bottom of a tank and gobble up the food that the other fish missed. Many types of catfish are nocturnal and like to hide in the sand, plants, toys or rock caves available to them.

CATFISH

If you're lucky enough to be the owner of a dog, follow these tips to help keep your pooch happy and healthy.

PLAYTIME

Dogs love exercise. It keeps them stimulated and in shape, it makes their brains sharper, and it even makes them behave better! So walk your dog around the block, play fetch or tug-of-war, or just run around your backyard together. Anything that gets it moving is good—and good for you!

NUTRITION

Like humans, dogs need to follow a well-balanced diet—with the right amount of proteins, vitamins, carbohydrates and fats—to stay healthy. (For more on nutrition, see page 92.) Top-quality dry food, which can be mixed with water or canned food, is best for dogs that are more than one year old, providing them with the protein they need for strong bones and muscles. Also, dogs like routines, so feed Fido at the same time every day. (Most dogs over one year old need just one or two meals a day.)

🐾 *Try not to share your "people food" with your pet. Not only will it upset your dog's balanced diet (canines' nutritional needs are different from humans'), but it might also give your pup behavioral problems. If you insist on giving people treats to your pooch, offer it small pieces of apple, carrot or broccoli.*

KEEP YOUR CANINE SAFE

Although you think your home is safe, it might be full of potentially dangerous pitfalls for your pet.

1 Keep electrical cords, kids' toys, books and any other chewable objects out of your pup's reach.

2 Make sure your kitchen garbage bin has a tight-fitting lid so your dog can't get its paws inside; that will help prevent a mess and protect your beloved pet from eating rotten food and becoming ill.

3 Pooches are good at breaking open bottles and boxes—put away all cleaning products so your pet won't get sick from them.

🐾 *Chocolate is pet poison! It contains theobromine, which can make your dog very ill. So keep those candy bars and chocolate chip cookies far away from little Max or Bailey.*

Guess what? Dogs have a sense of smell that is hundreds or thousands of times stronger than a human's.

Service Dogs

In addition to being sweet and reliable pets, dogs are also extremely helpful to law enforcement and to people with disabilities. K-9 dogs (usually German shepherds) work with police officers and are trained to sniff out illegal drugs or bombs and other explosives. Other dogs, such as bloodhounds, help track lost or missing persons by finding their scents based on an item of clothing or other belonging. Saint Bernard dogs are famous for their mountain rescue skills, and Labrador retrievers, as well as other breeds, are used as guides for blind people. Dogs also help the deaf by alerting them when a phone, bell or alarm rings. Some dogs can even sense if their epileptic owner is about to have a seizure. These animals can warn their owners, who can then take the necessary precautions.

Animals

SALAMANDER

VERTEBRATES AND

FLAMINGO

There are two basic kinds of animals: vertebrates, which have a backbone, and invertebrates, which don't.

MOOSE

Fish are cold-blooded, live in water and breathe using gills. Their skin is scaly and, with the exception of sharks (which give birth to live young), they lay eggs. Carp, clownfish, swordfish, tuna and eels are other examples of fish.

VERTEBRATES

Birds are warm-blooded and have wings and feathers. All birds lay eggs and most can fly (ostriches and penguins cannot). Other examples of birds are eagles, ducks, parrots, seagulls, storks and flamingos.

Amphibians are cold-blooded and begin life in the water, breathing through gills. When they are full grown, they breathe through lungs and can walk on land. They lay eggs. Some examples of amphibians are frogs, toads, newts and salamanders.

Mammals are warm-blooded and, with the exception of the platypus and the echidna, give birth to live young. Mammal mothers breast-feed their young. Most mammals have hair or fur and live on land (except for porpoises, dolphins and whales, which live in the water). Moose, bats, tigers, raccoons, bears, otters, gorillas and humans are all mammals.

Reptiles are cold-blooded and have lungs. Their skin is scaly. Most reptiles lay eggs. Reptiles include lizards, turtles, snakes, alligators and crocodiles.

TURTLE

Warm-Blooded or Cold-Blooded?

The temperature of an animal's body depends on whether that animal is warm-blooded or cold-blooded.

WARM-BLOODED ANIMALS (birds, mammals) are able to keep their body temperature constant. In cold weather, they turn the food they eat into energy that creates heat. In hot weather, they sweat, pant or do other things to help cool their outsides and insides. Most of the food warm-blooded animals take in is devoted to maintaining their body temperature.

The temperature of COLD-BLOODED ANIMALS (reptiles, fish, amphibians, invertebrates) is the same as that of their surroundings. Because of this, they are able to be very active in hot weather but are sluggish at low temperatures. When it is hot, chemicals in their bodies react quickly to help their muscles move, but these reactions slow down as the outside temperature drops. Most of the food cold-blooded animals take in is devoted to building their body mass.

WARM-BLOODED

COLD-BLOODED

INVERTEBRATES

SPONGE

SQUID

Sponges live in water and are immobile. They get their food by filtering tiny organisms that swim by.

Coelenterates use their mouths not only to eat with but also to eliminate waste. There are stinging tentacles around their mouths. Examples of coelenterates are corals, hydras, jellyfish and sea anemones.

Echinoderms live in the sea and have exoskeletons, which means that their skeleton or supporting structure is located on the outside of their bodies. Some echinoderms are sea urchins, brittle stars, starfish and sand dollars.

Worms live in a variety of places, including underwater, in the ground and even inside other living creatures. Examples of worms include tapeworms, flukes, pinworms, leeches, night crawlers and earthworms.

INVERTEBRATES

Mollusks have soft bodies. To protect themselves, some have hard shells. Clams, oysters, mussels, octopuses, scallops, squid and snails are all mollusks.

Arthropods have bodies that are divided into different parts or segments. They also have exoskeletons. Arthropods include crustaceans (such as lobsters, crabs, shrimp and barnacles); arachnids (spiders, scorpions and ticks); centipedes, millipedes and all insects (such as butterflies, ants, bees, dragonflies and beetles).

BEETLE

Endangered Animals

In 1973, the Endangered Species Act was passed by the U.S. Congress to protect various plants and animals from vanishing. The U.S. Fish and Wildlife Service keeps track of the populations of all known species in the United States, adding or removing their names from the list as their survival numbers change. Here are some endangered species on the list.

- **woodland caribou**
- **jaguar**
- **black-footed ferret**
- **bighorn sheep**
- **humpback whale**
- **red wolf**
- **grizzly bear**
- **whooping crane**
- **Florida panther**
- **ocelot**
- **Hawaiian coot**
- **ivory-billed woodpecker**
- **Atlantic salmon**
- **Puerto Rican boa**

Jaguar

TOP 5 Longest-Living Animals

In 2007, scientists dredging north of Iceland found a clam estimated to be at least 405 years old. Here are the animals that live the longest and the oldest-known age for each.

1.	QUAHOG CLAM	up to 410 years
2.	GIANT TORTOISE	up to 200 years
3.	HUMAN	up to 122
4.	STURGEON (type of fish)	up to 100
5.	BLUE WHALE AND GOLDEN EAGLE	up to 80

Bugs Are Animals Too

There are more insects on Earth than all other animals combined. Scientists have identified more than 1 million species of insects, including types of fleas, beetles, grasshoppers, butterflies, ants, earwigs, caterpillars and houseflies. Belonging to the class Insecta, insects have three different body parts: the head, the thorax and the abdomen. They also have three pairs of legs, two antennae and an exoskeleton (a tough outer skeleton). Get to know a few of these creepy, crawly critters.

guess what? At least 80 in every 100 animal species are insects.

TOE-BITERS One of the biggest and most vicious insects found in freshwater is the toe-biter. This large water bug lives in ponds, lakes and streams and attacks other insects, fish and even small birds. It has also bitten people. The toe-biter grabs its victim with its strong forelegs, injects it with a powerful venom, then sucks out its tissue through a hollow beak.

STINKBUGS, also known as shield bugs, secrete a smelly liquid when they sense danger.

GLOWWORMS are not really worms. They're actually beetles. Different glowworms produce light for different reasons. Some female glowworms emit a yellowish light from the underside of their bodies to attract male glowworms. Other glowworms shine to ward off potential predators.

LEAF-CUTTER ANTS, which often live in rain forests, use their strong jaws to clip pieces of leaves from plants and carry them to their underground colony. The pieces often weigh more than 10 times as much as the leaf-cutters do. Back at the colony, the leaf pieces are ground into a powder, then used to fertilize a special fungus, which becomes the leaf-cutters' food.

STICK INSECTS
If you're very patient and observant, you just might spot a stick insect in the forest or your yard. Usually long and thin, stick insects avoid predators by blending into their environment. They can be green and look like a leaf or turn brown to look like a twig.

SWALLOWTAIL CATERPILLARS When a swallowtail caterpillar senses danger, it extends from behind its head a Y-shaped hornlike gland, which secretes a foul-smelling chemical.

DRAGONFLIES Dragonflies have enormous eyes—bigger than any other insect's. These huge peepers enable dragonflies to see in front, below, above and behind at the same time.

GROSS-OUT FACT: A cockroach can survive up to a week without its head.

Little Critters

We all know about puppies and kittens, but what do you call other babies in the animal kingdom?

alligator	hatchling	cockroach	nymph
armadillo	pup	deer	fawn
bear	cub	duck	duckling
camel	calf	ferret	kit
		giraffe	calf
		goat	billy, kid
		goose	gosling
		gorilla	infant
		hyena	cub
		kangaroo	joey

koala	joey
mole	pup
oyster	spat
penguin	chick
pig	piglet, shoat
raccoon	pup
rhinoceros	calf
skunk	kit
turkey	poult
whale	calf

AWESOME ANIMAL FACTS

The bee hummingbird is the world's smallest bird. Even with its bill, it measures a mere 2 inches (5 cm) long.

The male African elephant has the largest ears in the animal kingdom—more than 3 feet (1 m) wide.

A chameleon's tongue can be longer than the length of its body.

Arctic terns make the longest migration of any animal. In the summer they live and breed in the Arctic. Then they fly to the Antarctic for the winter, before returning to the Arctic.

There are more chickens than people in the world.

The Saint Bernard is one of the heaviest dogs, often weighing more than 200 pounds (91 kg).

The strongest insect is the rhinoceros beetle. Also known as the Hercules beetle, it can lift more than 800 times its weight.

An electric eel can produce a shock of up to 650 volts.

The female black widow is one of the most poisonous animals in the world. A bite from it can cause terrible pain, dizziness and even death.

The sailfish is the fastest fish on Earth, clocking 68 miles (109 km) per hour.

The Australian box jellyfish, otherwise known as the sea wasp, is the world's most poisonous marine animal. Its sting is excruciatingly painful, and its venom can be fatal to humans, causing death within minutes.

Ostriches are Earth's largest bird. They can be more than 8 feet (2 m) tall and weigh about 300 pounds (136 kg).

Humpback whales create the loudest sound of any living creature.

TFK GAME

SLEEPY SEASON

Each winter, many animals settle down for a long winter's nap. Write the letter for each type of animal next to the clue that describes it.

1. This mom went to sleep alone. In spring, she will leave her den with cubs. _____

2. These reptiles hibernate to keep from freezing. _____

3. This little mammal wakes every few weeks to eat nuts it has stored. _____

4. Some say this tunneling animal can tell when spring will begin. _____

A chipmunk
B groundhog
C bear
D snakes

ANSWERS ON PAGE 244.

Animals

23

Color Theory

The three **primary colors** are red, blue and yellow. Painters can mix different amounts of these three colors to achieve the wide range of shades in their works of art. On the other hand, no blend of nonprimary colors can result in a primary color.

The **secondary colors**—violet, green and orange—are made by combining equal amounts of two primary colors. Blue and red mixed together make violet, blue and yellow make green and red and yellow make orange.

By arranging the three primary and three secondary colors on a color wheel, we can see how they relate to one another. Colors that are opposite from each other on the wheel are called **complementary colors**. Complementary colors contrast with each other and appear more vivid when placed side by side.

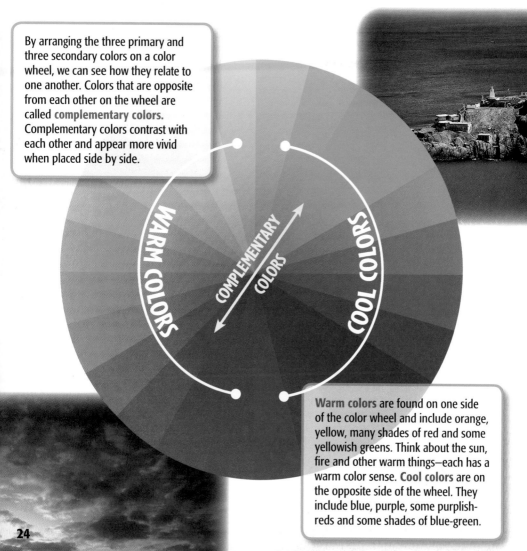

WARM COLORS

COMPLEMENTARY COLORS

COOL COLORS

Warm colors are found on one side of the color wheel and include orange, yellow, many shades of red and some yellowish greens. Think about the sun, fire and other warm things—each has a warm color sense. **Cool colors** are on the opposite side of the wheel. They include blue, purple, some purplish-reds and some shades of blue-green.

VISUAL ART MATERIALS

Artists create images by using many types of materials—paint, pencil, charcoal, pastels and ink, to name a few.

PAINTING

Painters have many kinds of paint to choose from. All paints are made with a colored powder known as pigment, which is mixed with a liquid base to form the paint. When the base dries, it acts like glue to stick the pigment to the canvas.

Tempera by Sandro Botticelli

- **Tempera paint** uses a base made of egg yolks. It dries quickly with a smooth matte finish and retains its color for a long time—which is a good thing, since tempera paint has been used for thousands of years.

- **Watercolors,** made by mixing pigment in water, have also been used by artists from all over the world in various forms since ancient times.

Oil by Edouard Manet

- **Oil paint** uses oil as a base and has a thick consistency. It has been around for hundreds of years and has been used for many famous paintings. Oil paint can create highly detailed and rich images, but it takes a long time to dry and tends to darken and yellow with age.

- **Acrylic** is a much newer type of paint. Acrylic paint uses a synthetic base and dries faster than oil, but it cannot be as easily altered or blended on the canvas.

While painting is most commonly done with a brush, many artists have also painted with other objects, including their fingers, a palette knife and airbrushes, or even thrown the paint at the canvas.

OTHER METHODS

The ordinary pencil is used by many artists and can create a wide range of shading and detail in drawings. Different kinds of pencils produce darker, lighter, softer or finer lines— and even different colors. An eraser can also come in handy!

Charcoal by Albrecht Dürer

Charcoal is great for sketches and for shading large areas of a drawing quickly. It can provide a strong, dark line, but also smudges easily.

Pastels have existed for hundreds of years and can be used to create brilliant colors or subtle textures. The pastel itself is almost like a crayon or piece of chalk, made of pigment held together with a binding material.

Pastel by Edgar Degas

In the hand of a skillful artist, **pen and ink** can be used to create quick sketches, detailed line drawings and more.

If none of the above are handy, use whatever you can find—markers, crayons and so on—to create your own masterpieces. You're limited only by your imagination!

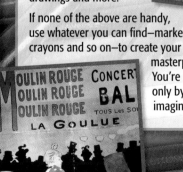

Pen and ink by Henri de Toulouse-Lautrec

Art

25

WHAT'S YOUR BODY MADE OF?

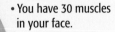

BONE UP ON BONES

BONES HAVE TWO MAJOR PURPOSES: to give shape and structure to your body and to protect internal organs.

At birth, people have more than 300 bones, but by the time you are an adult, you'll have just 206. Where do those additional bones go? Some bones fuse together, making one bone where there had been two.

WHERE ARE YOUR BONES FOUND?

YOU HAVE 30 MUSCLES IN YOUR FACE.

- 27 are in each hand.
- 26 are in each foot.
- 14 are in your face.

THE SKULL BONE

- 7 are in your neck—the same number as in a giraffe's. (Flamingoes, on the other hand, have 19 neck bones.)
- Your funny bone isn't a bone at all. It's a mass of nerves that runs along the long bone in your arm—a bone called the *humerus*.

The **LONGEST BONE** in your body is the thighbone, or femur. It's about 1/4 of your total height. It keeps growing as long as you do. Your spinal cord, however, stops growing when you are about five years old.

26 BONES ARE IN EACH FOOT.

MUSCLE MANIA

Muscles allow you to move by pulling and pushing your skeleton along. Some muscles, like your heart, are involuntary. That means they work without your doing anything about it. Other muscle movements are voluntary, like when you move your hand to pick up and clench a ball.

AAAAA-CHOOO!

- You have 30 muscles in your face.
  - Your largest muscle is called the *gluteus maxiumus* (another name for buttocks).
  - Your eye muscles move more than 100,000 times a day.
  - Your heart muscle beats about 70 times a minute.

TALK ABOUT USING YOUR MUSCLES

THE SKIN YOU'RE IN

Your skin is the largest organ of your body, and it does more than just hold you together. It forms a barrier to keep germs and water out.

- More than half of the dust you see in your house is made of shed skin. Over a lifetime, most people shed about 40 pounds (18 kg) of skin!
- An average-size adult has about 20 square feet (1.9 sq m) of skin.
- Skin gets its color from a pigment called *melanin*.

FUNNY FACTS

- Halitosis is the fancy name for bad breath.
- Most people pass gas about 15 times a day.
- Earwax can range in color from gray to yellow to orange.
- The acid in your stomach (hydrochloric acid) can eat through steel.
- While still in their mother's stomach, unborn babies can hiccup.
  - Sneezing sends air (and snot) out of your nose at about 100 miles (161 km) per hour.
  - There are billions of bacteria in your body and covering your skin.

WHY EXERCISE?

Exercising is one of the most important ways to keep your body healthy. When you exercise, you strengthen your bones, muscles and heart. You also burn off excess fat, improve your balance, regulate your body's metabolism (the process that turns the nutrients in food into energy and heat) and improve your mood.

Today, many kids don't get enough exercise. In fact, the average kid spends about three hours each day watching television and another two and a half hours sitting down using other kinds of media, such as video games or the Internet. Does that sound like you? If it does, it's time to get up and moving!

Whether you are playing soccer, dancing or challenging your neighbor to a game of tag, you can always find a workout that is fun for you. To stay healthy, everyone should try to do about one hour of exercise a day, in four 15-minute periods. And try not to be inactive for more than two hours at a time.

The Calorie Connection

People gain weight because they take in more calories through eating and drinking than they burn off through exercise. Calories are units of energy that you take in when you consume food (see "Food and Nutrition," page 92). Here are a few examples of activities and the number of calories they burn.

ACTIVITY	CALORIES BURNED IN 30 MINUTES
Running (10 minutes per mile)	300
Jumping rope	300
Climbing stairs	300
Swimming laps	225
Bicycling 5 miles	150
Shooting baskets	150
Walking 2 miles (15 minutes per mile)	150

Children, Teens and Obesity

One out of three American kids between ages 2 and 20 is overweight or obese—a scary trend. Being overweight cuts down on kids' energy levels and makes both playing and learning harder. Additional pounds can also lead to conditions such as high blood pressure and diabetes.

Here are some ways to stay healthy and avoid becoming overweight—or to help you start losing weight.

- **Read package labels** to find out what ingredients are in a product. Avoid foods that contain high-fructose corn syrup and a lot of chemicals.
- **Count calories.** But take note: The number of calories in a food depends on the portion size, not the contents of an entire package. A bag of chips might list 100 calories per portion on the nutrition facts label, but that's for just a few chips, not the whole bag.
- **Stock up on fruits and veggies.** The foods that have the fewest calories and are also the most healthful don't usually have labels. You can eat plenty of these. Fruit juice, however, can be loaded with calories, so drink it in moderation.
- **Switch to whole grains and low fat** when you are choosing bread, pasta and dairy products.
- **Keep sweets, highly salted foods and soda at a minimum.**
- **Don't skip meals, especially breakfast.** Breakfast is particularly important.
- **Get active.** Walk or bike instead of getting a ride. Join a sports team. Challenge yourself to be active every day.
- **Eat with your family at the table.** Eating while watching TV makes it easier to overeat or to keep munching long after you are full.

Body and Health

27

HOW DOES YOUR BODY WORK?

Your body is an amazing thing. It's made up of different systems, which consist of organs that have their own special functions. Some organs are the liver, kidneys and heart. Even your skin is an organ!

CARDIOVASCULAR SYSTEM

The cardiovascular system, or circulatory system, has one main job: to pump blood throughout the body. The system's major organ is the heart, which pumps blood through the arteries into all parts of the body. Blood contains oxygen, hormones and nutrients that cells need to grow, work and repair themselves. Cells take in these products and give off carbon dioxide and other waste materials, which the blood then carries through the veins to the organs that remove the waste from the body.

MUSCULAR SYSTEM

Different types of muscles are located throughout the body. Skeletal muscles are attached to the body's bones and move them by contracting and releasing. Smooth muscles line the digestive system and help move food and water through it. Cardiac muscles are found in the heart. They pump blood through the heart to the lungs and the rest of the body.

SKELETAL SYSTEM

The skeletal system is made up of bones, joints and cartilage, which is a flexible tissue that forms body parts like the nose and ears. Cartilage also helps bones and joints work together smoothly. The body's bones have four main functions. First, they support the body and work with muscles to help it move in different ways, as well as to carry weight. Second, they protect the other organs in the body from injury. For example, your skull protects your brain, and your ribs protect many of your soft internal organs. Third, bones store important minerals such as calcium and phosphorous, releasing them into the bloodstream when the body's other organs need them. Finally, bones produce blood cells.

Guess what? *Bones are actually living organs.*

IMMUNE SYSTEM

Diseases in the form of bacteria, viruses, toxins and microbes can attack the body. Your immune system fights off disease and helps to keep you healthy in many ways. Lymph, a liquid produced by lymph nodes in various parts of the body, is carried in the bloodstream to the cells to clean them of harmful bacteria and waste products. The center of bones, called the *bone marrow*, is where red and white blood cells are created. White blood cells are important because they produce antibodies, which kill toxins, bacteria and viruses. The thymus, which is located in the chest, produces special cells that fight disease. The spleen filters out old red blood cells and other foreign bodies, such as bacteria. The adenoids (behind the nose) and tonsils (in the throat) also trap and kill bacteria and viruses.

ENDOCRINE SYSTEM

The organs of this system are called *glands*. They produce hormones, which are chemicals that travel through your bloodstream and tell your organs what to do. For this reason, hormones are often referred to as the body's messengers. The endocrine system works to regulate mood, growth, body development, sleep, blood pressure and metabolism, which is the process by which the body changes food into energy.

NERVOUS SYSTEM

Your nervous system is made up of two parts: the central nervous system, which includes the brain and the spinal cord, and the peripheral nervous system, which consists of neurons found all over the body. The brain helps to regulate all the other systems of the body by sending signals down the spinal cord and through the body's nerves to all the other organs. Different parts of the brain specialize in processing thoughts, memories, feelings, dreams, speech, physical coordination, balance, hunger and sleep. Your nervous system is extremely complicated and helps the systems in your body to communicate.

guess what? *When you see a puppy, it is your brain that recognizes it and tells you that you like those sorts of critters. Your brain then tells your muscles to run over to it and pet the dog. Your brain also processes your senses, which tell you the puppy's fur is soft and its breath is stinky.*

DIGESTIVE SYSTEM

This system is responsible for taking in and digesting the food and liquids you consume and making sure you get the nutrients you need from what you eat. It also gets rid of solid waste. When food enters the mouth, glands under the tongue secrete saliva (or spit), which helps to moisten the food as you chew it. The food is swallowed into the esophagus, a tube that leads to the stomach. The stomach produces acid that turns the food into a thick liquid. This liquid enters the intestines, where enzymes, bile (made by the liver and stored in the gallbladder) and insulin (made in the pancreas) digest it even further. As the food moves through the small and then large intestine, its water and nutrients are absorbed into the bloodstream. Finally, the solid waste that's left is passed out of the body.

guess what? *At 20 feet (6 m) long, the small intestine is actually a lot larger than the large intestine. The large intestine is wider, but only about 5 feet (1.5 m) long.*

RESPIRATORY SYSTEM

The respiratory system supplies your body with oxygen. Air that enters the nose and mouth moves down the trachea, or windpipe, and into large bronchial tubes that are connected to each lobe, or side, of the lungs. The tubes branch into many smaller tubes that end in tiny passageways called *alveoli*. In these teeny spaces, oxygen enters the bloodstream and carbon dioxide is removed, sent back up the trachea and breathed out through the nose and mouth.

REPRODUCTIVE SYSTEM

This system is responsible for producing sperm cells in men and egg cells in women. The reproductive system allows sperm and egg cells to combine to form an embryo, which eventually becomes a baby.

URINARY SYSTEM

The urinary system is responsible for eliminating excess fluid from the body. The body's two kidneys remove toxins from the water flowing in the bloodstream. Those toxins then travel through tubes called *ureters* and into the bladder, where they remain until leaving the body as urine.

INTEGUMENTARY SYSTEM

This system is made up of skin, sweat and oil glands, nails, and hair. It protects the inside of the body by forming a barrier to the outside atmosphere. The skin senses touch, heat, cold and pain and sends signals to the brain. The brain then sends signals back to the appropriate body parts so they can react correctly to those sensations. Sweat glands in your skin help the body cool itself. The skin's oil glands keep the body from drying out. Nails provide defense, and hair provides protection and warmth.

Comics in Class

FROM TFK MAGAZINE

Picture this: You are sitting in class and *pow!* your teacher turns into Superman. *Thwak!* Garfield is chasing Mickey Mouse around your desk. What are comic book characters doing in class?

Maryland students share their hand-drawn comics.

In some places, they are part of the lesson. Schools around the country are using comic books as a way to teach reading, writing and other subjects.

Critics say comics are too simple for school. But many teachers give comics a good grade for getting their students to read.

A COLORFUL NEW WAY TO LEARN

Third-grade teachers in Maryland are using classic Disney comics. The department of education created lesson plans for the comics.

Maryland tested the program in eight classrooms. "The teachers love it. It captures students' interest," says Nancy Grasmick, superintendent of Maryland schools. She adds that they believe the comics have helped improve reading skills.

Another program, the Comic Book Project, is being used in 850 schools in the United States. Students write and draw their own comics. The project was started by Michael Bitz of Teachers College at Columbia University, in New York City. Bitz wanted to give kids the chance to "write their own stories and create their own characters," he told TFK, "while improving their reading and writing skills."

Katie Van Els, 11, from Hawaii, says the project has made her a better writer. "You need to use the right words and punctuation."

Teachers also give the program high marks. Bitz has heard stories of children who didn't like to read. "Suddenly, they're the star writers in their class," he says.

Classic Tales by Young Authors

Want to be a published novelist? You can! And you don't even have to wait until you're an adult to become one. Start writing now.

WALTER FARLEY began writing his famous novel while he was still in high school. *The Black Stallion*, published in 1941, is about a shipwrecked young boy named Alec Ramsay and a spirited stallion, who has become one of the most famous horses in fiction. Farley followed up with *The Black Stallion Returns, Son of the Black Stallion* and others.

S.E. HINTON sold *The Outsiders*, a modern classic of young adult literature, when she was 17 years old. Other popular books by Hinton are *That Was Then, This Is Now* and *Rumble Fish*.

ANNE FRANK One of the most famous and deeply moving books by a young author is not a novel but a diary started by a girl on her 13th birthday. Anne Frank's chronicles of her harrowing life in hiding during the Holocaust were published in 1947 (after her death) under the title *The Diary of a Young Girl*.

Graphic Novels

A graphic novel is a novel that is told through a combination of text and art. Some graphic novels look like comic strips, while others don't. Some of the most well-known examples of this type of book are Belgian artist Hergé's beloved Tintin stories, which were published in the 1930s.

Here are some recent graphic novels recommended by the Young Adult Library Services Association.

THE ARRIVAL BY SHAUN TAN Illustrated in black, white and sepia (yellowish) tones, this wordless novel explores the struggle of a man who leaves his country behind for a bizarre and unfamiliar land.

BLUE BEETLE: SHELLSHOCKED BY KEITH GIFFEN When teen Jaime Reyes discovers a strange artifact—which turns out to be the mystical Blue Beetle scarab—on the street one day, he brings it home and is suddenly thrust into the role of superhero. Now the third incarnation of the Blue Beetle, Jaime has to learn how to control and use his powers, which include the ability to generate a shell-like armor around his body.

LAIKA BY NICK ABADZIS In 1957, the Soviet Union sent the first living creature into outer space. It was a dog named Laika. This book is a fictionalized account of the life of the first brave space voyager, from her birth on the streets of Moscow to her ultimate death aboard a spaceship.

THE MAGICAL LIFE OF LONG TACK SAM BY ANN MARIE FLEMING This remarkable story explores the life of the writer's great-grandfather, a comic, acrobat and world traveler, who just happened to be China's greatest magician.

ROBOT DREAMS BY SARA VARON This touching tale revolves around the strange friendship between a dog and a robot. During a day at the beach, the robot jumps into the water, then rusts on the beach. Unsure of what to do, the dog abandons his friend. Many seasons go by and, as the robot dreams of rescue, the dog struggles with the guilt of leaving a friend behind.

WHAT IS MANGA?

Manga is the Japanese word for "comics." It refers to the distinct style of art found in Japanese comics. Characters often have oversize eyes and small mouths, and they usually express emotions in an exaggerated way. In recent years, manga has become very popular in the United States.

Guess what? Art Spiegelman's Maus: A Survivor's Tale *is probably the most critically acclaimed graphic novel. In it, Spiegelman replaces humans with animals to illustrate the horrors of the Holocaust. In the book, Jewish people are represented by mice—***maus*** *means "mouse" in German.*

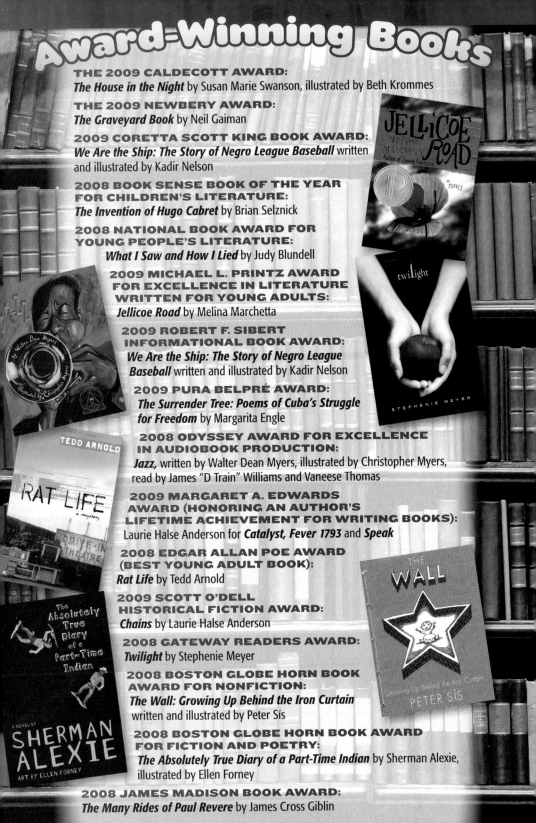

Award-Winning Books

THE 2009 CALDECOTT AWARD:
The House in the Night by Susan Marie Swanson, illustrated by Beth Krommes

THE 2009 NEWBERY AWARD:
The Graveyard Book by Neil Gaiman

2009 CORETTA SCOTT KING BOOK AWARD:
We Are the Ship: The Story of Negro League Baseball written and illustrated by Kadir Nelson

2008 BOOK SENSE BOOK OF THE YEAR FOR CHILDREN'S LITERATURE:
The Invention of Hugo Cabret by Brian Selznick

2008 NATIONAL BOOK AWARD FOR YOUNG PEOPLE'S LITERATURE:
What I Saw and How I Lied by Judy Blundell

2009 MICHAEL L. PRINTZ AWARD FOR EXCELLENCE IN LITERATURE WRITTEN FOR YOUNG ADULTS:
Jellicoe Road by Melina Marchetta

2009 ROBERT F. SIBERT INFORMATIONAL BOOK AWARD:
We Are the Ship: The Story of Negro League Baseball written and illustrated by Kadir Nelson

2009 PURA BELPRÉ AWARD:
The Surrender Tree: Poems of Cuba's Struggle for Freedom by Margarita Engle

2008 ODYSSEY AWARD FOR EXCELLENCE IN AUDIOBOOK PRODUCTION:
Jazz, written by Walter Dean Myers, illustrated by Christopher Myers, read by James "D Train" Williams and Vaneese Thomas

2009 MARGARET A. EDWARDS AWARD (HONORING AN AUTHOR'S LIFETIME ACHIEVEMENT FOR WRITING BOOKS):
Laurie Halse Anderson for *Catalyst, Fever 1793* and *Speak*

2008 EDGAR ALLAN POE AWARD (BEST YOUNG ADULT BOOK):
Rat Life by Tedd Arnold

2009 SCOTT O'DELL HISTORICAL FICTION AWARD:
Chains by Laurie Halse Anderson

2008 GATEWAY READERS AWARD:
Twilight by Stephenie Meyer

2008 BOSTON GLOBE HORN BOOK AWARD FOR NONFICTION:
The Wall: Growing Up Behind the Iron Curtain written and illustrated by Peter Sís

2008 BOSTON GLOBE HORN BOOK AWARD FOR FICTION AND POETRY:
The Absolutely True Diary of a Part-Time Indian by Sherman Alexie, illustrated by Ellen Forney

2008 JAMES MADISON BOOK AWARD:
The Many Rides of Paul Revere by James Cross Giblin

You've Got to Read This!

According to the Association for Library Service to Children, here is a sampling of great reads for middle schoolers.

***The Cat: Or, How I Lost Eternity* by Jutta Richter, illustrated by Rotraut Susanne Berner and translated by Anna Brailovsky.** With the help of a mysterious white alley cat, Christine learns some valuable lessons about life and friendship.

***Henry's Freedom Box: A True Story from the Underground Railroad* by Ellen Levine, illustrated by Kadir Nelson.** This is the true tale of how Henry "Box" Brown escaped slavery. He actually shipped himself to freedom—in a box! A 2008 Caldecott Honor Book.

***The Many Rides of Paul Revere* by James Cross Giblin.** Most of us know the name Paul Revere, but do we really know who he is? This book fills us in, from Revere's life as a French immigrant to his work as a silversmith, horse messenger, dentist, statesman and eventually hero of the American Revolution.

***The Mysterious Benedict Society* by Trenton Lee Stewart, illustrated by Carson Ellis.** Four brilliant young sleuths, aided by their benefactor Mr. Benedict, embark on a quest to infiltrate a mysterious organization and save the world from a scheming mad scientist.

***Nicholas and the Gang* by René Goscinny, illustrated by Jean-Jacques Sempé.** Young Nicholas is always getting himself into trouble. These 16 delightful stories about the French equivalent of Dennis the Menace are made even more charming by the pen-and-ink illustrations.

***One Thousand Tracings: Healing the Wounds of World War II* by Lita Judge.** This moving story describes how a young American girl's grandparents come to the aid of a needy German family following World War II, thus beginning a huge overseas relief project. The book is based on real-life events from the author's family history.

***Rainstorm* by Barbara Lehman.** No words are necessary in this beautifully illustrated book, in which a lonely boy discovers a key on a rainy day. The key opens a chest, which contains a ladder. Climbing down the ladder, the boy begins a wondrous and magical adventure that brings him fun and friends.

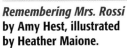

***Remembering Mrs. Rossi* by Amy Hest, illustrated by Heather Maione.** Eight-year-old Annie learns how to deal with the loss of her mother, with help from her adoring father and her mother's sixth-grade students.

MYSTERY PERSON

Clue 1: I was born in Topeka, Kansas, on June 7, 1917.

Clue 2: In 1950, I became the first African-American poet to win the Pulitzer Prize.

Clue 3: My poem "We Real Cool" is often studied in school.

Who am I? _____

ANSWER ON PAGE 244.

Books and Literature

Buildings and Architecture

Architecture Terms:
WHAT'S THAT?

Buildings use these basic features to create a structure and let in light and air: roof, walls, doorways and windows. Architects—people who design buildings—have figured out many ways to use these features to make buildings both strong and beautiful.

Notre Dame, Paris, France

Amiens Cathedral, Amiens, France

Arch of Constantine, Rome, Italy

GARGOYLE A carved face of a person or animal that is usually made of stone and is placed as an ornament on the gutters of a building. Sometimes gargoyles are placed just for ornamentation. Other gargoyles are actually spouts—rainwater flowing from the roof can escape through the mouths of these decorative beasts.

ARCH A curved or pointed ceiling that bridges a gap. An arch can bear more weight than a flat roof or a bridge can. Before 1100 A.D., arches were always shaped like rounded curves. In the Gothic period, architects first used pointed arches, which they found could support even more weight than rounded arches. This allowed them to use heavier materials and to design and build taller structures.

St. George's Chapel, Windsor Castle, London, England

BUTTRESS A stone support that projects outward from a wall

FLYING BUTTRESS A buttress that forms an arch, connecting a main wall with another structure

COLUMN A pillar made of stone or concrete that supports an arch or roof or that stands alone

Westminster Abbey, London, England

SPIRE A tower shaped like a cone that was developed in Europe and is usually the top of a place of worship

U.S. Capitol, Washington, D.C.

PORTICO An entrance porch, usually supported by columns

Batalha Monastery, Batalha, Portugal

Salisbury Cathedral, Salisbury, England

DOME A rounded roof of a building

VAULT An arched ceiling; the inside of a dome

The Duomo, Florence, Italy

Architecture Through the Ages

CLASSICAL A style developed by ancient Greeks and Romans. Classical buildings are made by layering stones on top of one another or by placing beams across columns. Classical buildings often include arches, domes and vaults.
Example: Pantheon; Rome, Italy; completed around 128 A.D.

GOTHIC A style that began in Europe in the 12th century and features pointed arches and windows. In Gothic architecture, window glass is often placed within fancy stonework.
Example: Reims Cathedral; Reims, France; built between 1211 and 1311

RENAISSANCE A style developed in the early 15th century that shows a return to the more classical styles of ancient times. Renaissance architecture was a move away from the fancier Gothic style and often includes carved statues built into the walls and within arches of buildings.
Example: St. Peter's Basilica; Rome, Italy; built between 1546 and 1590

BAROQUE Beginning in the early 17th century in Europe, architects and designers designed ornate buildings, which means that the buildings had flowery details and flashy decoration. This style was popular through the 18th century.
Example: The Palace of Versailles, France; built between 1661 and 1710

NEOCLASSICAL This style is yet another return to the classical style after the extreme decoration of the Baroque period.
Example: U.S. Capitol Building; Washington, D.C.; begun in 1793 and added to, rebuilt, repaired and renovated many times since

MODERN Popular in the 1920s, modern features include spare, useful designs made of steel and glass as well as sleek stone.
Example: Bauhaus Building; Dessau, Germany; built in 1925

ART DECO Developed in the 1930s, this style features stylized metalwork on stone.
Example: Chrysler Building; New York, New York; built in 1930

COOL CONSTRUCTIONS

The Guggenheim Museum in New York City, designed by Frank Lloyd Wright, completed in 1959
Fascinating Features:

- Most of the building's exterior was created without corners.
- Visitors never need to retrace their steps. They can take an elevator to the top floor and walk down a circular path, seeing each object of art just once.
- When it first opened, some artists criticized the building, saying that it was more exciting than the artwork inside.

The Guggenheim Museum in Bilbao, Spain, designed by Frank Gehry, completed in 1997
Fascinating Features:

- Its curved walls catch and reflect light. At any time of day, different sides of the building reflect sunlight.
- Situated in a port city, it is designed to resemble a ship.
- It's made of glass, titanium and limestone.

The Hearst Building in New York City, designed by Norman Foster and Partners, completed in 2006
Fascinating Features:

- The Hearst Building was built over a stone 1928 landmark building.
- It uses 25% less energy to run than other similar-size buildings. *going green*
- To create its gridlike design, builders used 20% less steel than is normally used for a building this size.

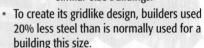

The Burj Dubai (Dubai Tower) in Dubai, United Arab Emirates, designed by Adrian Smith, under construction (expected completion date: late 2009)
Fascinating Features:

- At 2,684 feet (818 m), the Burj Dubai will be the world's tallest building—and the tallest human-made object ever. Its 78th-floor swimming pool is also the highest swimming pool in the world.
- More than 5,000 workers have taken part in the construction of the tower. Designed to house more than 35,000 people, the construction features hotel rooms, apartments, offices and other spaces.

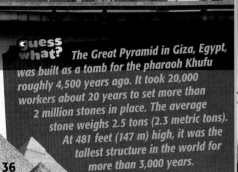

Guess what? *The Great Pyramid in Giza, Egypt, was built as a tomb for the pharaoh Khufu roughly 4,500 years ago. It took 20,000 workers about 20 years to set more than 2 million stones in place. The average stone weighs 2.5 tons (2.3 metric tons). At 481 feet (147 m) high, it was the tallest structure in the world for more than 3,000 years.*

Green Buildings

going green

Green buildings are not new. For thousands of years, humans built structures with local, natural materials. These structures did not use energy or damage the planet. When the people who lived in them moved on, the structures usually collapsed and their materials returned to the earth.

Before the 1930s, most buildings used far less energy than today's buildings. Instead of air conditioning, they had windows that opened to let in breezes. They weren't quite green, however. Coal-burning furnaces were used for heating. As a result, many buildings spewed dirty smoke into the air. Beginning in the 1970s in the United States and much of the world, air-pollution laws were passed to force builders to reduce or eliminate pollution caused by buildings.

Solar cells on the roof of a home

WHAT MAKES A BUILDING GREEN?

From the materials used in the construction to the placement of the windows, there are a number of things that make a building green. Ideally, it is made with materials that don't harm the people inside or the environment. Also, an eco-friendly building is only as big as it needs to be, so it doesn't use a lot of energy for heating or cooling.

- Green buildings use power made by sustainable resources such as sunlight and wind rather than relying on energy supplied by burning fossil fuels, which creates pollution. (For more information on energy sources, see pages 86–87.)

- To avoid using energy for air-conditioning systems, architects take advantage of natural cooling. Windows are placed in such a way that they can be opened to create indoor breezes, and designers include awnings or shades to keep sunlight from making buildings too warm.

- Eco-friendly buildings are built from materials that are plentiful. For example, they are not made with wood or other materials from endangered forests. Bamboo is one great option for builders. It grows quickly and is not an endangered plant.

- Builders avoid (or limit) the use of chemicals that can create indoor air pollution or harm occupants. To encourage healthy living, some buildings are designed with easy-to-use interior staircases and ramps so that people will walk more and use elevators or escalators less.

One Green Museum

going green

Opened in 2008, the California Academy of Sciences in San Francisco's Golden Gate Park is the world's greenest museum. Its 2.5-acre (1 hectare) roof is covered with about 1.7 million native plants, and the walls are insulated with recycled blue jeans. There are solar panels to help power the building, and skylights help air flow freely.

The architect, Renzo Piano, designed the building to fit into the natural landscape. To reduce the need for electrical lighting, the walls are mostly glass, which allows sunlight in. The museum's aquarium is also lit by natural sunlight. Much of the water used in the plumbing and for watering the plants is recycled waste water from the city of San Francisco.

The museum's "living roof" and skylights

Buildings and Architecture

JANUARY 1: NEW YEAR'S DAY

JANUARY 18: MARTIN LUTHER KING DAY (third Monday in January). This holiday commemorates the birthday of civil rights leader Martin Luther King Jr., who was born January 15, 1929.

FEBRUARY 2: Every **GROUNDHOG DAY,** people gather in Pennsylvania to watch a groundhog named Punxsutawney Phil emerge from his burrow. According to the legend, if he sees his shadow, there will be six more weeks of winter. If he doesn't, spring is on the way.

FEBRUARY 14: VALENTINE'S DAY

FEBRUARY 15: PRESIDENT'S DAY is a federal holiday set aside to honor two great U.S. Presidents: Abraham Lincoln, who was born on February 12, 1809, and George Washington, born on February 22, 1732.

FEBRUARY 16: MARDI GRAS, which means "Fat Tuesday" in French, is the last day of festivities before Lent begins. For Christians, Lent is a time of prayer, fasting and asking to be forgiven for one's sins. During Mardi Gras parades, beads are tossed into the crowd from spectacular floats. Participants wear colorful costumes and outrageous masks.

MARCH 14: DAYLIGHT SAVING TIME BEGINS

MARCH 17: ST. PATRICK'S DAY

APRIL 1: APRIL FOOL'S DAY

MARCH 30–APRIL 6: PASSOVER is an eight-day holiday during which Jews celebrate the Hebrews' liberation from slavery in Egypt.

APRIL 4: EASTER. On Easter, Christians celebrate the resurrection of Jesus Christ. In addition to attending church services, many children dye Easter eggs, participate in Easter egg hunts and receive baskets of goodies from the Easter Bunny.

APRIL 22: EARTH DAY

MAY 5: CINCO DE MAYO means "fifth of May" in Spanish. It commemorates a victory over the French during a battle in 1862. It is celebrated in Mexico and within Hispanic communities in the United States.

MAY 9: MOTHER'S DAY

MAY 31: MEMORIAL DAY. This day is reserved to remember those who died while serving their country in the armed forces.

JUNE 20: FATHER'S DAY

JULY 4: INDEPENDENCE DAY

SEPTEMBER 6: LABOR DAY, which honors the achievements of working people, has been on the calendar since 1882.

SEPTEMBER 9: ROSH HASHANAH
is the first day of the Jewish new year.

SEPTEMBER 18: YOM KIPPUR
is the Jewish Day of Atonement.

OCTOBER 11: COLUMBUS DAY
celebrates Columbus's discovery of the New World in 1492.

OCTOBER 31: HALLOWEEN

NOVEMBER 7: DAYLIGHT SAVING TIME ENDS

NOVEMBER 11: VETERANS DAY

NOVEMBER 25: THANKSGIVING

DECEMBER 2–9: HANUKKAH
is an eight-day Jewish holiday often referred to as
the Festival of Lights.

DECEMBER 25: CHRISTMAS
is the day on which Christians celebrate the birth
of Jesus.

DECEMBER 26–JANUARY 1: KWANZAA
People of African descent all over the world celebrate Kwanzaa,
a seven-day holiday that honors African heritage.

Earth Day going green

The first Earth Day was celebrated on April 22, 1970, in many cities and towns around the United States. This was the same year in which the Environmental Protection Agency (EPA) became part of the U.S. government. At that time, many people were just beginning to understand that their actions were having a negative effect on the environment. Some rivers were so polluted that they caught fire. The air in some places was so full of soot and smog that kids who played outside had trouble breathing.

People participate in a beach cleanup.

Since that first Earth Day, many laws have been passed to clean up the air and waterways. Today, America's air and water are much cleaner than they used to be, but the fight for a cleaner, greener planet continues.

Today, Earth Day is celebrated in many countries of the world. Every year, people look at the progress that has been made. They also think about and take actions that will help protect the environment. Some people celebrate Earth Day by attending concerts or events that raise money for environmental causes. Others plant trees or participate in cleanup days to remove litter from beaches, roadways or or parks. Talk to your class or your parents about fun and Earth-conscious ways to celebrate the day.

2010

JANUARY

S	M	T	W	T	F	S
					1	2
3	4	5	6	7	8	9
10	11	12	13	14	15	16
17	18	19	20	21	22	23
24	25	26	27	28	29	30
31						

FEBRUARY

S	M	T	W	T	F	S
	1	2	3	4	5	6
7	8	9	10	11	12	13
14	15	16	17	18	19	20
21	22	23	24	25	26	27
28						

MARCH

S	M	T	W	T	F	S
	1	2	3	4	5	6
7	8	9	10	11	12	13
14	15	16	17	18	19	20
21	22	23	24	25	26	27
28	29	30	31			

APRIL

S	M	T	W	T	F	S
				1	2	3
4	5	6	7	8	9	10
11	12	13	14	15	16	17
18	19	20	21	22	23	24
25	26	27	28	29	30	

MAY

S	M	T	W	T	F	S
						1
2	3	4	5	6	7	8
9	10	11	12	13	14	15
16	17	18	19	20	21	22
23	24	25	26	27	28	29
30	31					

JUNE

S	M	T	W	T	F	S
		1	2	3	4	5
6	7	8	9	10	11	12
13	14	15	16	17	18	19
20	21	22	23	24	25	26
27	28	29	30			

JULY

S	M	T	W	T	F	S
				1	2	3
4	5	6	7	8	9	10
11	12	13	14	15	16	17
18	19	20	21	22	23	24
25	26	27	28	29	30	31

AUGUST

S	M	T	W	T	F	S
1	2	3	4	5	6	7
8	9	10	11	12	13	14
15	16	17	18	19	20	21
22	23	24	25	26	27	28
29	30	31				

SEPTEMBER

S	M	T	W	T	F	S
			1	2	3	4
5	6	7	8	9	10	11
12	13	14	15	16	17	18
19	20	21	22	23	24	25
26	27	28	29	30		

OCTOBER

S	M	T	W	T	F	S
					1	2
3	4	5	6	7	8	9
10	11	12	13	14	15	16
17	18	19	20	21	22	23
24	25	26	27	28	29	30
31						

NOVEMBER

S	M	T	W	T	F	S
	1	2	3	4	5	6
7	8	9	10	11	12	13
14	15	16	17	18	19	20
21	22	23	24	25	26	27
28	29	30				

DECEMBER

S	M	T	W	T	F	S
			1	2	3	4
5	6	7	8	9	10	11
12	13	14	15	16	17	18
19	20	21	22	23	24	25
26	27	28	29	30	31	

SEASONS

What season is it? You might be surprised to know that the answer depends on where you live. Just imagine: As you are throwing snowballs in the Northern Hemisphere in January and playing tag in the July sunshine, kids in Australia and other Southern Hemisphere countries are on the opposite schedule.

Why aren't the seasons the same around the world?

• Earth travels around the sun, making a complete orbit every 365.26 days. Its path is elliptical, which means that it is closer to the sun during some parts of the year and farther away during other parts.

• As Earth spins on its axis, it's tilted at a 23.5° angle. Depending on where Earth is in its year-long journey around the sun, either the Northern or Southern Hemisphere is tilted toward the sun. When the Northern Hemisphere is tilted toward the sun, it's summer in the north. When the Southern Hemisphere is tilted toward the sun, it summer in the south.

• Places on Earth that are closer to the equator or the poles don't have as much of a difference in temperatures between winter and summer.

OCTOBER   SEPTEMBER
NOVEMBER   AUGUST
DECEMBER   JULY

Northern Autumn/Southern Spring

Northern Winter
Southern Summer

THE SUN

Northern Summer
Southern Winter

JANUARY   JUNE

Northern Spring/Southern Autumn

FEBRUARY   MAY
MARCH   APRIL

Why are there more hours of sunlight at some times of year than at other times?

• In the Northern Hemisphere, there are more hours of sunlight between March 21 and September 22. In the Southern Hemisphere, there are more hours of sunlight between September and March.

• On two days each year—September 22 and March 20—every place on Earth (except the poles) experiences 12 hours of sunlight and 12 hours of darkness. A day in which darkness and light are equal is called an **equinox.** The amount of sunlight and darkness are equal because Earth's position in its orbit is not tilted in relation to the sun.

• On two days each year—June 21 and December 21—Earth is positioned in its orbit so that either the North Pole or the South Pole is most inclined toward the sun. This happens when the Earth is farthest from the sun on its orbit. Each of these days is called the **solstice.** During the June solstice, the North Pole is tilted toward the sun and gets 24 hours of sunlight. During the December solstice, the North Pole is tilted away from the sun and gets 24 hours of darkness.

Computers and Communication

Webby Awards

Steven Colbert

Ben Huh, creator of icanhascheezburger?

We Has Too Webby ? KTHXBAI!!!

Will.i.am

ACTIVISM: loveisrespect.org loveisrespect.org

ART: Richard Serra Sculpture: Forty Years moma.org/serra

AUTOMOTIVE: Toyota FJ Cruiser yyzwork.com/VI/toyotafjcruiser/

BROADBAND: ABC.com Full Episode Player abc.go.com/player/index

CELEBRITY/FAN: Annie Lennox Official Website annielennox.com

EDUCATION: The Earth Institute at Columbia University earth.columbia.edu

FAMILY/PARENTING: KidsHealth kidshealth.org

FASHION: Louis Vuitton Core Values journeys.louisvuitton.com

GAMES: Kongregate kongregate.com

HUMOR: The Onion theonion.com

MAGAZINE: National Geographic Magazine Online ngm.com

MOVIE & FILM: Simpsons Movie simpsonsmovie.com

MUSIC: BBC Radio 1 Meet the DJs bbc.co.uk/radio1/djs

NEWS: NYTimes.com nytimes.com

PERSONAL WEB SITE: The Whale Hunt thewhalehunt.org

RADIO: BBC World Service channel site bbc.co.uk/worldservice

SCIENCE: nature.com nature.com

SOCIAL NETWORKING: Flock the Social Web Browser flock.com

SPORTS: Yahoo! Sports sports.yahoo.com

YOUTH: Scholastic Site Redesign scholastic.com

PEOPLE'S VOICE WINNER HUMOR CATEGORY:
I Can Has Cheezburger? icanhascheezburger.com

WEBBY PERSON OF THE YEAR: Steven Colbert

WEBBY ARTIST OF THE YEAR: Will.i.am

WEBBY LIFETIME ACHIEVEMENT AWARD: David Byrne

going green

THE ELECTRONIC JUNK PILE
E-waste is the world's fastest growing type of solid waste. Old cell phones, DVD players, computers and television sets are filling up landfills, and they might be a threat to our safety too. Some electronic waste can leak toxic materials into groundwater and endanger nearby communities. Visit mygreenelectronics.org to find more information about caring for and disposing of electronic equipment.

Surfing Safe and Sound

The Internet is a great place to find information, learn new things and communicate with others. But like any other resource, it has its downside. Protect yourself from being a cyber-victim by following these simple tips.

 Tech-Savvy Countries

Companies around the world compete to come up with the next big thing in computers and technology.

These new applications are used in schools, in different jobs and industries, and also just for fun. *BusinessWeek* took a look at the major tech-producing countries and rated them on how well they use new technology to benefit their citizens and their economies. Here are the countries that came out on top.

1. Denmark
2. Sweden
3. Switzerland
4. United States
5. Singapore
6. Finland
7. The Netherlands
8. Iceland
9. Republic of Korea
10. Norway

- Talk with your parents about when and how you will use the Internet and send e-mails and instant messages. Together create a pledge all of you can sign. Review this pledge from time to time to see if any changes are needed.

- Never give out personal information—such as your name, address, phone number, school, a photo, where you like to hang out or whether you are home alone—to anyone who contacts you unless your parents say it's okay.

- If you ever receive a message that frightens you or makes you uncomfortable, tell your parents (or your teacher, if you're at school).

- Don't make plans to meet in person anyone you've met online unless your parents give you permission and accompany you.

- Never share your password with anyone except your parents.

- Treat everyone on the Internet the same way you want to be treated. Don't be rude or a bully. And don't send a message when you're angry—wait until you calm down.

- Don't open any e-mails from senders you don't recognize. To see if an e-mail is from a sender who is safe, learn how to view the message's source without opening the message itself.

Internet Resource Sites for Kids

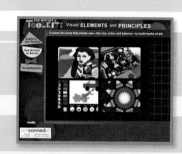

General

TIME For Kids **timeforkids.com**
4Kids.org **4kids.org**
Smithsonian Education **smithsonianeducation.org/students**
Brain Pop **brainpop.com**
Homework Help Yahoo! Kids **kids.yahoo.com/learn**
Internet Public Library **ipl.org/div/kidspace; www.ipl.org/div/teen**

Art

The Artist's Toolkit **artsconnected.org/toolkit**
Museum Kids **metmuseum.org/explore/museumkids.htm**
NGA (National Gallery of Art) Kids **nga.gov/kids**
WebMuseum, Paris **ibiblio.org/wm**

Biography

Biography.com **biography.com**
Academy of Achievement **achievement.org/galleryachieve.html**

Ecology and the Environment

EPA Environmental Kids Club **epa.gov/kids**
Illinois EPA Envirofun **epa.state.il.us/kids/index.html**
National Institute of Environmental Health Sciences (NIEHS) Kids' Pages **kids.niehs.nih.gov**

Geography

National Geographic Kids **kids.nationalgeographic.com**
The CIA World Factbook **cia.gov/library/publications/the-world-factbook/index.html**
50states.com **50states.com**

Government and Politics

Kids.gov **kids.gov**
Congress for Kids **congressforkids.net**
White House Kids **whitehouse.gov/kids**

Health

KidsHealth **kidshealth.org/kid; kidshealth.org/teen**
BAM! Body and Mind **bam.gov**
Kidnetic.com **kidnetic.com**

History

History.com This Day in History **history.com/this-day-in-history.do**
Women in World History **womeninworldhistory.com**
America's Library **americaslibrary.gov**
PBS African American World **pbs.org/wnet/aaworld**
NativeWeb **nativeweb.org/resources/history**

Literature, Language and Communication

FCC Kids Zone **fcc.gov/cgb/kidszone**
Aaron Shepard's Home Page **aaronshep.com/index.html**
Sylvan Book Adventure **bookadventure.org/ki/bs/ki_bs_helpfind.asp**
ABC's of the Writing Process **angelfire.com/wi/writingprocess/index.html**
RIF Reading Planet **rif.org/readingplanet**
The Blue Book of Grammar and Punctuation **grammarbook.com**

Music, Games and Entertainment

Zoom: By Kids for Kids **pbskids.org/zoom/games/index.html**
Dallas Symphony Orchestra (DSO) Kids **dsokids.com/2001/rooms/musicroom.asp**
San Francisco Symphony (SFS) Kids **sfskids.org**
A Game a Day **agameaday.com**
PBS Kids Games **pbskids.org/games/index.html**
FunBrain.com **funbrain.com/kidscenter.html**
Club Penguin **clubpenguin.com**

Nature

Animal Corner **animalcorner.co.uk**
Kids' Planet **kidsplanet.org**
National Wildlife Federation **nwf.org/kids**

News and Current Events

TIME For Kids News **timeforkids.com/TFK/kids/news**

Science, Technology and Mathematics

The Exploratorium, San Francisco **exploratorium.edu**
Ask Dr. Universe **wsu.edu/DrUniverse**
The Yuckiest Site on the Internet **yucky.discovery.com/flash**
Discovery Kids **kids.discovery.com**
CoolMath.com **coolmath.com**
Webmath.com **webmath.com**
Ask Dr. Math **mathforum.org/dr.math**

Sports

Sports Illustrated Kids **sikids.com**
Major League Baseball **mlb.com**
Major League Soccer **mlsnet.com**
National Basketball Association **nba.com**
Women's National Basketball Association **wnba.com**
National Football League **nfl.com**
National Hockey League **nhl.com**

Cool Computer Facts

• The earliest electronic computers were a bit different from what we use today. The ENIAC computer (1946) cost more than $400,000, was 8 feet (3 m) tall and more than 100 feet (305 m) long, and weighed 60,000 lbs (27,216 kg)—not exactly a laptop!

BIGGEST COMPUTER EVER?

• The first Web page was put online on August 6, 1991.

• The first Apple computer, the Apple I, was made in 1976 and sold for just under $700. Only around 200 were made—by hand—by Steve Wozniak and Steve Jobs.

STEVE JOBS AND IPOD

• An average new computer today is about 4,000 times faster than the Apple I.

Shape Up Your Photos with Special Software

Computer programs like Adobe Photoshop are used to change digital photos, either to fix a problem in the picture or to make it look different. Here are some of the basic things that can be done with a photo-editing program.

- cropping, or cutting, a picture down to a different size or shape
- making the photo darker or lighter
- reducing that annoying red-eye effect that sometimes happens when you use a flash

You can also do more interesting things—say, taking your dog from one picture and placing her in front of the pyramids in Egypt in another photo. Special effects are also possible; you can make your photos look like they were painted with a brush or even carved out of stone!

Using Computers for Making Movies

One of the most exciting things computers are used for today is animation and special effects in movies. In the old days, moviemakers would create animated films by drawing a picture for each frame by hand. The film would then be played back at 20 or 24 frames per second. So that's a lot of drawing! Today, this work can be done by computers, and the results are amazing. *Toy Story* (1995) was the first completely computer-animated feature film. Since then, computer effects and animation have continued to wow audiences in movies like *WALL-E* (2008).

Computer-generated effects aren't just for animated movies. Sometimes what looks like a crazy costume is really the result of computer special effects, like the octopus-faced Davy Jones in the Pirates of the Caribbean series. Many movies have used effects and animation to create characters that aren't really there. *Jurassic Park* (1993) was one of the first movies to use CG (computer graphics) to simulate realistic-looking dinosaurs "acting" alongside actual people.

Filming in front of a blue screen allows CG effect makers to place actors in to virtual sets.

Cellular Technology

CELL PHONES are much more than voice-communication devices. Depending on the model you use, a cell phone can do many kinds of tasks, including sending and receiving e-mail and text messages, surfing the Internet, taking photographs, keeping track of appointments, flashing reminders, transmitting TV programs, navigating using global positioning and downloading music. How can a small handheld device do so much? It's all in the technology that supports it. Here are the basics.

Cell phones These are sophisticated radios that tune in to frequencies transmitted by towers that are located everywhere and cover a range of about 10 square miles (26 sq km) each.

Towers
These are usually made of steel and are hundreds of feet tall. Sometimes they are disguised to look like other structures, such

as flagpoles, bell towers and even trees. The towers have antennae and transmitters that are often shared by several different phone companies. As a cell phone user moves from place to place, a different tower picks up the phone's signal and transmits to it.

Technology Unlike a walkie-talkie or CB radio, with which only one person can speak at a time, cell phones have a dual-frequency capacity. They can send signals and receive them at the same time. Inside the phone is a microprocessor similar to one inside a computer. This is what enables the phone to act like a computer and do such a wide variety of tasks.

SATELLITE PHONES use a different technology. They bypass landlines and cellular networks by relying on "low Earth-orbiting" satellites to receive and relay phone messages. This technology is especially valuable during weather disasters, which can break land wires and topple cellular towers. The signal of a satellite call is sent to the satellites of the caller's phone company. The satellites receive the call and send it back to Earth using a ground station, or gateway. The gateway then uses regular landlines or cellular networks to send the call to the recipient.

WIRELESS FIDELITY (WiFi), or **BROADBAND SERVICE,** is a means of communication that uses low-power microwave radio signals to connect computers to other computers or Web sites using wireless network cards and hubs. The advantage of this system is that a computer need not be connected to an electrical or telephone outlet or cable line. Instead, a laptop can be carried from room to room without being plugged in.

TOP 5 Wi-Fi Friendly American Cities

1. **Seattle, Washington**
2. **San Francisco, California**
3. **Austin, Texas**
4. **Portland, Oregon**
5. **Atlanta, Georgia**

Source: Microsoft Small Business Center

Clue 1: I was born in Houston, Texas, in 1965.

Clue 2: In 1984, while in college, I launched a computer company called PC's Limited.

Clue 3: Today, my company, which carries my name, is a top seller of computers.

Who am I? _____

ANSWER ON PAGE 244.

Computers and Communication

47

Can India Save Its Working Kids?

FROM TFK MAGAZINE

Kailash Satyarthi speaking at the United Nations

Haldiram's Restaurant, in New Delhi, India, is crowded. Happy families enjoy dinner at large tables. At smaller tables sit girls called *ayahs*. They are the children's nannies. These girls are not much older than the kids they care for. Ayahs make very little money.

In India, putting children to work as maids and servants is a way of life. It is also against the law. Girls and boys do a variety of household chores. They also work in tea shops, hotels and restaurants. Working kids do not go to school.

The Indian government has a law that prohibits children under age 14 from working in dangerous jobs. In 2006, leaders added a ban on jobs in hotels, restaurants and homes. An Indian government agency estimates that nearly 13 million children under age 14 are working in India. But the real number may be between 75 million and 90 million.

The ban was a "positive step forward," says Farida Lambay, a children's rights worker. But many kids work to survive. The poor can't afford to send their kids to school.

A HELPING HAND

Kailash Satyarthi (*kay*-lash suth-*yar*-thee) has rescued more than 67,000 child workers. He has built three centers that teach the kids important life skills. Hundreds of these former laborers have become champions for change in their communities.

Satyarthi has also spoken to Indian officials and world leaders. Indian businesses are realizing that the country's future lies in educating its youth. One large company has set up 10,000 libraries in rural areas across the country. Another will help pay for 7,500 schools. Changes such as these will bring about a future in which all children will work side by side in school.

Young children working at an embroidery shop in India.

THE WORLD'S NATIONS
FROM A TO Z

On the following pages you will find information about the world's nations. Here's an example.

This tells the main languages and the official languages (if any) spoken in a nation.

This is the type of currency, or money, used in the nation.

Life expectancy is the number of years a person can expect to live. It's affected by heredity, a person's health and nutrition, the health care and wealth of a nation, and a person's occupation.

This tells the percentage of people who can read and write.

If you divide the population by the area, you can find out the population density—how many people there are per square mile.

INDIA
LOCATION: Asia
CAPITAL: New Delhi
AREA: 1,269,338 sq mi (3,287,590 sq km)
POPULATION ESTIMATE (2009): 1,166,079,217
GOVERNMENT: Federal Republic
LANGUAGES: Hindi (national), English; 14 other official languages
MONEY: Indian rupee
LIFE EXPECTANCY: 69.9
LITERACY RATE: 61%

guess what? *Every fall, thousands of people travel to Pushkar for the annual camel fair, which is thought to be the largest livesto...*

This is an interesting fact about the country.

AFGHANISTAN
LOCATION: Asia
CAPITAL: Kabul
AREA: 251,737 sq mi (647,500 sq km)
POPULATION ESTIMATE (2009): 33,609,937
GOVERNMENT: Islamic republic
LANGUAGES: Pushto and Dari (both official), others
MONEY: Afghani
LIFE EXPECTANCY: 44.6
LITERACY RATE: 28%

guess what? *Afghanistan is slightly smaller than the U.S. state of Texas.*

ALBANIA
LOCATION: Europe
CAPITAL: Tirana
AREA: 11,100 sq mi (28,750 sq km)
POPULATION ESTIMATE (2009): 3,639,453
GOVERNMENT: Emerging democracy
LANGUAGES: Albanian (Tosk is the official dialect), Greek
MONEY: Lek
LIFE EXPECTANCY: 78
LITERACY RATE: 99%

guess what? *Albania is the only European country in which a majority of its citizens practice Islam.*

ALGERIA
LOCATION: Africa
CAPITAL: Algiers
AREA: 919,590 sq mi (2,381,740 sq km)
POPULATION ESTIMATE (2009): 34,178,188
GOVERNMENT: Republic
LANGUAGES: Arabic (official), French, Berber dialects
MONEY: Dinar
LIFE EXPECTANCY: 74
LITERACY RATE: 70%

guess what? *Algeria became independent from France in 1962 after 130 years of French occupation.*

ANDORRA
LOCATION: Europe
CAPITAL: Andorra la Vella
AREA: 181 sq mi (468 sq km)
POPULATION ESTIMATE (2009): 83,888
GOVERNMENT: Parliamentary democracy
LANGUAGES: Catalan (official), French, Castilian, Portuguese
MONEY: Euro (formerly French franc and Spanish peseta)
LIFE EXPECTANCY: 82.5
LITERACY RATE: 100%

guess what? *Many tourists visit Andorra for the great skiing that can be found there.*

ANGOLA

LOCATION: Africa
CAPITAL: Luanda
AREA: 481,350 sq mi
(1,246,700 sq km)
POPULATION ESTIMATE (2009):
12,799,293
GOVERNMENT: Republic
LANGUAGES: Bantu, Portuguese
(official)
MONEY: Kwanza
LIFE EXPECTANCY: 38.2
LITERACY RATE: 67%

guess what? *After many years of civil war, Angola's countryside is filled with many dangerous land mines.*

ANTIGUA AND BARBUDA

LOCATION: Caribbean
CAPITAL: St. John's
AREA: 171 sq mi (443 sq km)
POPULATION ESTIMATE (2009): 85,632
GOVERNMENT: Constitutional
monarchy
LANGUAGE: English
MONEY: East Caribbean dollar
LIFE EXPECTANCY: 74.8
LITERACY RATE: 86%

guess what? *In 1995, Hurricane Luis hit Antigua and Barbuda. The winds, which blew at more than 125 mph (210 km/h), damaged every hotel on Barbuda and nearly 75% of the houses on Antigua.*

ARGENTINA

LOCATION: South America
CAPITAL: Buenos Aires
AREA: 1,068,296 sq mi
(2,766,890 sq km)
POPULATION ESTIMATE (2009):
40,913,584
GOVERNMENT: Republic
LANGUAGES: Spanish (official),
English, Italian, German, French
MONEY: Argentine peso
LIFE EXPECTANCY: 76.6
LITERACY RATE: 97%

guess what? *Argentina's Parque Nacional Laguna Blanca is one of two swan sanctuaries in the Western Hemisphere.*

ARMENIA

LOCATION: Asia
CAPITAL: Yerevan
AREA: 11,487 sq mi
(29,750 sq km)
POPULATION ESTIMATE (2009):
2,967,004
GOVERNMENT: Republic
LANGUAGE: Armenian
MONEY: Dram
LIFE EXPECTANCY: 72.7
LITERACY RATE: 99%

guess what? *Armenia was the smallest Soviet Republic from 1920 until the breakup of the Soviet Union in 1991.*

AUSTRALIA

LOCATION: Oceania
CAPITAL: Canberra
AREA: 2,967,893 sq mi
(7,686,850 sq km)
POPULATION ESTIMATE (2009):
21,262,641
GOVERNMENT: Democracy
LANGUAGE: English
MONEY: Australian dollar
LIFE EXPECTANCY: 81.6
LITERACY RATE: 99%

guess what? *Images carved into rocks by aborigines can be found in Australia. Some of these **engravings** are more than 40,000 years old.*

AUSTRIA

LOCATION: Europe
CAPITAL: Vienna
AREA: 32,382 sq mi
(83,870 sq km)
POPULATION ESTIMATE (2009):
8,210,281
GOVERNMENT: Federal Republic
LANGUAGE: German
MONEY: Euro (formerly schilling)
LIFE EXPECTANCY: 79.5
LITERACY RATE: 98%

guess what? *Austria is made up of nine federal provinces, each with its own government. On May 15, 1955, the country declared its permanent neutrality in future wars.*

AZERBAIJAN

LOCATION: Asia
CAPITAL: Baku
AREA: 33,400 sq mi
(86,600 sq km)
POPULATION ESTIMATE (2009):
8,238,672
GOVERNMENT: Republic
LANGUAGES: Azerbaijani, Lezgi,
Russian, Armenian
MONEY: Azerbaijani manat
LIFE EXPECTANCY: 66.7
LITERACY RATE: 99%

Guess what? *Azerbaijan was a major stop on the trade routes that ran from Europe to Asia in the 13th, 14th and 15th centuries.*

BAHAMAS

LOCATION: North America
CAPITAL: Nassau
AREA: 5,380 sq mi
(13,940 sq km)
POPULATION ESTIMATE (2009): 309,156
GOVERNMENT: Parliamentary
democracy
LANGUAGES: English, Creole
MONEY: Bahamian dollar
LIFE EXPECTANCY: 65.8
LITERACY RATE: 96%

Guess what? ***Christopher Columbus*** *landed on the islands of the Bahamas in 1492 during his quest to find a new route to India. He called the area* Baja Mar, *or Shallow Sea.*

BAHRAIN

LOCATION: Middle East
CAPITAL: Manama
AREA: 257 sq mi (665 sq km)
POPULATION ESTIMATE (2009): 727,785
GOVERNMENT: Constitutional
monarchy
LANGUAGES: Arabic, English,
Farsi, Urdu
MONEY: Bahraini dinar
LIFE EXPECTANCY: 75.2
LITERACY RATE: 87%

Guess what? *The earliest recorded reference to what is now Bahrain dates to around 3000 B.C. when the country was known as Dilmun.*

BANGLADESH

LOCATION: Asia
CAPITAL: Dhaka
AREA: 55,598 sq mi
(144,000 sq km)
POPULATION ESTIMATE (2009):
156,050,883
GOVERNMENT: Parliamentary
democracy
LANGUAGES: Bangla (official),
English
MONEY: Taka
LIFE EXPECTANCY: 60.3
LITERACY RATE: 43%

Guess what? *Most of Bangladesh was originally called East Bengal and was a province of Pakistan from 1955 until 1971. Every year, about one-third of the country floods during the rainy season.*

BARBADOS

LOCATION: Caribbean
CAPITAL: Bridgetown
AREA: 166 sq mi (431 sq km)
POPULATION ESTIMATE (2009): 284,589
GOVERNMENT: Parliamentary
democracy
LANGUAGE: English
MONEY: Barbadian dollar
LIFE EXPECTANCY: 73.9
LITERACY RATE: 100%

Guess what? *Sugar production was the main industry of Barbados until the 1990s, when tourism became more important to the economy.*

BELARUS

LOCATION: Europe
CAPITAL: Minsk
AREA: 80,154 sq mi
(207,600 sq km)
POPULATION ESTIMATE (2009):
9,648,533
GOVERNMENT: Republic
LANGUAGES: Belarusian, Russian
MONEY: Belarusian ruble
LIFE EXPECTANCY: 70.6
LITERACY RATE: 100%

Guess what? *In 1887, the painter **Marc Chagall** was born in what is now Belarus.*

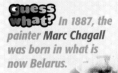

BELGIUM

LOCATION: Europe
CAPITAL: Brussels
AREA: 11,787 sq mi
(30,528 sq km)
POPULATION ESTIMATE (2009):
10,414,336
GOVERNMENT: Parliamentary
democracy under a
constitutional monarchy
LANGUAGES: Dutch (Flemish),
French, German (all official)
MONEY: Euro (formerly
Belgian franc)
LIFE EXPECTANCY: 79.2
LITERACY RATE: 99%

Guess what? *Belgium has more castles per square mile than anywhere else in the world.*

BELIZE

LOCATION: Central America
CAPITAL: Belmopan
AREA: 8,867 sq mi
(22,966 sq km)
POPULATION ESTIMATE (2009): 307,899
GOVERNMENT: Parliamentary
democracy
LANGUAGES: English (official),
Creole, Spanish, Garifuna,
Mayan
MONEY: Belizean dollar
LIFE EXPECTANCY: 68.2
LITERACY RATE: 77%

Guess what? *There are more than 125 species of animals native to Belize, including three species of turtles and five species of wild cats.*

BENIN

LOCATION: Africa
CAPITAL: Porto-Novo
AREA: 43,483 sq mi
(112,620 sq km)
POPULATION ESTIMATE (2009):
8,791,832
GOVERNMENT: Republic
LANGUAGES: French (official),
Fon, Yoruba, other African
languages
MONEY: CFA franc
LIFE EXPECTANCY: 59
LITERACY RATE: 35%

Guess what? *Benin is made up of 42 African ethnic groups, with the majority living in the south.*

BHUTAN

LOCATION: Asia
CAPITAL: Thimphu
AREA: 18,147 sq mi
(47,000 sq km)
POPULATION ESTIMATE (2009): 691,141
GOVERNMENT: Constitutional
monarchy
LANGUAGE: Dzongkha
MONEY: Ngultrum
LIFE EXPECTANCY: 66.1
LITERACY RATE: 47%

Guess what? *The national animal of Bhutan is the takin. Herds of takin live at altitudes higher than 13,000 feet (3,962 m).*

BOLIVIA

LOCATION: South America
CAPITALS: La Paz (seat of
government), Sucre
(legal capital)
AREA: 424,162 sq mi
(1,098,580 sq km)
POPULATION ESTIMATE (2009):
9,775,246
GOVERNMENT: Republic
LANGUAGES: Spanish, Quechua,
Aymara (all official)
MONEY: Boliviano
LIFE EXPECTANCY: 66.9
LITERACY RATE: 87%

Guess what? *Bolivia and Paraguay are the only two landlocked countries in South America.*

BOSNIA AND HERZEGOVINA

LOCATION: Europe
CAPITAL: Sarajevo
AREA: 19,772 sq mi (51,209 sq km)
POPULATION ESTIMATE (2009): 4,613,414
GOVERNMENT: Emerging democracy
LANGUAGE: The language is called
Serbian, Croatian or Bosnian
depending on the speaker.
MONEY: Convertible mark
LIFE EXPECTANCY: 78.5
LITERACY RATE: 96.7%

Guess what? *The Bridge of Mostar is one of the country's most famous landmarks. The 400-year-old bridge was destroyed during the civil war in the 1990s and rebuilt in 2004.*

BOTSWANA

LOCATION: Africa
CAPITAL: Gaborone
AREA: 231,800 sq mi (600,370 sq km)
POPULATION ESTIMATE (2009): 1,990,876
GOVERNMENT: Parliamentary republic
LANGUAGES: English (official), Setswana, Kalanga, Sekgalagadi
MONEY: Pula
LIFE EXPECTANCY: 61.9
LITERACY RATE: 81%

guess what? *Diamonds were found in Botswana in 1967. It is currently one of the world's biggest diamond producers.*

BRAZIL

LOCATION: South America
CAPITAL: Brasília
AREA: 3,286,470 sq mi (8,511,965 sq km)
POPULATION ESTIMATE (2009): 198,739,269
GOVERNMENT: Federal republic
LANGUAGES: Portuguese (official), Spanish, English
MONEY: Real
LIFE EXPECTANCY: 72
LITERACY RATE: 89%

guess what? *The official language of Brazil is Portuguese, unlike the rest of South America, whose residents speak Spanish.*

BRUNEI

LOCATION: Asia
CAPITAL: Bandar Seri Begawan
AREA: 2,228 sq mi (5,770 sq km)
POPULATION ESTIMATE (2009): 388,190
GOVERNMENT: Constitutional sultanate
LANGUAGES: Malay (official), Chinese, English
MONEY: Bruneian dollar
LIFE EXPECTANCY: 75.7
LITERACY RATE: 93%

guess what? *The buildings in Kampong Ayer (Water Village) are constructed on stilts above the Brunei River. About 30,000 people live in this area of the capital.*

BULGARIA

LOCATION: Europe
CAPITAL: Sofia
AREA: 48,822 sq mi (110,910 sq km)
POPULATION ESTIMATE (2009): 7,204,687
GOVERNMENT: Parliamentary democracy
LANGUAGES: Bulgarian, Turkish
MONEY: Lev
LIFE EXPECTANCY: 73.1
LITERACY RATE: 98%

guess what? *There are more than 600 mineral springs in Bulgaria.*

BURKINA FASO

LOCATION: Africa
CAPITAL: Ouagadougou
AREA: 105,870 sq mi (274,200 sq km)
POPULATION ESTIMATE (2009): 15,746,232
GOVERNMENT: Parliamentary republic
LANGUAGES: French (official), tribal languages
MONEY: CFA franc
LIFE EXPECTANCY: 53
LITERACY RATE: 22%

guess what? *The Black Volta, or Mouhoun River, is home to a large population of hippos.*

BURUNDI

LOCATION: Africa
CAPITAL: Bujumbura
AREA: 10,745 sq mi (27,830 sq km)
POPULATION ESTIMATE (2009): 8,988,091
GOVERNMENT: Republic
LANGUAGES: Kirundi and French (both official), Swahili
MONEY: Burundi franc
LIFE EXPECTANCY: 52.1
LITERACY RATE: 59%

guess what? *Almost all of Burundi is located at more than 3,000 feet (914 m) above sea level.*

CAMBODIA

LOCATION: Asia
CAPITAL: Phnom Penh
AREA: 69,900 sq mi
(181,040 sq km)
POPULATION ESTIMATE (2009):
14,494,293
GOVERNMENT: Multiparty
democracy under a
constitutional monarchy
LANGUAGES: Khmer (official),
French, English
MONEY: Riel
LIFE EXPECTANCY: 62.1
LITERACY RATE: 74%

guess what? *Every fall, the
end of the rainy season is
celebrated with a festival
called Bon Om Tuk. Millions of
people come to Phnom Penh to
participate in the festivities.*

CAMEROON

LOCATION: Africa
CAPITAL: Yaoundé
AREA: 183,567 sq mi
(475,440 sq km)
POPULATION ESTIMATE (2009):
18,879,301
GOVERNMENT: Republic
LANGUAGES: French and
English (both official),
African languages
MONEY: CFA franc
LIFE EXPECTANCY: 53.7
LITERACY RATE: 68%

guess what? *Cameroon's name
comes from the giant shrimp
that Portuguese explorers
found off its coast when they
landed in 1472. The Portuguese
word for shrimp is camerão.*

CANADA

LOCATION: North America
CAPITAL: Ottawa, Ontario
AREA: 3,855,081 sq mi
(9,984,670 sq km)
POPULATION ESTIMATE (2009):
33,487,208
GOVERNMENT: Parliamentary
democracy
LANGUAGES: English and French
(both official)
MONEY: Canadian dollar
LIFE EXPECTANCY: 81.2
LITERACY RATE: 99%

guess what? *There are an
estimated 500,000
to 1 million moose in Canada.
They are found in every
province of the country and
live to be 15 to 25 years old.*

CAPE VERDE

LOCATION: Africa
CAPITAL: Praia
AREA: 1,557 sq mi (4,033 sq km)
POPULATION ESTIMATE (2009): 429,474
GOVERNMENT: Republic
LANGUAGES: Portuguese, Crioulo
MONEY: Cape Verdean escudo
LIFE EXPECTANCY: 71.6
LITERACY RATE: 77%

guess what? *These islands off
the west coast of Africa were
formed by volcanoes.*

CENTRAL AFRICAN REPUBLIC

LOCATION: Africa
CAPITAL: Bangui
AREA: 240,534 sq mi
(622,984 sq km)
POPULATION ESTIMATE (2009):
4,511,488
GOVERNMENT: Republic
LANGUAGES: French (official),
Sangho, other African
languages
MONEY: CFA franc
LIFE EXPECTANCY: 44.4
LITERACY RATE: 49%

guess what? *Two species of
mouse, the oubangui and the
gounda, are native to the
Central African Republic.*

CHAD

LOCATION: Africa
CAPITAL: N'Djamena
AREA: 495,752 sq mi
(1,284,000 sq km)
POPULATION ESTIMATE (2009):
10,329,208
GOVERNMENT: Republic
LANGUAGES: French and Arabic
(both official), Sara, others
MONEY: CFA franc
LIFE EXPECTANCY: 47.7
LITERACY RATE: 26%

guess what? *Archaeologists
have found many fossils and
ancient hunting tools in the
dried-up lakes and riverbeds
throughout Chad, including a
skull that is between 6 million
and 7 million years old.*

CHILE

LOCATION: South America
CAPITAL: **Santiago**
AREA: 292,258 sq mi
(756,950 sq km)
POPULATION ESTIMATE (2009):
16,601,707
GOVERNMENT: Republic
LANGUAGES: Spanish (official),
Mapudungun, German, English
MONEY: Chilean peso
LIFE EXPECTANCY: 77.3
LITERACY RATE: 96%

 *Chile is the longest country on Earth. Its length (2,700 miles/4,300 km) is 18 times the country's widest point (150 miles/ 240 km).*

CHINA

LOCATION: Asia
CAPITAL: Beijing
AREA: 3,705,386 sq mi
(9,596,960 sq km)
POPULATION ESTIMATE (2009):
1,338,612,968
GOVERNMENT: Communist state
LANGUAGES: Chinese (Mandarin),
Yue (Cantonese), local dialects
MONEY: Renminbi, Yuan
LIFE EXPECTANCY: 73.5
LITERACY RATE: 91%

 A terrible earthquake struck China's Sichuan province in May 2008, killing nearly 70,000 people.

COLOMBIA

LOCATION: South America
CAPITAL: Bogotá
AREA: 439,733 sq mi
(1,138,910 sq km)
POPULATION ESTIMATE (2009):
45,644,023
GOVERNMENT: Republic
LANGUAGE: Spanish
MONEY: Colombian peso
LIFE EXPECTANCY: 72.8
LITERACY RATE: 93%

Colombia is the only country in South America with coastlines on both the Pacific Ocean and Caribbean Sea.

COMOROS

LOCATION: Africa
CAPITAL: Moroni
AREA: 838 sq mi (2,170 sq km)
POPULATION ESTIMATE (2009): 752,438
GOVERNMENT: Republic
LANGUAGES: French and Arabic
(both official), Shikomoro
MONEY: Comoran franc
LIFE EXPECTANCY: 63.5
LITERACY RATE: 57%

From 1997 to 2001, each island of Comoros was a separate country. They reunified in December 2001 and became the Union of Comoros.

CONGO, DEMOCRATIC REPUBLIC OF THE

LOCATION: Africa
CAPITAL: Kinshasa
AREA: 905,562 sq mi
(2,345,410 sq km)
POPULATION ESTIMATE (2009):
68,692,542
GOVERNMENT: Republic
LANGUAGES: French (official),
Lingala, Kingwana, others
MONEY: Congolese franc
LIFE EXPECTANCY: 54.4
LITERACY RATE: 67%

Kinshasa is directly across the Congo River from Brazzaville, the capital of the Republic of Congo. This is the only place where two capitals face each other in this way.

CONGO, REPUBLIC OF THE

LOCATION: Africa
CAPITAL: Brazzaville
AREA: 132,046 sq mi
(342,000 sq km)
POPULATION ESTIMATE (2009):
4,012,809
GOVERNMENT: Republic
LANGUAGES: French (official),
Lingala, Kikongo, others
MONEY: CFA franc
LIFE EXPECTANCY: 54.2
LITERACY RATE: 84%

*The Republic of the Congo is home to one of the world's largest populations of **chimpanzees.***

COSTA RICA

LOCATION: Central America
CAPITAL: San José
AREA: 19,730 sq mi
(51,100 sq km)
POPULATION ESTIMATE (2009):
4,253,877
GOVERNMENT: Democratic republic
LANGUAGES: Spanish, English
MONEY: Colón
LIFE EXPECTANCY: 77.6
LITERACY RATE: 95%

guess what? *Four of the world's seven species of **marine turtles** nest on Costa Rica's Pacific coast, including the leatherback, which is the largest marine turtle in the world.*

CÔTE D'IVOIRE

LOCATION: Africa
CAPITAL: Yamoussoukro
AREA: 124,502 sq mi
(322,460 sq km)
POPULATION ESTIMATE (2009):
20,617,068
GOVERNMENT: Republic
LANGUAGES: French (official),
African languages
MONEY: CFA franc
LIFE EXPECTANCY: 55.5
LITERACY RATE: 49%

guess what? *Côte D'Ivoire boasts a diverse tribal mixture including peoples of the Dan, Lobi, Baoulé and Senoufo ethnic groups.*

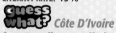

CROATIA

LOCATION: Europe
CAPITAL: Zagreb
AREA: 21,831 sq mi
(56,542 sq km)
POPULATION ESTIMATE (2009):
4,489,409
GOVERNMENT: Parliamentary
democracy
LANGUAGES: Croatian, Serbian
MONEY: Kuna
LIFE EXPECTANCY: 75.4
LITERACY RATE: 98%

guess what? *The city of **Dubrovnik** is entirely enclosed by stone walls, some of which date from the 13th century.*

CUBA

LOCATION: Caribbean
CAPITAL: Havana
AREA: 42,803 sq mi
(110,860 sq km)
POPULATION ESTIMATE (2009):
11,451,652
GOVERNMENT: Communist state
LANGUAGE: Spanish
MONEY: Peso
LIFE EXPECTANCY: 77.5
LITERACY RATE: 100%

guess what? *The Cuevas de Punta del Este (Caves of the Easter Point) on Cuba's Isla de la Juventud contain about 200 drawings made by Indians in pre-Columbian times.*

CYPRUS

LOCATION: Europe
CAPITAL: Nicosia
AREA: 3,571 sq mi (9,250 sq km)
POPULATION ESTIMATE (2009): 796,740
GOVERNMENT: Republic
LANGUAGES: Greek, Turkish,
English
MONEY: Euro (formerly Cyprus
pound), Turkish new lira
LIFE EXPECTANCY: 78.3
LITERACY RATE: 98%

guess what? *The island of Cyprus gets its name from the Greek word for copper, kypros.*

CZECH REPUBLIC

LOCATION: Europe
CAPITAL: Prague
AREA: 30,450 sq mi
(78,866 sq km)
POPULATION ESTIMATE (2009):
10,221,904
GOVERNMENT: Parliamentary
democracy
LANGUAGES: Czech, Slovak
MONEY: Koruna
LIFE EXPECTANCY: 76.8
LITERACY RATE: 99%

guess what? *The Czech Republic is nicknamed the Heart of Europe.*

DENMARK

LOCATION: Europe
CAPITAL: Copenhagen
AREA: 16,639 sq mi
(43,094 sq km)
POPULATION ESTIMATE (2009):
5,500,510
GOVERNMENT: Constitutional
monarchy
LANGUAGES: Danish, Faroese,
Greenlandic, German
MONEY: Krone
LIFE EXPECTANCY: 78.3
LITERACY RATE: 99%

guess what? *Denmark's Jesperhus Flower Park is the largest flower park in Scandinavia. It contains thousands of flowers, a zoo and an amusement park.*

DJIBOUTI

LOCATION: Africa
CAPITAL: Djibouti
AREA: 8,800 sq mi
(23,000 sq km)
POPULATION ESTIMATE (2009): 516,055
GOVERNMENT: Republic
LANGUAGES: Arabic and French
(both official), Somali, Afar
MONEY: Djiboutian franc
LIFE EXPECTANCY: 43.4
LITERACY RATE: 68%

guess what? *Flocks of flamingos gather every day to drink and feed at Lac Abbé, located on Djibouti's Ethiopian border.*

DOMINICA

LOCATION: Caribbean
CAPITAL: Roseau
AREA: 291 sq mi (754 sq km)
POPULATION ESTIMATE (2009): 72,660
GOVERNMENT: Parliamentary
democracy
LANGUAGES: English (official),
French patois
MONEY: East Caribbean dollar
LIFE EXPECTANCY: 75.5
LITERACY RATE: 94%

guess what? *The world's second-largest boiling lake is located in Dominica. The boiling is caused by hot gases escaping from a crack in Earth's crust.*

DOMINICAN REPUBLIC

LOCATION: Caribbean
CAPITAL: Santo Domingo
AREA: 18,815 sq mi
(48,730 sq km)
POPULATION ESTIMATE (2009):
9,650,054
GOVERNMENT: Democratic republic
LANGUAGE: Spanish
MONEY: Dominican peso
LIFE EXPECTANCY: 73.7
LITERACY RATE: 87%

guess what? *Restoration Day marks the day that reestablished the Dominican Republic's independence from Haiti in 1865.*

EAST TIMOR

LOCATION: Asia
CAPITAL: Dili
AREA: 5,794 sq mi
(15,007 sq km)
POPULATION ESTIMATE (2009):
1,131,612
GOVERNMENT: Republic
LANGUAGES: Tetum and
Portuguese (both official),
Indonesian, English
MONEY: U.S. dollar
LIFE EXPECTANCY: 67
LITERACY RATE: 59%

guess what? *Tetum, a Malayo-Polynesian language influenced by Portuguese, is the national language of East Timor.*

ECUADOR

LOCATION: South America
CAPITAL: Quito
AREA: 109,483 sq mi
(283,560 sq km)
POPULATION ESTIMATE (2009):
14,573,101
GOVERNMENT: Republic
LANGUAGES: Spanish (official),
Quechua
MONEY: U.S. dollar
LIFE EXPECTANCY: 75.3
LITERACY RATE: 91%

guess what? *Cuy, or guinea pig, is a traditional food in Ecuador.*

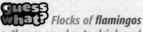

Countries

EGYPT

LOCATION: Africa
CAPITAL: Cairo
AREA: 386,660 sq mi
(1,001,450 sq km)
POPULATION ESTIMATE (2009):
83,082,869
GOVERNMENT: Republic
LANGUAGE: Arabic
MONEY: Egyptian pound
LIFE EXPECTANCY: 72.2
LITERACY RATE: 71%

 In ancient Egypt, onions were considered symbols of eternity and were often buried with pharaohs.

EL SALVADOR

LOCATION: Central America
CAPITAL: San Salvador
AREA: 8,124 sq mi
(21,040 sq km)
POPULATION ESTIMATE (2009):
7,185,218
GOVERNMENT: Republic
LANGUAGE: Spanish
MONEY: U.S. dollar
LIFE EXPECTANCY: 72.3
LITERACY RATE: 80%

 The Santa Ana Volcano, El Salvador's highest peak, erupted in 2005, causing surprisingly few fatalities.

EQUATORIAL GUINEA

LOCATION: Africa
CAPITAL: Malabo
AREA: 10,830 sq mi
(28,051 sq km)
POPULATION ESTIMATE (2009): 633,441
GOVERNMENT: Republic
LANGUAGES: Spanish (official),
French (second official),
Fang, Bubi
MONEY: CFA franc
LIFE EXPECTANCY: 61.6
LITERACY RATE: 87%

 Equatorial Guinea is one of Africa's smallest countries. It is made up of a mainland area and five small islands off the west coast of the continent.

ERITREA

LOCATION: Africa
CAPITAL: Asmara
AREA: 46,842 sq mi
(121,320 sq km)
POPULATION ESTIMATE (2009):
5,647,168
GOVERNMENT: Transitional
LANGUAGES: Afar, Arabic, Tigre,
Kunama, Tigrinya, others
MONEY: Nakfa
LIFE EXPECTANCY: 61.8
LITERACY RATE: 59%

 *Eritrea and Ethiopia have been involved in a border dispute since 1998.*

ESTONIA

LOCATION: Europe
CAPITAL: Tallinn
AREA: 17,462 sq mi
(45,226 sq km)
POPULATION ESTIMATE (2009):
1,299,371
GOVERNMENT: Parliamentary
republic
LANGUAGES: Estonian (official),
Russian
MONEY: Kroon
LIFE EXPECTANCY: 72.8
LITERACY RATE: 100%

*The **Tahkuna Lighthouse** on the island of Hiiumaa is 140 feet (42.6 m) high. Its light can be seen for 12 nautical miles.*

ETHIOPIA

LOCATION: Africa
CAPITAL: Addis Ababa
AREA: 435,184 sq mi
(1,127,127 sq km)
POPULATION ESTIMATE (2009):
85,237,338
GOVERNMENT: Federal republic
LANGUAGES: Amharic (official),
Oromigna, Tigrigna, Somaligna,
others
MONEY: Birr
LIFE EXPECTANCY: 55.4
LITERACY RATE: 43%

Muslims consider Harar to be the fourth Holy City, following Mecca, Medina and Jerusalem.

FIJI

LOCATION: Oceania
CAPITAL: Suva
AREA: 7,054 sq mi
(18,270 sq km)
POPULATION ESTIMATE (2009): 944,720
GOVERNMENT: Republic
LANGUAGES: Fijian and English
(both official), Hindustani
MONEY: Fijian dollar
LIFE EXPECTANCY: 68.2
LITERACY RATE: 94%

Guess what? *The Fijian monkey-faced bat is native to a single mountain on Taveuni Island in Fiji.*

FINLAND

LOCATION: Europe
CAPITAL: Helsinki
AREA: 130,127 sq mi
(337,030 sq km)
POPULATION ESTIMATE (2009):
5,250,275
GOVERNMENT: Republic
LANGUAGES: Finnish and Swedish
(both official)
MONEY: Euro (formerly markka)
LIFE EXPECTANCY: 75.5
LITERACY RATE: 100%

Guess what? *Some Finns say their country is the home of **Santa Claus**. In the town of Rovaniemi, tourists can visit Santa Claus Village.*

FRANCE

LOCATION: Europe
CAPITAL: Paris
AREA: 211,208 sq mi
(547,030 sq km)
POPULATION ESTIMATE (2009):
64,057,792
GOVERNMENT: Republic
LANGUAGE: French
MONEY: Euro (formerly franc)
LIFE EXPECTANCY: 77.8
LITERACY RATE: 99%

Guess what? *France is the largest nation in western Europe. It shares borders with eight countries: Italy, Switzerland, Germany, Luxembourg, Belgium, Spain, Andorra and Monaco.*

GABON

LOCATION: Africa
CAPITAL: Libreville
AREA: 103,346 sq mi
(267,667 sq km)
POPULATION ESTIMATE (2009):
1,514,993
GOVERNMENT: Republic
LANGUAGES: French (official),
Fang, Myene, Nzebi,
Bapounou/Eschira, Bandjabi
MONEY: CFA franc
LIFE EXPECTANCY: 52.2
LITERACY RATE: 63%

Guess what? *Gabon is home to 200 mammal species, more than 670 species of birds and an estimated 8,000 to 10,000 types of plants.*

THE GAMBIA

LOCATION: Africa
CAPITAL: Banjul
AREA: 4,363 sq mi
(11,300 sq km)
POPULATION ESTIMATE (2009):
1,782,893
GOVERNMENT: Republic
LANGUAGES: English (official),
Mandinka, Wolof, Fula, others
MONEY: Dalasi
LIFE EXPECTANCY: 55.4
LITERACY RATE: 40%

Guess what? *President Franklin D. Roosevelt spent the night in Banjul in 1943—the first time a U.S. President visited the African continent while in office.*

GEORGIA

LOCATION: Asia
CAPITAL: Tbilisi
AREA: 26,911 sq mi
(69,700 sq km)
POPULATION ESTIMATE (2009):
4,615,807
GOVERNMENT: Republic
LANGUAGES: Georgian (official),
Russian, Armenian, Azeri
MONEY: Lari
LIFE EXPECTANCY: 76.7
LITERACY RATE: 100%

Guess what? *Georgia was invaded by Russia in August 2008.*

GERMANY

LOCATION: Europe
CAPITAL: Berlin
AREA: 137,846 sq mi
(357,021 sq km)
POPULATION ESTIMATE (2009):
82,329,758
GOVERNMENT: Federal republic
LANGUAGE: German
MONEY: Euro (formerly
deutsche mark)
LIFE EXPECTANCY: 79.3
LITERACY RATE: 99%

Guess what? *The garden gnome was invented in Thuringia, Germany, in the mid-1800s.*

GHANA

LOCATION: Africa
CAPITAL: Accra
AREA: 92,456 sq mi
(239,460 sq km)
POPULATION ESTIMATE (2009):
23,832,495
GOVERNMENT: Constitutional
democracy
LANGUAGES: Asante, Ewe, Fante,
others
MONEY: Cedi
LIFE EXPECTANCY: 59.9
LITERACY RATE: 58%

Guess what? *Lake Volta, in the southeast region of Ghana, is the largest man-made lake in the world.*

GREECE

LOCATION: Europe
CAPITAL: Athens
AREA: 50,942 sq mi
(131,940 sq km)
POPULATION ESTIMATE (2009):
10,737,428
GOVERNMENT: Parliamentary
republic
LANGUAGE: Greek
MONEY: Euro (formerly drachma)
LIFE EXPECTANCY: 79.7
LITERACY RATE: 96%

Guess what? *The ancient Olympics began in Greece in 776 B.C. and ended in A.D. 393. The modern Olympic Games launched in Athens in 1896.*

GRENADA

LOCATION: Caribbean
CAPITAL: Saint George's
AREA: 133 sq mi (344 sq km)
POPULATION ESTIMATE (2009): 90,739
GOVERNMENT: Parliamentary
democracy
LANGUAGES: English (official),
French patois
MONEY: East Caribbean dollar
LIFE EXPECTANCY: 66
LITERACY RATE: 96%

Guess what? *The small nation of Grenada is made up of three islands: Grenada, Carriacou and Petit Martinique.*

GUATEMALA

LOCATION: Central America
CAPITAL: Guatemala City
AREA: 42,042 sq mi
(108,890 sq km)
POPULATION ESTIMATE (2009):
13,276,517
GOVERNMENT: Republic
LANGUAGES: Spanish, Amerindian
languages
MONEY: Quetzal
LIFE EXPECTANCY: 70.3
LITERACY RATE: 69%

Guess what? *Guatemala City is actually Guatemala's third capital city. Its first, Ciudad Vieja, and second, Antigua, were destroyed by floods and earthquakes in 1542 and 1773.*

GUINEA

LOCATION: Africa
CAPITAL: Conakry
AREA: 94,925 sq mi
(245,860 sq km)
POPULATION ESTIMATE (2009):
10,057,975
GOVERNMENT: Republic
LANGUAGES: French (official),
native tongues
MONEY: Guinean franc
LIFE EXPECTANCY: 57.1
LITERACY RATE: 30%

Guess what? *This is one of the wettest places on Earth. Conakry gets about 169 inches (430 cm) of rain per year!*

GUINEA-BISSAU

LOCATION: Africa
CAPITAL: Bissau
AREA: 13,946 sq mi
(36,120 sq km)
POPULATION ESTIMATE (2009):
1,533,964
GOVERNMENT: Republic
LANGUAGES: Portuguese (official),
Crioulo, African languages
MONEY: CFA franc
LIFE EXPECTANCY: 47.9
LITERACY RATE: 42%

Guess what? *The islands off the coast of Guinea-Bissau make up the Bijagós Archipelago. These islands are home to sharks, manatees, turtles and other wildlife, including an incredibly rare type of hippopotamus.*

GUYANA

LOCATION: South America
CAPITAL: Georgetown
AREA: 83,000 sq mi
(214,970 sq km)
POPULATION ESTIMATE (2009): 772,298
GOVERNMENT: Republic
LANGUAGES: English (official),
Amerindian dialects, Creole
MONEY: Guyanese dollar
LIFE EXPECTANCY: 66.7
LITERACY RATE: 99%

Guess what? *Guyana is the only South American country in which English is the primary language.*

HAITI

LOCATION: Caribbean
CAPITAL: Port-au-Prince
AREA: 10,714 sq mi
(27,750 sq km)
POPULATION ESTIMATE (2009):
9,035,536
GOVERNMENT: Republic
LANGUAGES: Creole and French
(both official)
MONEY: Gourde
LIFE EXPECTANCY: 60.8
LITERACY RATE: 53%

Guess what? *Etang Saumâtre (Brackish Pond) is Haiti's largest saltwater lake and home to more than 100 species of animals, including flamingos and crocodiles.*

HONDURAS

LOCATION: Central America
CAPITAL: Tegucigalpa
AREA: 43,278 sq mi
(112,090 sq km)
POPULATION ESTIMATE (2009):
7,792,854
GOVERNMENT: Republic
LANGUAGES: Spanish, Amerindian
dialects
MONEY: Lempira
LIFE EXPECTANCY: 69.4
LITERACY RATE: 80%

Guess what? *This country was given its name, which means "the depths" (referring to the deep Caribbean waters off the east coast) by a Spanish explorer in the 16th century.*

HUNGARY

LOCATION: Europe
CAPITAL: Budapest
AREA: 35,919 sq mi
(93,030 sq km)
POPULATION ESTIMATE (2009):
9,905,596
GOVERNMENT: Parliamentary
democracy
LANGUAGE: Magyar (Hungarian)
MONEY: Forint
LIFE EXPECTANCY: 73.4
LITERACY RATE: 99%

Guess what? *Goulash, Hungary's national dish, is named after the herdsman, or gulyas, who used to eat it while out in the fields.*

ICELAND

LOCATION: Europe
CAPITAL: Reykjavík
AREA: 39,768 sq mi
(103,000 sq km)
POPULATION ESTIMATE (2009): 306,694
GOVERNMENT: Constitutional
republic
LANGUAGES: Icelandic, English
MONEY: Icelandic krona
LIFE EXPECTANCY: 80.7
LITERACY RATE: 99%

Guess what? *Formed from an explosion of an underwater volcano, Surtsey, the youngest island on Earth, became part of Iceland in 1963.*

INDIA

LOCATION: Asia
CAPITAL: New Delhi
AREA: 1,269,338 sq mi
(3,287,590 sq km)
POPULATION ESTIMATE (2009):
1,166,079,217
GOVERNMENT: Federal Republic
LANGUAGES: Hindi (national),
English; 14 other official
languages
MONEY: Indian rupee
LIFE EXPECTANCY: 69.9
LITERACY RATE: 61%

guess what? *Every fall, thousands of people travel to Pushkar for the annual* **camel fair,** *which is thought to be the largest livestock market on Earth.*

INDONESIA

LOCATION: Asia
CAPITAL: Jakarta
AREA: 741,096 sq mi
(1,919,440 sq km)
POPULATION ESTIMATE (2009):
240,271,522
GOVERNMENT: Republic
LANGUAGES: Bahasa Indonesia
(official), Dutch, English;
many local dialects
MONEY: Rupiah
LIFE EXPECTANCY: 70.8
LITERACY RATE: 90%

guess what? *Indonesia is home to the world's largest Muslim population. Nearly 90% of the population is Muslim. Christians and Hindus make up most of the remainder.*

IRAN

LOCATION: Middle East
CAPITAL: Tehran
AREA: 636,293 sq mi
(1,648,000 sq km)
POPULATION ESTIMATE (2009):
66,429,284
GOVERNMENT: Islamic theocracy
LANGUAGES: Persian, Turkic,
Kurdish
MONEY: Rial
LIFE EXPECTANCY: 71.1
LITERACY RATE: 77%

guess what? *Some villages in Iran are 6,000 years old.*

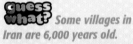

IRAQ

LOCATION: Middle East
CAPITAL: Baghdad
AREA: 168,753 sq mi
(437,072 sq km)
POPULATION ESTIMATE (2009):
28,945,647
GOVERNMENT: Parliamentary
democracy
LANGUAGES: Arabic, Kurdish
MONEY: New Iraqi dinar
LIFE EXPECTANCY: 69.9
LITERACY RATE: 74%

guess what? *The ancient city of Ur is now an archaeological site with buildings dating as far back as 4000 B.C.*

IRELAND

LOCATION: Europe
CAPITAL: Dublin
AREA: 27,136 sq mi
(70,280 sq km)
POPULATION ESTIMATE (2009):
4,203,200
GOVERNMENT: Republic
LANGUAGES: Irish (Gaelic), English
(both official)
MONEY: Euro (formerly Irish
pound, or punt)
LIFE EXPECTANCY: 78.2
LITERACY RATE: 99%

guess what? *The failure of potato crops in Ireland in the mid-1800s led to the Great Famine, during which nearly 1 million people died.*

ISRAEL

LOCATION: Middle East
CAPITAL: Jerusalem
AREA: 8,020 sq mi
(20,770 sq km)
POPULATION ESTIMATE (2009):
7,233,701
GOVERNMENT: Parliamentary
democracy
LANGUAGES: Hebrew (official),
Arabic, English
MONEY: Shekel
LIFE EXPECTANCY: 80.7
LITERACY RATE: 97%

guess what? *The water of the Dead Sea is roughly 10 times saltier than the water in Earth's oceans.*

ITALY

LOCATION: Europe
CAPITAL: Rome
AREA: 116,305 sq mi
(301,230 sq km)
POPULATION ESTIMATE (2009):
58,126,212
GOVERNMENT: Republic
LANGUAGES: Italian (official),
German, French, Slovene
MONEY: Euro (formerly lira)
LIFE EXPECTANCY: 80.2
LITERACY RATE: 98%

guess what? *The Duomo in Milan is one of the world's largest Gothic cathedrals.*

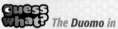

JAMAICA

LOCATION: Caribbean
CAPITAL: Kingston
AREA: 4,244 sq mi
(10,991 sq km)
POPULATION ESTIMATE (2009):
2,825,928
GOVERNMENT: Parliamentary
democracy
LANGUAGES: English, English patois
MONEY: Jamaican dollar
LIFE EXPECTANCY: 73.5
LITERACY RATE: 88%

guess what? *In 2006, Jamaica elected its first female prime minister, Portia Simpson Miller.*

JAPAN

LOCATION: Asia
CAPITAL: Tokyo
AREA: 145,882 sq mi
(377,835 sq km)
POPULATION ESTIMATE (2009):
127,078,679
GOVERNMENT: Constitutional
monarchy with a
parliamentary government
LANGUAGE: Japanese
MONEY: Yen
LIFE EXPECTANCY: 82.1
LITERACY RATE: 99%

guess what? *Japan is actually an archipelago made up of more than 3,000 islands.*

JORDAN

LOCATION: Middle East
CAPITAL: Amman
AREA: 35,637 sq mi
(92,300 sq km)
POPULATION ESTIMATE (2009):
6,342,948
GOVERNMENT: Constitutional
monarchy
LANGUAGES: Arabic (official)
MONEY: Jordanian dinar
LIFE EXPECTANCY: 78.8
LITERACY RATE: 90%

guess what? *Queen Noor of Jordan was born in Washington, D.C.*

KAZAKHSTAN

LOCATION: Asia
CAPITAL: Astana
AREA: 1,049,150 sq mi
(2,717,300 sq km)
POPULATION ESTIMATE (2009):
15,399,437
GOVERNMENT: Republic
LANGUAGES: Kazakh (Qazaq) and
Russian (both official)
MONEY: Tenge
LIFE EXPECTANCY: 67.9
LITERACY RATE: 100%

guess what? *Kazakhstan was once used for nuclear testing, so parts of the country are highly contaminated with radiation.*

KENYA

LOCATION: Africa
CAPITAL: Nairobi
AREA: 224,960 sq mi
(582,650 sq km)
POPULATION ESTIMATE (2009):
39,002,772
GOVERNMENT: Republic
LANGUAGES: English, Kiswahili
(both official), others
MONEY: Kenyan shilling
LIFE EXPECTANCY: 57.8
LITERACY RATE: 85%

guess what? *Elephants gather every night at Kitum, an underground cave near Mount Elgon on the Ugandan border. There, they feed on the cave's rich salt deposits.*

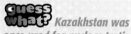

Countries

KIRIBATI

LOCATION: Oceania
CAPITAL: Tarawa
AREA: 313 sq mi (811 sq km)
POPULATION ESTIMATE (2009): 112,850
GOVERNMENT: Republic
LANGUAGES: English (official), I-Kiribati (Gilbertese)
MONEY: Australian dollar
LIFE EXPECTANCY: 63.2
LITERACY RATE: Not available

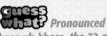 *Pronounced keer-uh-bhass, the 32 atolls that make up Kiribati cross the equator and are found between Hawaii and Australia. Atolls are ring-shaped coral islands with lagoons in the center.*

KOREA, NORTH

LOCATION: Asia
CAPITAL: Pyongyang
AREA: 46,540 sq mi (120,540 sq km)
POPULATION ESTIMATE (2009): 22,665,345
GOVERNMENT: Communist dictatorship
LANGUAGE: Korean
MONEY: North Korean Won
LIFE EXPECTANCY: 63.8
LITERACY RATE: 99%

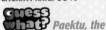 *Paektu, the country's highest mountain, is an extinct volcano with a huge crater lake at its summit.*

KOREA, SOUTH

LOCATION: Asia
CAPITAL: Seoul
AREA: 38,023 sq mi (98,480 sq km)
POPULATION ESTIMATE (2009): 48,508,972
GOVERNMENT: Republic
LANGUAGE: Korean
MONEY: South Korean Won
LIFE EXPECTANCY: 78.7
LITERACY RATE: 98%

 *Many kings have lived at the grand **Gyeongbokgung** palace, also known as the Northern Palace. It is now a museum and tourist destination.*

KOSOVO

LOCATION: Europe
CAPITAL: **Pristina**
AREA: 4,203 sq mi (10,887 sq km)
POPULATION ESTIMATE (2009): 1,804,838
GOVERNMENT: Republic
LANGUAGES: Albanian and Serbian (both official), Bosnian, Turkish, Roma
MONEY: Euro, Serbian dinar
LIFE EXPECTANCY: 75.1
LITERACY RATE: 96.4%

 *Kosovo's name means "field of blackbirds."*

KUWAIT

LOCATION: Middle East
CAPITAL: Kuwait
AREA: 6,880 sq mi (17,820 sq km)
POPULATION ESTIMATE (2009): 2,691,158
GOVERNMENT: Constitutional monarchy (emirate)
LANGUAGES: Arabic (official), English
MONEY: Kuwaiti dinar
LIFE EXPECTANCY: 77.7
LITERACY RATE: 93%

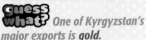 *On average, it rains only about two days a year in Kuwait.*

KYRGYZSTAN

LOCATION: Asia
CAPITAL: Bishkek
AREA: 76,641 sq mi (198,500 sq km)
POPULATION ESTIMATE (2009): 5,431,747
GOVERNMENT: Republic
LANGUAGES: Kyrgyz and Russian (official), Uzbek
MONEY: Som
LIFE EXPECTANCY: 69.4
LITERACY RATE: 99%

*One of Kyrgyzstan's major exports is **gold**.*

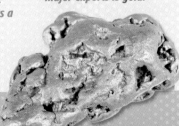

LAOS

LOCATION: Asia
CAPITAL: Vientiane
AREA: 91,429 sq mi
(236,800 sq km)
POPULATION ESTIMATE (2009):
6,834,942
GOVERNMENT: Communist state
LANGUAGES: Lao (official), French,
English
MONEY: Kip
LIFE EXPECTANCY: 56.7
LITERACY RATE: 69%

guess what? *The **Plain of
Jars** is located near the
northern city of Phongsavan.
Archaeologists have
yet to determine
the purpose of the
hundreds of stone
jars found there.*

LATVIA

LOCATION: Europe
CAPITAL: Riga
AREA: 24,938 sq mi
(64,589 sq km)
POPULATION ESTIMATE (2009):
2,231,503
GOVERNMENT: Parliamentary
democracy
LANGUAGES: Latvian, Russian
MONEY: Lats
LIFE EXPECTANCY: 72.1
LITERACY RATE: 100%

guess what? *According to
legend, the first decorated
evergreen tree was used
in a Christmas
celebration in Riga,
Latvia, in 1510.*

LEBANON

LOCATION: Middle East
CAPITAL: Beirut
AREA: 4,015 sq mi
(10,400 sq km)
POPULATION ESTIMATE (2009):
4,017,095
GOVERNMENT: Republic
LANGUAGES: Arabic (official),
French, English, Armenian
MONEY: Lebanese pound
LIFE EXPECTANCY: 73.7
LITERACY RATE: 87%

guess what? *Ancient
Lebanese people, known as
Phoenicians, developed the
first phonetic alphabet in
1100 B.C.*

LESOTHO

LOCATION: Africa
CAPITAL: Maseru
AREA: 11,720 sq mi
(30,355 sq km)
POPULATION ESTIMATE (2009):
2,130,819
GOVERNMENT: Parliamentary
constitutional monarchy
LANGUAGES: English and Sesotho
(both official), Zulu, Xhosa
MONEY: Maluti
LIFE EXPECTANCY: 40.4
LITERACY RATE: 85%

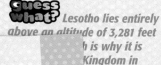
*Lesotho lies entirely
above an altitude of 3,281 feet
...h is why it is
...Kingdom in*

LIBERIA

LOCATION: Africa
CAPITAL: Monrovia
AREA: 43,000 sq mi
(111,370 sq km)
POPULATION ESTIMATE (2009):
3,441,790
GOVERNMENT: Republic
LANGUAGES: English (official),
ethnic dialects
MONEY: Liberian dollar
LIFE EXPECTANCY: 41.8
LITERACY RATE: 58%

guess what? *Firestone
Plantation, in the eastern
city of Harbel, is the world's
largest rubber plantation.*

LIBYA

LOCATION: Africa
CAPITAL: Tripoli
AREA: 679,358 sq mi
(1,759,540 sq km)
POPULATION ESTIMATE (2009):
6,310,434
GOVERNMENT: Military
dictatorship
LANGUAGES: Arabic, Italian,
English
MONEY: Libyan dinar
LIFE EXPECTANCY: 77.3
LITERACY RATE: 83%

guess what? *Libya was
under Italian rule from
1911 until 1947.*

Countries

LIECHTENSTEIN

LOCATION: Europe
CAPITAL: Vaduz
AREA: 62 sq mi (160 sq km)
POPULATION ESTIMATE (2009): 34,761
GOVERNMENT: Constitutional monarchy
LANGUAGES: German (official), Alemannic dialect
MONEY: Swiss franc
LIFE EXPECTANCY: 80.1
LITERACY RATE: 100%

Guess what? *Liechtenstein is one of only two doubly landlocked countries in the world, which means it is entirely surrounded by other landlocked countries. The other one is Uzbekistan.*

LITHUANIA

LOCATION: Europe
CAPITAL: Vilnius
AREA: 25,174 sq mi (65,200 sq km)
POPULATION ESTIMATE (2009): 3,555,179
GOVERNMENT: Parliamentary democracy
LANGUAGES: Lithuanian (official), Polish, Russian
MONEY: Litas
LIFE EXPECTANCY: 74.9
LITERACY RATE: 100%

Guess what? *The* **Hill of Crosses** *near Siauliai is covered with thousands of different-size crosses, some dating to the 14th century.*

LUXEMBOURG

LOCATION: Europe
CAPITAL: Luxembourg
AREA: 998 sq mi (2,586 sq km)
POPULATION ESTIMATE (2009): 491,775
GOVERNMENT: Constitutional monarchy
LANGUAGES: Luxembourgish, French, German
MONEY: Euro (formerly Luxembourg franc)
LIFE EXPECTANCY: 79.3
LITERACY RATE: 100%

Guess what? *The Ardennes region, which covers nearly half of the country, was where the historic Battle of the Bulge took place in World War II.*

MACEDONIA

LOCATION: Europe
CAPITAL: Skopje
AREA: 9,928 sq mi (25,713 sq km)
POPULATION ESTIMATE (2009): 2,066,718
GOVERNMENT: Parliamentary democracy
LANGUAGES: Macedonian, Albanian
MONEY: Denar
LIFE EXPECTANCY: 74.7
LITERACY RATE: 96%

Guess what? *The golden sun on Macedonia's flag represents the freedom of the country and its people.*

MADAGASCAR

LOCATION: Africa
CAPITAL: Antananarivo
AREA: 226,656 sq mi (587,040 sq km)
POPULATION ESTIMATE (2009): 20,653,556
GOVERNMENT: Republic
LANGUAGES: Malagasy, French, English (all official)
MONEY: Malagasy ariary
LIFE EXPECTANCY: 62.9
LITERACY RATE: 69%

Guess what? *Bands of pirates once used Madagascar as a base from which to attack ships traveling around the* **Cape of Good Hope.**

MALAWI

LOCATION: Africa
CAPITAL: Lilongwe
AREA: 45,745 sq mi (118,480 sq km)
POPULATION ESTIMATE (2009): 14,268,711
GOVERNMENT: Multiparty democracy
LANGUAGES: Chichewa (official), Chinyanja, Chiyao, Chitumbuka
MONEY: Kwacha
LIFE EXPECTANCY: 43.8
LITERACY RATE: 63%

Guess what? *More than 20% of Malawi's total area is water.*

MALAYSIA

LOCATION: Asia
CAPITAL: Kuala Lumpur
AREA: 127,316 sq mi
(329,750 sq km)
POPULATION ESTIMATE (2009):
25,715,819
GOVERNMENT: Constitutional
monarchy
LANGUAGES: Bahasa Malay
(official), Chinese, Tamil,
English, others
MONEY: Ringgit
LIFE EXPECTANCY: 73.3
LITERACY RATE: 89%

Guess what? *Most restaurants in Malaysia are small roadside diners called kedai kopi, which means "coffee café."*

MALDIVES

LOCATION: Asia
CAPITAL: Male
AREA: 116 sq mi
(300 sq km)
POPULATION ESTIMATE (2009): 396,334
GOVERNMENT: Republic
LANGUAGES: Dhivehi (official),
English
MONEY: Rufiyaa
LIFE EXPECTANCY: 74
LITERACY RATE: 96%

Guess what? *The cargo ship Victory hit a reef and sank off the coast of the Maldives in 1981. The wreck, now inhabited by a variety of marine life, is a popular scuba diving spot.*

MALI

LOCATION: Africa
CAPITAL: Bamako
AREA: 478,764 sq mi
(1,240,000 sq km)
POPULATION ESTIMATE (2009):
12,666,987
GOVERNMENT: Republic
LANGUAGES: French (official),
Bambara, African languages
MONEY: CFA franc
LIFE EXPECTANCY: 50.4
LITERACY RATE: 46%

Guess what? *The Cattle Crossing Festival occurs every year in December, when the Fulani people celebrate the return of the young men who have been tending cattle along the Niger River.*

MALTA

LOCATION: Europe
CAPITAL: Valletta
AREA: 122 sq mi (316 sq km)
POPULATION ESTIMATE (2009): 405,165
GOVERNMENT: Republic
LANGUAGES: Maltese and English
(both official)
MONEY: Euro (formerly
Maltese lira)
LIFE EXPECTANCY: 79.4
LITERACY RATE: 93%

Guess what? *Malta is an archipelago, or group of islands, in the Mediterranean Sea. The country's name is also the name of the largest island in the group.*

MARSHALL ISLANDS

LOCATION: Oceania
CAPITAL: Majuro
AREA: 70 sq mi (181.3 sq km)
POPULATION ESTIMATE (2009): 64,522
GOVERNMENT: Constitutional
government
LANGUAGES: Marshallese and
English (both official)
MONEY: U.S. dollar
LIFE EXPECTANCY: 71.2
LITERACY RATE: 94%

Guess what? *Bikini bathing suits are named after the Bikini Atoll, which is part of the Marshall Islands.*

MAURITANIA

LOCATION: Africa
CAPITAL: Nouakchott
AREA: 397,953 sq mi
(1,030,700 sq km)
POPULATION ESTIMATE (2009):
3,129,486
GOVERNMENT: Military junta
LANGUAGES: Arabic (official),
French, Pulaar, Soninke, others
MONEY: Ouguiya
LIFE EXPECTANCY: 60.4
LITERACY RATE: 51%

Guess what? *Mauritania, a Saharan Desert nation, has some of the world's most abundant fishing areas off its Atlantic coast.*

Countries

MAURITIUS

LOCATION: Africa
CAPITAL: Port Louis
AREA: 788 sq mi
(2,040 sq km)
POPULATION ESTIMATE (2009):
1,284,264
GOVERNMENT: Parliamentary
democracy
LANGUAGES: English (official),
Creole, Bhojpuri, French
MONEY: Mauritian rupee
LIFE EXPECTANCY: 74
LITERACY RATE: 84%

 *During Holi, the Hindu spring festival of colors, people throw colored water on one another.*

MEXICO

LOCATION: North America
CAPITAL: Mexico City
AREA: 761,602 sq mi
(1,972,550 sq km)
POPULATION ESTIMATE (2009):
111,211,789
GOVERNMENT: Republic
LANGUAGES: Spanish, indigenous
languages
MONEY: Peso
LIFE EXPECTANCY: 76.1
LITERACY RATE: 91%

 *The artist **Frida Kahlo** (1907–54) spent most of her life in Coyoacán, a neighborhood in Mexico City. Her house, known as the Blue House, is now a museum.*

MICRONESIA

LOCATION: Oceania
CAPITAL: Palikir
AREA: 271 sq mi (702 sq km)
POPULATION ESTIMATE (2009): 107,434
GOVERNMENT: Constitutional
government
LANGUAGES: English (official),
Chukese, Pohnpeian, Yapase,
Kosrean, Ulithian, others
MONEY: U.S. dollar
LIFE EXPECTANCY: 70.9
LITERACY RATE: 89%

Many historians think the first settlers on Micronesia traveled there from the Philippines and Indonesia in canoes.

MOLDOVA

LOCATION: Europe
CAPITAL: Chisinau
AREA: 13,067 sq mi
(33,843 sq km)
POPULATION ESTIMATE (2009):
4,320,748
GOVERNMENT: Republic
LANGUAGES: Moldovan (official),
Russian, Gagauz
MONEY: Leu
LIFE EXPECTANCY: 70.8
LITERACY RATE: 99%

Throughout its history, Moldova has often been involved in border disputes between Russia and Romania.

MONACO

LOCATION: Europe
CAPITAL: Monaco
AREA: 0.75 sq mi (1.95 sq km)
POPULATION ESTIMATE (2009): 32,965
GOVERNMENT: Constitutional
monarchy
LANGUAGES: French (official),
English, Italian, Monégasque
MONEY: Euro (formerly French
franc)
LIFE EXPECTANCY: 80.1
LITERACY RATE: 99%

*Prince Rainier III was the ruler of Monaco from 1949 until his death in 2005. In 1956, the Prince married movie star **Grace Kelly**, who then became known as Princess Grace.*

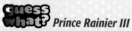

MONGOLIA

LOCATION: Asia
CAPITAL: Ulaanbaatar
AREA: 604,247 sq mi
(1,565,000 sq km)
POPULATION ESTIMATE (2009):
3,041,142
GOVERNMENT: Parliamentary
republic
LANGUAGES: Khalkha Mongol,
Turkic, Russian
MONEY: Togrog/tugriks
LIFE EXPECTANCY: 67.7
LITERACY RATE: 98%

Mongolia is called the Land of Blue Sky because it is sunny nearly all year.

MONTENEGRO

LOCATION: Europe
CAPITAL: Podgorica
AREA: 5,333 sq mi
(13,812 sq km)
POPULATION ESTIMATE (2009): 672,180
GOVERNMENT: Republic
LANGUAGES: Montenegrin (official),
Serbian, Bosnian, Albanian
MONEY: Euro (formerly
deutsche mark)
LIFE EXPECTANCY: 72.8
LITERACY RATE: 94%

 St. John Fortress, in the seaside village of Kotor, protected the city from pirate attacks for centuries.

MOROCCO

LOCATION: Africa
CAPITAL: Rabat
AREA: 172,413 sq mi
(446,550 sq km)
POPULATION ESTIMATE (2009):
34,859,364
GOVERNMENT: Constitutional
monarchy
LANGUAGES: Arabic (official),
French, Berber dialects
MONEY: Dirham
LIFE EXPECTANCY: 71.8
LITERACY RATE: 52%

 *You can eat most Moroccan food with your hands, but be sure to eat only with your right hand—the left hand is supposed to be used to clean yourself in the bathroom!*

MOZAMBIQUE

LOCATION: Africa
CAPITAL: Maputo
AREA: 309,494 sq mi
(801,590 sq km)
POPULATION ESTIMATE (2009):
21,669,278
GOVERNMENT: Republic
LANGUAGES: Portuguese (official),
Emakhuwa, Xichangana,
others
MONEY: Metical
LIFE EXPECTANCY: 41.2
LITERACY RATE: 48%

 *The flag of Mozambique features an open book, a hoe and a rifle, which stand for education, the peasants and the ability to defend the country.*

MYANMAR (BURMA)

LOCATION: Asia
CAPITAL: Rangoon
AREA: 261,969 sq mi
(678,500 sq km)
POPULATION ESTIMATE (2009):
48,137,741
GOVERNMENT: Military junta
LANGUAGES: Burmese, minority
languages
MONEY: Kyat
LIFE EXPECTANCY: 63
LITERACY RATE: 90%

 The highest point in Myanmar is Hkakabo Razi, a mountain in the north on the Chinese border.

NAMIBIA

LOCATION: Africa
CAPITAL: Windhoek
AREA: 318,694 sq mi
(825,418 sq km)
POPULATION ESTIMATE (2009):
2,108,665
GOVERNMENT: Republic
LANGUAGES: Afrikaans, German,
English (official), native
languages
MONEY: Namibian dollar
LIFE EXPECTANCY: 51.2
LITERACY RATE: 85%

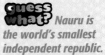 *The eastern coast of Namibia is called the Skeleton Coast because of the large number of **shipwrecks** that have occurred there.*

NAURU

LOCATION: Oceania
CAPITAL: Yaren District (unofficial)
AREA: 8.11 sq mi (21 sq km)
POPULATION ESTIMATE (2009): 14,019
GOVERNMENT: Republic
LANGUAGES: Nauruan (official),
English
MONEY: Australian dollar
LIFE EXPECTANCY: 64.2
LITERACY RATE: Not available

Nauru is the world's smallest independent republic.

NEPAL

LOCATION: Asia
CAPITAL: Kathmandu
AREA: 56,827 sq mi
(147,181 sq km)
POPULATION ESTIMATE (2009):
28,563,377
GOVERNMENT: Republic
LANGUAGES: Nepali (official),
Maithali, Bhojpuri, Tharu,
Tamang
MONEY: Nepalese rupee
LIFE EXPECTANCY: 65.5
LITERACY RATE: 49%

Guess what? *Nepal's national flag is the only one in the world that isn't rectangular or square.*

THE NETHERLANDS

LOCATION: Europe
CAPITAL: **Amsterdam**
AREA: 16,033 sq mi
(41,526 sq km)
POPULATION ESTIMATE (2009):
16,715,999
GOVERNMENT: Constitutional
monarchy
LANGUAGES: Dutch and Frisian
(both official)
MONEY: Euro (formerly guilder)
LIFE EXPECTANCY: 79.4
LITERACY RATE: 99%

Guess what? *The Netherlands is also known as Holland, and its citizens are called Dutch.*

NEW ZEALAND

LOCATION: Oceania
CAPITAL: Wellington
AREA: 103,737 sq mi
(268,680 sq km)
POPULATION ESTIMATE (2009):
4,213,418
GOVERNMENT: Parliamentary
democracy
LANGUAGES: English, Maori, sign
language (all official)
MONEY: New Zealand dollar
LIFE EXPECTANCY: 80.4
LITERACY RATE: 99%

Guess what? *There are about 4 million people— and 40 million sheep—in New Zealand.*

NICARAGUA

LOCATION: Central America
CAPITAL: Managua
AREA: 49,998 sq mi
(129,494 sq km)
POPULATION ESTIMATE (2009):
5,891,199
GOVERNMENT: Republic
LANGUAGE: Spanish (official)
MONEY: Gold córdoba
LIFE EXPECTANCY: 71.5
LITERACY RATE: 68%

Guess what? *The most popular sport in Nicaragua is **baseball**.*

NIGER

LOCATION: Africa
CAPITAL: Niamey
AREA: 489,189 sq mi
(1,267,000 sq km)
POPULATION ESTIMATE (2009):
15,306,252
GOVERNMENT: Republic
LANGUAGES: French (official),
Hausa, Djerma
MONEY: CFA franc
LIFE EXPECTANCY: 52.6
LITERACY RATE: 29%

Guess what? *The remains of a dinosaur, now called the Nigersaurus, were found in Niger in 1997.*

NIGERIA

LOCATION: Africa
CAPITAL: Abuja
AREA: 356,667 sq mi
(923,768 sq km)
POPULATION ESTIMATE (2009):
149,229,090
GOVERNMENT: Republic
LANGUAGES: English (official),
Hausa, Yoruba, Igbo, Fulani
MONEY: Naira
LIFE EXPECTANCY: 46.9
LITERACY RATE: 68%

Guess what? *Nicknamed Nollywood, Nigeria has a big film industry. In fact, it is the world's third-largest moviemaker, following the United States and India.*

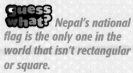

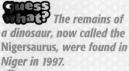

NORWAY

LOCATION: Europe
CAPITAL: Oslo
AREA: 125,021 sq mi
(323,802sq km)
POPULATION ESTIMATE (2009):
4,660,539
GOVERNMENT: Constitutional
monarchy
LANGUAGES: Two official forms
of Norwegian, Bokmal and
Nynorsk
MONEY: Krone
LIFE EXPECTANCY: 80
LITERACY RATE: 100%

Guess What? *The Viking Age, a time of great Norwegian Sea exploration, lasted from the 8th to the 11th century.*

OMAN

LOCATION: Middle East
CAPITAL: **Muscat**
AREA: 82,031 sq mi
(212,460 sq km)
POPULATION ESTIMATE (2009):
3,418,085
GOVERNMENT: Monarchy
LANGUAGES: Arabic (official),
English, others
MONEY: Omani rial
LIFE EXPECTANCY: 74.2
LITERACY RATE: 81%

Guess What? *Oman is known for the breeding of prized Arabian horses.*

PAKISTAN

LOCATION: Asia
CAPITAL: Islamabad
AREA: 310,401 sq mi
(803,940 sq km)
POPULATION ESTIMATE (2009):
176,242,949
GOVERNMENT: Republic
LANGUAGES: Punjabi, Sindhi,
Siraiki, Pashtu, Urdu (official),
others
MONEY: Pakistani rupee
LIFE EXPECTANCY: 64.5
LITERACY RATE: 50%

Guess What? *The world's second-highest mountain is in Pakistan. It's called K2 and stands at 28,250 feet (8,610 m).*

PALAU

LOCATION: Oceania
CAPITAL: Melekeok
AREA: 177 sq mi (458 sq km)
POPULATION ESTIMATE (2009): 20,796
GOVERNMENT: Constitutional
government
LANGUAGES: Palauan, English,
Sonsoralese, Tobi, Anguar,
Filipino, Chinese
MONEY: U.S. dollar
LIFE EXPECTANCY: 71.2
LITERACY RATE: 92%

Guess What? *Thousands of jellyfish live in Palau's Jellyfish Lake. Unlike jellyfish found elsewhere, they don't sting.*

PANAMA

LOCATION: Central America
CAPITAL: Panama City
AREA: 30,193 sq mi
(78,200 sq km)
POPULATION ESTIMATE (2009):
3,360,474
GOVERNMENT: Constitutional
democracy
LANGUAGES: Spanish (official),
English
MONEY: Balboa, U.S. dollar
LIFE EXPECTANCY: 77.3
LITERACY RATE: 92%

Guess What? *More than 60 million pounds (27 million kg) of dynamite were used during the* **construction of the Panama Canal.**

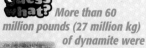

PAPUA NEW GUINEA

LOCATION: Oceania
CAPITAL: Port Moresby
AREA: 178,703 sq mi
(462,840 sq km)
POPULATION ESTIMATE (2009):
6,057,263
GOVERNMENT: Parliamentary
democracy
LANGUAGES: Melanesian
pidgin, more than 820
native languages
MONEY: Kina
LIFE EXPECTANCY: 66.3
LITERACY RATE: 57%

Guess What? *This island is so densely forested that groups of locals living near one another may have little or no contact.*

PARAGUAY

LOCATION: South America
CAPITAL: Asunción
AREA: 157,046 sq mi
(406,750 sq km)
POPULATION ESTIMATE (2009):
6,995,655
GOVERNMENT: Republic
LANGUAGES: Spanish and Guaraní
(both official)
MONEY: Guaraní
LIFE EXPECTANCY: 75.8
LITERACY RATE: 94%

Guess what? *One of the world's largest hydroelectric dams, the*

Itaipu, is on the border of Paraguay and Brazil.

PERU

LOCATION: South America
CAPITAL: Lima
AREA: 496,223 sq mi
(1,285,220 sq km)
POPULATION ESTIMATE (2009):
29,546,963
GOVERNMENT: Republic
LANGUAGES: Spanish and Quechua
(both official), Aymara, other
native languages
MONEY: Nuevo sol
LIFE EXPECTANCY: 70.7
LITERACY RATE: 88%

Guess what? *The potato was first grown in Peru.*

THE PHILIPPINES

LOCATION: Asia
CAPITAL: Manila
AREA: 115,830 sq mi
(300,000 sq km)
POPULATION ESTIMATE (2009):
97,976,603
GOVERNMENT: Republic
LANGUAGES: Filipino (based on
Tagalog) and English (both
official), regional languages
MONEY: Philippine peso
LIFE EXPECTANCY: 71.1
LITERACY RATE: 93%

Guess what?  *Most of the Philippines's imports and exports pass through the island's capital, Manila.*

POLAND

LOCATION: Europe
CAPITAL: Warsaw
AREA: 120,728 sq mi
(312,685 sq km)
POPULATION ESTIMATE (2009):
38,482,919
GOVERNMENT: Republic
LANGUAGE: Polish
MONEY: Zloty
LIFE EXPECTANCY: 75.6
LITERACY RATE: 100%

Guess what? *Scientist Marie Curie was born in Warsaw on November 7, 1867. She won two Nobel Prizes—one for physics (1903) and one for chemistry (1911).*

PORTUGAL

LOCATION: Europe
CAPITAL: Lisbon
AREA: 35,672 sq mi
(92,391 sq km)
POPULATION ESTIMATE (2009):
10,707,924
GOVERNMENT: Republic
LANGUAGES: Portuguese and
Mirandese (both official)
MONEY: Euro (formerly escudo)
LIFE EXPECTANCY: 78.2
LITERACY RATE: 93%

Guess what? *Portuguese is an official language of nine countries: Portugal, Brazil, Mozambique, Angola, Guinea-Bissau, East Timor, Equatorial Guinea, Cape Verde, and São Tomé and Principe.*

QATAR

LOCATION: Middle East
CAPITAL: **Doha**
AREA: 4,416 sq mi
(11,437 sq km)
POPULATION ESTIMATE (2009): 833,285
GOVERNMENT: Traditional
monarchy (emirate)
LANGUAGES: Arabic (official),
English
MONEY: Qatari rial
LIFE EXPECTANCY: 75.4
LITERACY RATE: 89%

Guess what? *Qatar's Northfield oil reservoir is the largest in the world. It's about half the size of the entire country.*

ROMANIA

LOCATION: Europe
CAPITAL: Bucharest
AREA: 91,699 sq mi (237,500 sq km)
POPULATION ESTIMATE (2009): 22,215,421
GOVERNMENT: Republic
LANGUAGES: Romanian (official), Hungarian, Romany
MONEY: Leu
LIFE EXPECTANCY: 72.5
LITERACY RATE: 97%

 *Monks and nuns at the Painted Monasteries strike wooden beams as a call to prayer, a tradition that started when invading Turks forbade the ringing of bells.*

RUSSIA

LOCATION: Europe and Asia
CAPITAL: Moscow
AREA: 6,592,735 sq mi (17,075,200 sq km)
POPULATION ESTIMATE (2009): 140,041,247
GOVERNMENT: Federation
LANGUAGES: Russian, others
MONEY: Ruble
LIFE EXPECTANCY: 66
LITERACY RATE: 99%

 *According to legend, **Viking Rurik** founded the first Russian dynasty in Novgorod in 862 A.D.*

RWANDA

LOCATION: Africa
CAPITAL: Kigali
AREA: 10,169 sq mi (26,338 sq km)
POPULATION ESTIMATE (2009): 10,473,282
GOVERNMENT: Republic
LANGUAGES: Kinyarwanda, French, English (all official)
MONEY: Rwandan franc
LIFE EXPECTANCY: 50.5
LITERACY RATE: 70%

 Rwanda's nickname is Land of a Thousand Hills.

SAINT KITTS AND NEVIS

LOCATION: Caribbean
CAPITAL: Basseterre
AREA: 101 sq mi (261 sq km)
POPULATION ESTIMATE (2009): 40,131
GOVERNMENT: Parliamentary democracy
LANGUAGE: English
MONEY: East Caribbean dollar
LIFE EXPECTANCY: 73.2
LITERACY RATE: 98%

Saint Kitts and Nevis's bustling sugar industry closed down in 2005. The government is now looking into developing biofuels from sugarcane.

SAINT LUCIA

LOCATION: Caribbean
CAPITAL: Castries
AREA: 238 sq mi (616 sq km)
POPULATION ESTIMATE (2009): 160,267
GOVERNMENT: Parliamentary democracy
LANGUAGES: English (official), French patois
MONEY: East Caribbean dollar
LIFE EXPECTANCY: 76.5
LITERACY RATE: 90%

*The Caribbean's leading **banana** exporter is Saint Lucia. The country grows six varieties.*

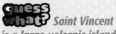

SAINT VINCENT AND THE GRENADINES

LOCATION: Caribbean
CAPITAL: Kingstown
AREA: 150 sq mi (389 sq km)
POPULATION ESTIMATE (2009): 104,574
GOVERNMENT: Parliamentary democracy
LANGUAGES: English, French patois
MONEY: East Caribbean dollar
LIFE EXPECTANCY: 73.7
LITERACY RATE: 96%

Saint Vincent is a large volcanic island. The Grenadines are made up of 32 smaller islands and cays, which are low islands made of sand or coral.

SAMOA

LOCATION: Oceania
CAPITAL: Apia
AREA: 1,137 sq mi (2,944 sq km)
POPULATION ESTIMATE (2009): 219,998
GOVERNMENT: Parliamentary democracy
LANGUAGES: Samoan, English
MONEY: Tala
LIFE EXPECTANCY: 71.9
LITERACY RATE: 100%

Robert Louis Stevenson, author of Treasure Island, is buried on Mount Vaea, above the Samoan capital of Apia.

SAN MARINO

LOCATION: Europe
CAPITAL: San Marino
AREA: 24 sq mi (61 sq km)
POPULATION ESTIMATE (2009): 30,324
GOVERNMENT: Republic
LANGUAGE: Italian
MONEY: Euro (formerly Italian lira)
LIFE EXPECTANCY: 82
LITERACY RATE: 96%

Guess what? San Marino is only 24 square miles (61 sq km) and is completely surrounded by Italy. Its capital city is perched atop Mount Titano. Three towers sit atop the three peaks of Mount Titano.

SÃO TOMÉ AND PRÍNCIPE

LOCATION: Africa
CAPITAL: São Tomé
AREA: 386 sq mi (1,001 sq km)
POPULATION ESTIMATE (2009): 212,679
GOVERNMENT: Republic
LANGUAGE: Portuguese (official)
MONEY: Dobra
LIFE EXPECTANCY: 68.3
LITERACY RATE: 85%

Guess what? Made up of the islands of São Tomé and Príncipe, this is Africa's smallest country.

SAUDI ARABIA

LOCATION: Middle East
CAPITAL: Riyadh
AREA: 830,000 sq mi (2,149,690 sq km)
POPULATION ESTIMATE (2009): 28,686,633
GOVERNMENT: Monarchy
LANGUAGE: Arabic
MONEY: Saudi riyal
LIFE EXPECTANCY: 76.3
LITERACY RATE: 79%

Guess what? People who live in Saudi Arabia refer to their country simply as Saudi.

SENEGAL

LOCATION: Africa
CAPITAL: Dakar
AREA: 75,749 sq mi (196,190 sq km)
POPULATION ESTIMATE (2009): 13,711,597
GOVERNMENT: Republic
LANGUAGES: French (official), Wolof, Pulaar, Jola, Mandinka
MONEY: CFA franc
LIFE EXPECTANCY: 59
LITERACY RATE: 39%

Guess what? One of Senegal's major sports is canoe racing.

SERBIA

LOCATION: Europe
CAPITAL: Belgrade
AREA: 29,913 sq mi (77,474 sq km)
POPULATION ESTIMATE (2009): 10,159,046
GOVERNMENT: Republic
LANGUAGES: Serbian, Hungarian, others
MONEY: Serbian dinar
LIFE EXPECTANCY: 75.3
LITERACY RATE: 96.4%

Guess what? Serbia grows about one-third of the world's raspberries.

SEYCHELLES

LOCATION: Africa
CAPITAL: Victoria
AREA: 176 sq mi (455 sq km)
POPULATION ESTIMATE (2009): 87,476
GOVERNMENT: Republic
LANGUAGES: Creole, English (official), other
MONEY: Seychelles rupee
LIFE EXPECTANCY: 73
LITERACY RATE: 92%

 *An archipelago, or group of islands, in the Indian Ocean, Seychelles was once a **pirate hideout.***

SIERRA LEONE

LOCATION: Africa
CAPITAL: Freetown
AREA: 27,699 sq mi (71,740 sq km)
POPULATION ESTIMATE (2009): 6,440,053
GOVERNMENT: Constitutional democracy
LANGUAGES: English (official), Mende, Temne, Krio
MONEY: Leone
LIFE EXPECTANCY: 41.2
LITERACY RATE: 35%

 The name Sierra Leone means "lion mountain."

SINGAPORE

LOCATION: Asia
CAPITAL: Singapore
AREA: 267 sq mi (692.7 sq km)
POPULATION ESTIMATE (2009): 4,657,542
GOVERNMENT: Parliamentary republic
LANGUAGES: Chinese (Mandarin), English, Malay, Hokkien, Cantonese, others
MONEY: Singapore dollar
LIFE EXPECTANCY: 82
LITERACY RATE: 93%

 Singapore has some extremely strict laws. It is illegal to bring chewing gum into the country, and litterbugs are subject to stiff penalties and fines.

SLOVAKIA

LOCATION: Europe
CAPITAL: Bratislava
AREA: 18,859 sq mi (48,845 sq km)
POPULATION ESTIMATE (2009): 5,463,046
GOVERNMENT: Parliamentary democracy
LANGUAGES: Slovak (official), Hungarian, Roma, Ukranian
MONEY: Koruna
LIFE EXPECTANCY: 75.4
LITERACY RATE: 99%

*The inventor of the **modern parachute**, Stefan Banic, was born in Slovakia in 1870. He patented his creation in 1914.*

SLOVENIA

LOCATION: Europe
CAPITAL: Ljubljana
AREA: 7,827 sq mi (20,273 sq km)
POPULATION ESTIMATE (2009): 2,005,692
GOVERNMENT: Parliamentary republic
LANGUAGES: Slovenian, Serbo-Croatian
MONEY: Euro (formerly Slovenian tolar)
LIFE EXPECTANCY: 76.9
LITERACY RATE: 100%

*Slovenia has the **lowest marriage rate** in the European Union.*

SOLOMON ISLANDS

LOCATION: Oceania
CAPITAL: Honiara
AREA: 10,985 sq mi (28,450 sq km)
POPULATION ESTIMATE (2009): 595,613
GOVERNMENT: Parliamentary democracy
LANGUAGES: Melanesian pidgin, English, more than 120 local languages
MONEY: Solomon Islands dollar
LIFE EXPECTANCY: 73.7
LITERACY RATE: Not available

The Solomon Islands is made up of about 900 separate islands.

Countries

SOMALIA

LOCATION: Africa
CAPITAL: Mogadishu
AREA: 246,199 sq mi
(637,657 sq km)
POPULATION ESTIMATE (2009):
9,832,017
GOVERNMENT: Transitional
government
LANGUAGES: Somali (official),
Arabic, English, Italian
MONEY: Somali shilling
LIFE EXPECTANCY: 49.6
LITERACY RATE: 38%

 Many of Somalia's people are nomads, people who travel with their cattle rather than settle down.

SOUTH AFRICA

LOCATION: Africa
CAPITALS: Pretoria (adminis-
trative), Cape Town (legislative)
AREA: 471,008 sq mi
(1,219,912 sq km)
POPULATION ESTIMATE (2009):
49,052,489
GOVERNMENT: Republic
LANGUAGES: Zulu, Xhosa, Afrikaans,
Sepedi, English, Setswana,
Sesotho, Tsonga, others
MONEY: Rand
LIFE EXPECTANCY: 49
LITERACY RATE: 86%

 South Africa is home to many of wildlife's wonders, including elephants, lions, rhinos and leopards.

SPAIN

LOCATION: Europe
CAPITAL: Madrid
AREA: 194,896 sq mi
(504,782 sq km)
POPULATION ESTIMATE (2009):
40,525,002
GOVERNMENT: Parliamentary
monarchy
LANGUAGES: Castilian Spanish
(official), Catalan, Galician,
Basque
MONEY: Euro (formerly peseta)
LIFE EXPECTANCY: 80.1
LITERACY RATE: 98%

 The first recorded **bullfight** *took place in 711.*

SRI LANKA

LOCATION: Asia
CAPITAL: Colombo
AREA: 25,332 sq mi
(65,610 sq km)
POPULATION ESTIMATE (2009):
21,324,791
GOVERNMENT: Republic
LANGUAGES: Sinhala (official),
Tamil, English
MONEY: Sri Lankan rupee
LIFE EXPECTANCY: 75.1
LITERACY RATE: 91%

 Because Sri Lanka is home to **more than 400 species of birds**, *it has declared December National Bird Month.*

SUDAN

LOCATION: Africa
CAPITAL: Khartoum
AREA: 967,493 sq mi
(2,505,810 sq km)
POPULATION ESTIMATE (2009):
41,087,825
GOVERNMENT: Authoritarian
regime
LANGUAGES: Arabic, English (both
official), Nubian, Ta Bedawie,
others
MONEY: Sudanese pound
LIFE EXPECTANCY: 51.4
LITERACY RATE: 61%

At almost 970,000 square miles (2.5 million sq km), Sudan is Africa's largest country.

SURINAME

LOCATION: South America
CAPITAL: Paramaribo
AREA: 63,039 sq mi
(163,270 sq km)
POPULATION ESTIMATE (2009): 481,267
GOVERNMENT: Constitutional
democracy
LANGUAGES: Dutch (official),
Surinamese, English, others
MONEY: Surinamese dollar
LIFE EXPECTANCY: 73.7
LITERACY RATE: 90%

Some of Suriname's exports include bananas, rice, shrimp and fish, and lumber.

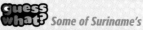

SWAZILAND

LOCATION: Africa
CAPITAL: Mbabane
AREA: 6,704 sq mi
(17,360 sq km)
POPULATION ESTIMATE (2009):
1,123,913
GOVERNMENT: Monarchy
LANGUAGES: Swati and English
(both official)
MONEY: Lilangeni
LIFE EXPECTANCY: 31.9
LITERACY RATE: 82%

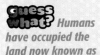 *Humans
have occupied the
land now known as
Swaziland since the
Stone Age.*

SWEDEN

LOCATION: Europe
CAPITAL: Stockholm
AREA: 173,731 sq mi
(449,964 sq km)
POPULATION ESTIMATE (2009):
9,059,651
GOVERNMENT: Constitutional
monarchy
LANGUAGE: Swedish
MONEY: Krona
LIFE EXPECTANCY: 80.9
LITERACY RATE: 99%

 *Sweden's **Ice Hotel**
in the village of
Jukkasjarvi is made
entirely of snow
and ice.*

SWITZERLAND

LOCATION: Europe
CAPITAL: Bern
AREA: 15,942 sq mi
(41,290 sq km)
POPULATION ESTIMATE (2009):
7,604,467
GOVERNMENT: Federal republic
LANGUAGES: German, French,
Italian, Romansch (all official)
MONEY: Swiss franc
LIFE EXPECTANCY: 80.9
LITERACY RATE: 99%

 *The Red Cross
was founded in Geneva,
Switzerland, in 1863. Its
world headquarters are
still there.*

SYRIA

LOCATION: Middle East
CAPITAL: **Damascus**
AREA: 71,498 sq mi
(185,180 sq km)
POPULATION ESTIMATE (2009):
20,178,485
GOVERNMENT: Republic under an
authoritarian regime
LANGUAGES: Arabic (official),
Kurdish, Armenian, Aramaic,
Circassian
MONEY: Syrian pound
LIFE EXPECTANCY: 71.2
LITERACY RATE: 80%

*Satellite images
of Syria show
evidence of
4,000-year-old
roads.*

TAIWAN

LOCATION: Asia
CAPITAL: Taipei
AREA: 13,892 sq mi
(35,980 sq km)
POPULATION ESTIMATE (2009):
22,974,347
GOVERNMENT: Multiparty
democracy
LANGUAGES: Chinese (Mandarin),
Taiwanese, Hakka dialects
MONEY: New Taiwan dollar
LIFE EXPECTANCY: 78
LITERACY RATE: 96%

 *Taipei, the most
populous city in Taiwan,
has an average of more
than 9,000 people per
square mile.*

TAJIKISTAN

LOCATION: Asia
CAPITAL: Dushanbe
AREA: 55,251 sq mi
(143,100 sq km)
POPULATION ESTIMATE (2009):
7,349,145
GOVERNMENT: Republic
LANGUAGES: Tajik (official), Russian
MONEY: Somoni
LIFE EXPECTANCY: 65.3
LITERACY RATE: 100%

*Mountains
cover more than 90% of
this country.*

TANZANIA

LOCATION: Africa
CAPITAL: Dar es Salaam
AREA: 364,898 sq mi (945,087 sq km)
POPULATION ESTIMATE (2009): 41,048,532
GOVERNMENT: Republic
LANGUAGES: Swahili and English (both official), Arabic, local languages
MONEY: Tanzanian shilling
LIFE EXPECTANCY: 52
LITERACY RATE: 69%

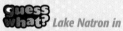 *Lake Natron in Tanzania is the breeding ground for lesser flamingos. Every year, more than 1 million flamingos come here from all over Africa.*

THAILAND

LOCATION: Asia
CAPITAL: Bangkok
AREA: 198,455 sq mi (514,000 sq km)
POPULATION ESTIMATE (2009): 65,905,410
GOVERNMENT: Constitutional monarchy
LANGUAGES: Thai (Siamese), English, regional dialects
MONEY: Baht
LIFE EXPECTANCY: 73.1
LITERACY RATE: 93%

 There are an estimated 2,000 wild Asian elephants in Thailand.

TOGO

LOCATION: Africa
CAPITAL: Lomé
AREA: 21,925 sq mi (56,785 sq km)
POPULATION ESTIMATE (2009): 6,019,877
GOVERNMENT: Republic (under transition)
LANGUAGES: French (official), Ewe, Mina, Kabye, Dagomba
MONEY: CFA franc
LIFE EXPECTANCY: 58.7
LITERACY RATE: 61%

 In the Ewe language spoken here, the word Togo means "house of sea," though only a small part of the country touches the ocean.

TONGA

LOCATION: Oceania
CAPITAL: Nuku'alofa
AREA: 289 sq mi (748 sq km)
POPULATION ESTIMATE (2009): 120,898
GOVERNMENT: Constitutional monarchy
LANGUAGES: Tongan, English
MONEY: Pa'anga
LIFE EXPECTANCY: 70.7
LITERACY RATE: 99%

 The Kingdom of Tonga is known as the Friendly Islands.

TRINIDAD AND TOBAGO

LOCATION: Caribbean
CAPITAL: Port-of-Spain
AREA: 1,980 sq mi (5,128 sq km)
POPULATION ESTIMATE (2009): 1,229,953
GOVERNMENT: Parliamentary democracy
LANGUAGES: English (official), Hindi, French, Spanish, Chinese
MONEY: Trinidad and Tobago dollar
LIFE EXPECTANCY: 70.9
LITERACY RATE: 99%

Cricket is the most popular sport in this island country.

TUNISIA

LOCATION: Africa
CAPITAL: Tunis
AREA: 63,170 sq mi (163,610 sq km)
POPULATION ESTIMATE (2009): 10,486,339
GOVERNMENT: Republic
LANGUAGES: Arabic (official), French
MONEY: Tunisian dinar
LIFE EXPECTANCY: 75.8
LITERACY RATE: 74%

Scenes of the planet Tatooine in the movie Star Wars were shot in Tunisia.

TURKEY

LOCATION: Europe and Asia
CAPITAL: Ankara
AREA: 301,382 sq mi
(780,580 sq km)
POPULATION ESTIMATE (2009):
76,805,524
GOVERNMENT: Parliamentary
democracy
LANGUAGES: Turkish (official),
Kurdish, Dimli, Azeri
MONEY: New Turkish lira
LIFE EXPECTANCY: 72
LITERACY RATE:
87%

Istanbul,
is the only
city in the world that is on two
continents, Europe and Asia.

TURKMENISTAN

LOCATION: Asia
CAPITAL: Ashgabat (Ashkhabad)
AREA: 188,455 sq mi
(488,100 sq km)
POPULATION ESTIMATE (2009):
4,884,887
GOVERNMENT: Republic
LANGUAGES: Turkmen, Russian,
Uzbek, others
MONEY: Manat
LIFE EXPECTANCY: 68.9
LITERACY RATE: 99%

 The rocks in
Turkmenistan's Kugitang State
Nature Reserve are embedded
with dinosaur footprints.

TUVALU

LOCATION: Oceania
CAPITAL: Funafuti
AREA: 10 sq mi (26 sq km)
POPULATION ESTIMATE (2009): 12,373
GOVERNMENT: Constitutional
monarchy with a
parliamentary democracy
LANGUAGES: Tuvaluan, English,
Samoan, Kiribati
MONEY: Australian dollar,
Tuvaluan dollar
LIFE EXPECTANCY: 69.3
LITERACY RATE: Not available

Tourists visiting
Tuvalu can purchase fans,
mats, baskets, necklaces,
woodcarvings and fishhooks
that are highly regarded
throughout the Pacific.

UGANDA

LOCATION: Africa
CAPITAL: Kampala
AREA: 91,135 sq mi
(236,040 sq km)
POPULATION ESTIMATE (2009):
32,369,558
GOVERNMENT: Republic
LANGUAGES: English (official),
Luganda, Swahili, others
MONEY: Ugandan shilling
LIFE EXPECTANCY: 52.7
LITERACY RATE: 67%

Uganda's
national bird is the
crested crane. *Its black,*
yellow and red
feathers match
the colors of the
country's flag.

UKRAINE

LOCATION: Europe
CAPITAL: Kyiv (Kiev)
AREA: 233,089 sq mi
(603,700 sq km)
POPULATION ESTIMATE (2009):
45,700,395
GOVERNMENT: Republic
LANGUAGES: Ukrainian, Russian
MONEY: Hryvnia
LIFE EXPECTANCY: 68.3
LITERACY RATE: 99%

 A cathedral in Kiev
dates to the 11th century. It
now belongs to the Russian
Orthodox Church.

UNITED ARAB EMIRATES

LOCATION: Middle East
CAPITAL: **Abu Dhabi**
AREA: 32,000 sq mi
(82,880 sq km)
POPULATION ESTIMATE (2009):
4,798,491
GOVERNMENT: Federation
LANGUAGES: Arabic (official),
Persian, English, Hindi, Urdu
MONEY: U.A.E. dirham
LIFE EXPECTANCY: 76.1
LITERACY RATE: 78%

The UAE is
made up of seven Arab
sheikhdoms
that came
together
in 1971.

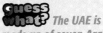

Countries

UNITED KINGDOM

LOCATION: Europe
CAPITAL: London
AREA: 94,525 sq mi
(244,820 sq km)
POPULATION ESTIMATE (2009):
61,113,205
GOVERNMENT: Constitutional
monarchy
LANGUAGES: English, Welsh,
Scottish Gaelic
MONEY: British pound
LIFE EXPECTANCY: 79
LITERACY RATE: 99%

 *The world's oldest
scientific zoo, The London Zoo,
opened in 1828.*

UNITED STATES

LOCATION: North America
CAPITAL: Washington, D.C.
AREA: 3,794,083 sq mi
(9,826,630 sq km)
POPULATION ESTIMATE (2009):
307,212,123
GOVERNMENT: Republic
LANGUAGES: English, Spanish
(spoken by a sizable minority)
MONEY: U.S. dollar
LIFE EXPECTANCY: 78.1
LITERACY RATE: 99%

 *Horses are not
native to the
U.S. They were
first brought
to America
by Spanish
conquistadors in 1519.*

URUGUAY

LOCATION: South America
CAPITAL: Montevideo
AREA: 68,039 sq mi
(176,220 sq km)
POPULATION ESTIMATE (2009):
3,494,382
GOVERNMENT: Republic
LANGUAGES: Spanish, Portunol,
Brazilero
MONEY: Uruguayan peso
LIFE EXPECTANCY: 76.4
LITERACY RATE: 98%

 *Uruguay has one
of the highest literacy rates
and the lowest poverty rates
in South America.*

UZBEKISTAN

LOCATION: Asia
CAPITAL: Tashkent
AREA: 172,741 sq mi
(447,400 sq km)
POPULATION ESTIMATE (2009):
27,606,007
GOVERNMENT: Republic
LANGUAGES: Uzbek, Russian,
Tajik, others
MONEY: Uzbekistani soum
LIFE EXPECTANCY: 72
LITERACY RATE: 99%

*Uzbekistan is
Central Asia's most populous
country.*

VANUATU

LOCATION: Oceania
CAPITAL: Port-Vila
AREA: 4,710 sq mi (12,200 sq km)
POPULATION ESTIMATE (2009): 218,519
GOVERNMENT: Republic
LANGUAGES: Most people speak
one of more than 100 local
languages; Bislama, English
MONEY: Vatu
LIFE EXPECTANCY: 64
LITERACY RATE: 74%

*Vanuatu is located
within the Pacific Basin's Ring
of Fire. This area includes about
75% of the world's
volcanoes. **Mount Yasur**
is one of Vanuatu's
active volcanoes.*

VATICAN CITY (HOLY SEE)

LOCATION: Europe
CAPITAL: Vatican City
AREA: 0.17 sq mi (0.44 sq km)
POPULATION ESTIMATE (2009): 826
GOVERNMENT: Ecclesiastical
LANGUAGES: Italian, Latin, French
MONEY: Euro
LIFE EXPECTANCY: 77.5
LITERACY RATE: 100%

*Vatican
City is actually a
city-state with a
noncommercial
economy. It is
supported by
contributions known as Peter's
Pence, which come mostly
from tourism and donations
from Roman Catholics
throughout the world.*

VENEZUELA

LOCATION: South America
CAPITAL: Caracas
AREA: 352,143 sq mi
(912,050 sq km)
POPULATION ESTIMATE (2009):
26,814,843
GOVERNMENT: Republic
LANGUAGES: Spanish (official),
native languages
MONEY: Bolivar
LIFE EXPECTANCY: 73.6
LITERACY RATE: 93%

Because of Venezuela's proximity to the equator, it experiences only two seasons, dry and wet.

VIETNAM

LOCATION: Asia
CAPITAL: Hanoi
AREA: 127,243 sq mi
(329,560 sq km)
POPULATION ESTIMATE (2009):
86,967,524
GOVERNMENT: Communist state
LANGUAGES: Vietnamese (official),
French, English, Khmer, Chinese
MONEY: Dong
LIFE EXPECTANCY: 71.6
LITERACY RATE: 90%

Instead of counting by their birthdays, the Vietnamese count their ages from the number of New Year holidays they have celebrated. On Têt (New Year), everyone becomes one year older.

YEMEN

LOCATION: Middle East
CAPITAL: Sanaa
AREA: 203,849 sq mi
(527,970 sq km)
POPULATION ESTIMATE (2009):
23,822,783
GOVERNMENT: Republic
LANGUAGE: Arabic
MONEY: Yemeni rial
LIFE EXPECTANCY: 63.3
LITERACY RATE: 50%

Ancient Greeks and Romans traveled to India through the ports of Yemen.

ZAMBIA

LOCATION: Africa
CAPITAL: Lusaka
AREA: 290,584 sq mi
(752,614 sq km)
POPULATION ESTIMATE (2009):
11,862,740
GOVERNMENT: Republic
LANGUAGES: English (official), local
dialects
MONEY: Kwacha
LIFE EXPECTANCY: 38.6
LITERACY RATE: 81%

*Milewide **Victoria Falls**, on the border of Zambia and Zimbabwe, is among the Seven Natural Wonders of the World.*

ZIMBABWE

LOCATION: Africa
CAPITAL: Harare
AREA: 150,803 sq mi
(390,580 sq km)
POPULATION ESTIMATE (2009):
11,392,629
GOVERNMENT: Parliamentary
democracy
LANGUAGES: English (official),
Shona, Ndebele (Sindebele)
MONEY: Zimbabwean dollar
LIFE EXPECTANCY: 45.8
LITERACY RATE: 91%

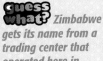

Zimbabwe gets its name from a trading center that operated here in medieval times.

Top 10 Most Livable Countries

Every year, the United Nations releases a list of the most livable countries. The order is based on life expectancy, adult literacy, education, income and other quality-of-life factors. These nations came out on top.

RANK	COUNTRY
1.	Iceland
2.	Norway
3.	Australia
4.	Canada
5.	Ireland
6.	Sweden
7.	Switzerland
8.	Japan
9.	Netherlands
10.	France

Source: *Human Development Report*, 2007-08, United Nations

Countries

Dance
Step Right Up!

There's a dance step for every time in history, every age group and every level of physical strength. Here are a few types of dance that have stood the test of time.

BREAK DANCING
A cross between acrobatics and dancing, this style began in U.S. cities in the late 1970s and early 1980s.

TANGO
A ballroom dance that originated in Buenos Aires, Argentina, includes sweeping movements and abrupt stops.

PASO DOBLE
Created in Spain, its movements resemble those of a bullfighter. The name means "double step" in Spanish.

FOX-TROT
A ballroom dance that consists of two slow steps followed by two quick movements.

WALTZ
A dance in which partners follow steps to work their way entirely around the dance floor.

CHA-CHA
A Latin-rhythm dance that includes hip and foot movements done to the beat of "one-two-cha-cha-cha!"

RUMBA
Created in Cuba, this dance is a mix of Spanish and African moves.

Dance Crazes and Crazy Dances

Some dances, like tap, began as crazes and went on to become classics. Other dance crazes are remembered for how ridiculous they were. Their names often give a clue as to what the dances looked like in motion.

• THE MASHED POTATO originated in 1962. In this dance, people move their feet as if they are trying to mash a potato under the balls of their feet.

• THE WATUSI takes its name from the Batutsi tribe of Rwanda. It features head bobbing and hand movements while the feet stay firmly planted on the floor.

• THE ROBOT, invented by Charles Washington in the 1960s, is a type of "popping," in which dancers imitate the jerky movements of a robot.

• Introduced in 1987, THE CABBAGE PATCH is named for a series of stuffed dolls. Dancers hold their hands like fists and move them in a circular motion.

• THE MOONWALK, popularized by pop icon Michael Jackson in 1983, includes a slow foot slide that makes the dancer appear to float backward across the floor.

• During THE CHICKEN DANCE, a circle of dancers imitate the movements of a chicken. For many, no wedding reception is complete without the chicken dance!

Dancing with the Stars

Since it premiered on June 1, 2005, *Dancing with the Stars* has been a hit for ABC. Based on the British show *Strictly Come Dancing,* it has regularly attracted at least 13 million viewers per episode and sometimes as many as 22 million! It has also developed a reputation for producing more injuries than any other prime-time program. Celebrities and competitors have suffered sprained ankles, scratched eyes and dislocated shoulders. Here are the show's winners and runners-up.

SEASON	WINNERS	RUNNERS-UP
Season 1 – Summer 2005	Kelly Monaco and Alec Mazo	John O'Hurley and Charlotte Jorgensen
Season 2 – Winter 2006	Drew Lachey and Cheryl Burke	Jerry Rice and Anna Trebunskaya
Season 3 – Fall 2006	Emmitt Smith and Cheryl Burke	Mario Lopez and Karina Smirnoff
Season 4 – Spring 2007	Apolo Anton Ohno and Julianne Hough	Joey Fatone and Kym Johnson
Season 5 – Fall 2007	Helio Castroneves and Julianne Hough	Mel B and Maksim Chmerkovskiy
Season 6 – Spring 2008	Kristi Yamaguchi and Mark Ballas	Jason Taylor and Edyta Sliwinska
Season 7 – Fall 2008	Brooke Burke and Derek Hough	Warren Sapp and Kym Johnson

America's Best Dance Crew

In 2008, Randy Jackson launched *America's Best Dance Crew* on MTV. He wanted to showcase a younger, hipper range of dancers than those featured on network shows, and, judging from audience response, he has succeeded. In each episode, hosted by Mario Lopez, groups of five to seven dancers compete for a chance to win a $100,000 cash prize—and a touring contract. Winners are chosen by the television audience.

In season one, the JabbaWockeeZ defeated Status Quo to become the first group named America's Best Dance Crew. For the second season, Super Cr3W took the top prize.

Energy and the Environment

A Green Meeting

FROM TFK MAGAZINE

EXPERTS SHARE THEIR IDEAS FOR CREATING AN ENVIRONMENTALLY FRIENDLY WORLD

By TFK Kid Reporter Erin Wiens St. John

Architects, designers, builders, home owners and people interested in creating an Earth-friendly world met at the San Jose Convention Center in California in September 2008. They were there to attend the West Coast Green conference. At the meeting, leaders in the green innovation movement showed off their designs and products. The conference aimed to expand people's thinking about how they can make a positive impact on the planet. About 14,000 people attended.

Harbinger House

A CHALLENGE TO AMERICANS

There were many speakers at the meeting, including former **Vice President Al Gore.** He challenged Americans to think about the country's use of energy. Gore told the audience that national security, the economy and the environment are all linked to U.S. dependence on foreign oil. Gore said he was optimistic that Americans can create cheap, carbon-free renewable resources.

Al Gore

Christi Graham, the founder of West Coast Green, agrees with Gore that Americans can make a difference. She sees kids as future decision makers and wants to empower the younger generation to make a green world. Celia Canfield, the development director for West Coast Green, also agreed, saying, "Your (generation) is going to look at us and say, 'You used to chip stone off of mountains? Why would you do that?' Let's just reuse stuff, and make it into cooler products."

REVOLUTIONARY DESIGNS

Visitors to the conference viewed numerous exciting new technologies. Event organizers hope that these products will change the way we build and live in our homes, offices and communities. That is what the Lawrence Group hopes to do with something called the **Harbinger House.** It is a two-story home made entirely of steel shipping containers, just like the ones you see on trains. Inside, it features countertops made of recycled paper and reused glass.

Another innovative product is the **Coolerado air conditioner.** It uses up to 90% less energy than a conventional unit and does not use environmentally dangerous chemicals. Other new technologies included:

- a zero-emissions car that runs on compressed air and a green battery
- a solar-powered coffee table that recharges electronics
- a bike that purifies water as you pedal
- a solar-powered radio that generates electricity and music

With products like these, it may be easy being green!

The Coolerado

FOSSIL FUELS AND THE GREENHOUSE EFFECT

Most of the energy people use to heat buildings and run machines comes from coal, oil or natural gas. These are called fossil fuels, because they are made from the remains of animals and plants that lived long ago. Burning fossil fuels provides energy for industry (electric power plants, manufacturing plants), transportation (cars, planes, boats) and households (lights, computers, televisions, dishwashers). But it also results in the release of carbon dioxide (CO_2) and other gases into Earth's atmosphere. Scientists believe that we are producing far more carbon dioxide than the atmosphere needs and, as a result, the planet is getting warmer.

WHAT IS GLOBAL WARMING?

Earth is surrounded by an atmosphere—layers of gases that protect it from extreme heat or cold. Gases such as carbon dioxide (CO_2) and methane trap the sun's heat in the atmosphere (just like the walls of a greenhouse trap heat and moisture). These gases help to keep the temperature of the planet warm enough for all living things. But in recent years, human activity has increased the concentration of greenhouse gases in the atmosphere. As a result, Earth's temperature is rising, which could spell disaster for the entire planet. From planting trees to decreasing the amount of energy we use every day, there are many things we can do to reduce those greenhouse gases and therefore lessen our **carbon footprint**.

WHAT IS A CARBON FOOTPRINT?
Your carbon footprint is not an actual footprint. It refers to the total amount of greenhouse gas emissions that result from your activities.

Energy Use at Home

The average U.S. household produces more than 26,000 pounds of carbon dioxide per year. Here's how.

Heating the home **34%**

Appliances and lighting **34%**

Heating water **13%**

Air-conditioning **11%**

Refrigerator **8%**

Electricity Used by Appliances

Ever wonder how much energy your appliances use? Watts are the units of measure for electrical power. They refer to the amount of total electrical power drawn by an item.

Ceiling fan	65–175 watts
Clock radio	10 watts
Clothes dryer (standard)	1,800–5,000 watts
Coffeemaker	900–1,200 watts
Computer (desktop CPU)	120 watts; 30 or less when "asleep"
Hair dryer	1,200–1,875 watts
Refrigerator	725 watts
Toaster	800–1,400 watts
TV (36 inch)	133 watts
TV (flat screen)	120 watts

Source: Department of Energy

10 WATTS

1,200-1,875 WATTS

800-1,400 WATTS

guess what? Coal-burning power plants contribute more to global warming than anything else, producing 2.5 billion tons of CO_2 every year. Cars are the second worst culprits, emitting 1.5 billion tons of CO_2 yearly.

Energy and the Environment

SOURCES OF ENERGY

The entire world relies on creating and using energy to heat homes, manufacture goods, grow and harvest food, transport products and complete many other processes. There are two kinds of energy sources: renewable and nonrenewable. Renewable energy sources are created repeatedly by nature and can be used repeatedly by people. Nonrenewable sources, also called fossil fuels, are in limited supply and will eventually be used up entirely.

RENEWABLE SOURCES

BIOMASS is an energy source found in plants and animals. It includes such natural products as wood, corn, sugarcane, manure, and plant and animal fats, and can also be found in organic trash. Biomass energy can be used in three ways:

- When burned, it creates steam that can be converted into electricity or captured to heat homes.
- Sources such as manure and organic trash give off a gas called **methane,** which can be used as fuel.
- Plant crops and plant and animal fats can be made into **ethanol** and **biodiesel,** two fuels used in transportation vehicles.

SUNLIGHT can be converted into heat and electricity.

- Solar cells absorb the heat from the sun and convert it into energy. They are used in calculators, watches and some highway signs.
- Solar power plants collect the sun's heat on huge **solar panels,** which then heat water to produce steam. The steam, in turn, moves electrical generators. A similar system is used on a smaller scale in solar-powered homes.

WIND has been used as an energy source for centuries. For example, windmills were used to help grind grain. Today, wind towers much taller than those windmills—usually about 20 stories high—are used to capture the power of wind. The wind turns giant blades connected to a long shaft that moves up and down to power an electrical generator.

WATER can produce energy called **hydropower.** Water pressure can turn the shafts of powerful electrical generators, making electricity. Waterfalls and fast-running rivers are major sources of hydropower because their natural flow creates pressure. Another way to harness hydropower is the storage method, in which dams are used to trap water in large reservoirs. When power is needed, the dams are opened and the water flows out. The water pressure created is then converted into energy.

GEOTHERMAL ENERGY uses the heat that rises from Earth's core, which is located about 4,000 miles (6,400 km) under the planet's surface. The most common way of harnessing geothermal energy involves capturing steam that comes from deep in the Earth and emerges in volcanoes, hot springs, fumaroles (vents in the Earth's surface that give off steam) and geysers (fountainlike bursts of water). This steam, heat or hot water can be trapped in pipes that lead directly to electrical power plants and even to homes.

HYDROGEN is the most common element in the universe. It is everywhere, but it doesn't exist on its own. Instead, hydrogen atoms bind with the atoms of other elements to form such compounds as water (hydrogen and oxygen), methane (hydrogen and carbon) and ammonia (hydrogen and nitrogen). Up-to-date technology is being used to separate hydrogen molecules and turn the hydrogen gas into a liquid that can be used in fuel cells. These fuel cells can power vehicles and electrical generators.

NONRENEWABLE SOURCES

COAL is a hard rock made of carbon. It started out as decaying plant matter that was covered with many layers of earth. Over the course of millions of years, the pressure of all this dirt, as well as Earth's heat, transformed the matter into coal. Because coal takes so long to form, it cannot be manufactured. Coal is the largest source of fossil fuel in the United States.

PETROLEUM is found deep within the Earth and has to be drilled and piped to the surface. It is made of decaying plant and animal remains that were trapped or covered with mud. Like coal, it was formed from pressure and heat over millions of years. In its crude state—before it is refined—it is known as petroleum. Petroleum can be refined into **oil, gasoline** or **diesel fuel,** which are used to power engines in vehicles, machines in factories and furnaces in homes.

NATURAL GAS was formed in the same way and over the same amount of time as coal and oil, except that it is the odorless by-product of decaying matter. The bubbles of gas are trapped underground and can be piped to the surface. Natural gas is used as a source of home heating as well as for cooking.

NUCLEAR ENERGY was developed in the 20th century. It relies on the heat given off when an atom is split (nuclear fission). In **nuclear fission,** the atoms of an element, Uranium-235, are hit with atomic particles called neutrons. The uranium atoms are split and give off a lot of heat, which is used to boil water. The steam from this water powers electrical generators.

Leading by Example

going green

New York State has vowed that, by 2013, its utilities (gas, water, telephone, electric and cable companies) will provide 25% of their electricity from renewable sources. California has passed a law requiring its largest utility companies to get 20% of their electricity from renewable sources by 2017. Hopefully, other states will follow New York's and California's lead.

Be Energy Smart

going green

USING ENERGY-EFFICIENT PRODUCTS NOT ONLY HELPS THE ENVIRONMENT, BUT CAN ALSO SAVE YOUR FAMILY MONEY. Make sure your parents purchase Energy Star appliances, including air conditioners, washers and dryers, dishwashers, televisions and DVD players. The Energy Star label is government approved, and it guarantees that an appliance meets high standards of energy efficiency.

CHOOSE COMPACT FLUORESCENT LIGHTBULBS (CFLs). A CFL, usually a small bulb with spiraled tubes, generates far less heat than standard incandescent lightbulbs.

SWITCH IT OFF TO SAVE!

CFLs are 75% more energy efficient than standard incandescent lightbulbs. Each time you use a CFL instead of an incandescent bulb, you keep almost 700 pounds of CO_2 out of the air.

MOST OF YOUR ELECTRONICS, INCLUDING STEREOS, TV SETS AND DVD PLAYERS, SUCK UP ENERGY EVEN WHEN THEY'RE TURNED OFF. In a typical American household, 5% to 15% of all electricity is consumed by electronics left on standby. So unplug them when they're not in use. If it sounds like a lot of unplugging, buy a power strip and plug everything into it. Then you'll only need to flip one switch.

POWERING CARS

Most automobiles run on internal combustion engines, which use large quantities of petroleum and pollute the air with harmful gases. To remedy this problem, engineers have been developing alternative types of fuel and engine systems.

BIOFUELS blend petroleum with plant materials. One type of biofuel is ethanol, made from grains, grasses or tree material. Using ethanol made from corn can reduce greenhouse gases by 40% to 60% compared with gasoline. Using ethanol made from grass or tree materials might reduce greenhouse gases by 100% when compared with gasoline.

BIODIESEL fuel uses oil from such plants as soybeans, as well as other oils—including vegetable oil left over from restaurant deep fryers! This fuel, which is mixed with varying amounts of petroleum, is popular in some European countries.

ELECTRIC CAR

ELECTRIC VEHICLES (EVs) are powered entirely by electricity, but often they can cover only a short distance before needing their batteries recharged. Because EVs emit no nasty tailpipe gases, some people think they are less damaging to the environment than standard-engine cars. But many researchers believe that the electricity needed to propel these cars might ultimately result in more pollution. Engineers are hopeful that solar batteries will some day be strong enough to power automobiles.

ELECTRIC-GASOLINE HYBRIDS combine a small gas engine with an electric motor. Hybrids, such as Toyota's Prius and Honda's Civic Hybrid, use the gas engine to supplement the electric motor only when necessary. Electric-gas hybrid engines can help cut down on global warming pollution.

Engineers are also experimenting with solar-powered cars, compressed-air cars and steam-powered engines. Keep your eyes out for new eco-friendly transportation in the near future.

What Vehicles Use the Most Energy?

According to the U.S. Department of Energy, trains are more energy efficient than cars and airplanes. British thermal units, or BTUs, are used to measure energy.

- Passenger trains use 2,978 BTUs per passenger mile.
- Cars use 3,496 BTUs per passenger mile.
- Airplanes use 3,959 BTUs per passenger mile.

Here's your best bet for getting around: a bicycle. It uses 0 BTUs per passenger mile.

WHERE DOES ALL YOUR TRASH GO?

On average, Americans produce about 1,600 pounds (726 kg) of garbage per person per year. To cut down on all that trash, make sure that you and your family are following the three Rs: reduce, reuse and recycle.

What happens to the waste that garbage trucks collect? In the United States, most trash is taken to landfills. Other trash is transported to incinerators, where it is burned for energy.

LANDFILLS are sites that are carefully designed to prevent dangerous waste from escaping into the soil and getting into groundwater. A thick layer of clay or plastic separates the garbage from the ground, and every day workers add a layer of soil to cover the trash on top. Liquid waste, called *leachate*, is pumped to the surface, where it is treated and made safe.

Sadly, landfills are expensive and can be bad for the environment. Materials deposited in landfills often do not decompose quickly, and the waste releases harmful methane gas into the environment as it breaks down. *Stinky fact: Some landfills collect the methane gas produced from their trash, treat it and then sell it as fuel.*

Boat carrying trash to a landfill

WASTE-TO-ENERGY PLANTS burn garbage to create energy. The trash is put into the plants' incinerators, where it burns down to about 10% of its original volume. The energy generated by this process heats water, which is turned into steam, which generates electricity. Because burning waste results in harmful CO_2 gases, the Environmental Protection Agency (EPA) requires that waste-to-energy plants comply with certain rules about capturing those emissions.

going green

What Does Biodegradable Really Mean?

A biodegradable product has the ability to break down (decompose) safely, quickly and naturally. Many biodegradable products that are sent to landfills, however, do not decompose quickly, because there's too much trash there and not enough air.

SOME OF THE LEAST BIODEGRADABLE PRODUCTS INCLUDE:
• Disposable diapers
• Aluminum cans (You can recycle these.)
• Tin cans
• Plastic bags
• Film canisters
• Glass bottles (You can recycle these too!)
• Styrofoam cups

Incinerator

Tips to Reduce Trash

• Try not to buy more than you need.
• Avoid products with a lot of packaging.
• Try to fix broken items rather than immediately replacing them.
• Donate your old toys and clothes to charity or community organizations.

A Waste-Wise City

Hamburg, Germany, provides a good example of what a city can do to decrease waste. The city has invested money in incinerators that have special filters to prevent harmful gases from escaping. The energy generated by the burning of trash is used to heat nearby homes. Ten years ago, Hamburg produced 1.6 million tons of waste and recycled less than 3% of it. Today, the city generates only 1.4 million tons and recycles nearly 60% of its waste.

Energy and the Environment

The landmasses on Earth consist of six different kinds of large regions called biomes. The environment of each biome reflects the climate, temperature and geographical features that exist there. Within a biome are many smaller areas called habitats. Wildlife thrive in their own habitats. For example, thick-furred animals live in the Arctic Circle, and color-changing chameleons thrive in lush forests filled with colorful plants. The relationship among various species of plants, animals and other creatures within their habitat is called an ecosystem.

BIOME	CLIMATE AND GEOGRAPHICAL FEATURES	EXAMPLES OF WILDLIFE
TROPICAL RAIN FOREST	Hot, humid, rainy; lush, dense trees and thick undergrowth	Monkeys, jaguars, anteaters, toucans, snakes, frogs, parrots
TEMPERATE FOREST	Four seasons, moderate amount of rain; evergreen and deciduous trees, mushrooms	Deer, foxes, squirrels, frogs, rabbits, eagles, sparrows, black bears
DESERT	Can be hot (Sahara in Africa) or cold (Antarctica), very little rain; sandy dunes and cacti or pure ice	Snakes, scorpions, camels, penguins
GRASSLAND	Savannah: rainy and dry seasons; dusty soil, some trees. Prairie: hot summers, cold winters; rich soil, wildflowers, no trees. Steppe: cool winters, hot summers; dry soil	Zebras, elephants, lions, tigers, giraffes, buffalo, cattle, sheep, horses, gophers, coyotes
TAIGA	Snowy, cold winters; short, wet summers; many evergreen or coniferous trees, rocky soil covered with twigs and evergreen needles, fungus	Elk, grizzly bears, moose, caribou, lynx, wolverines, rabbits, sparrows
TUNDRA	Very cold year-round, windy winters, short summers, hardly any precipitation; treeless plain, moss, lichen, grasses, low shrubs, permafrost layer (soil that never gets soft enough to cultivate)	Small rodents, polar bears, wolves, owls, foxes, seals

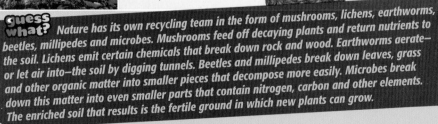

guess what? Nature has its own recycling team in the form of mushrooms, lichens, earthworms, beetles, millipedes and microbes. Mushrooms feed off decaying plants and return nutrients to the soil. Lichens emit certain chemicals that break down rock and wood. Earthworms aerate—or let air into—the soil by digging tunnels. Beetles and millipedes break down leaves, grass and other organic matter into smaller pieces that decompose more easily. Microbes break down this matter into even smaller parts that contain nitrogen, carbon and other elements. The enriched soil that results is the fertile ground in which new plants can grow.

WHAT IS COMPOST?

Compost is organic matter that decomposes, resulting in a crumbly material called *mulch* that helps fertilize soil and replenish nutrients. Mulch can be added to your plant and vegetable gardens, lawns, greenhouses and flower beds to help them grow.

WHAT GOES IN A COMPOST PILE?

- Toss all your leftover fruits and vegetables and their peelings into the pile. You can also throw in eggshells, nutshells, coffee grounds and tea bags, along with hay, straw, leaves, grass and even shredded newspaper.
- Don't put in any meat or meat products, cheese, oils, chemically-treated plants or grass, or pet waste.

HOW TO BUILD A COMPOST PILE

- Choose a location, preferably close to your kitchen or garden. A sunny spot will speed up the process.
- Use a shovel to remove some grass to create a good base, then pile on branches, leaves, grass clippings or hay. This should be about 3 feet (1 m) square and 3 feet (1 m) high.
- Start composting! Make sure you chop or shred larger pieces of matter.
- Turn your compost pile with a shovel every week or so to keep it moist and to distribute air.
- Your compost should be ready in one to four months!

Unspoiled Places

Today, it's rare to find a truly wild part of the world, but there are still pockets of relatively unspoiled land. Conservation International (conservation.org) compiled a list of 37 of the Earth's last wild places. These are places that cover at least 3,860 square miles (10,000 sq km) and have fewer than five humans per square kilometer. In these areas, the majority of the original vegetation exists and has not been cut down. Here are a few of these environment wonders.

AMAZONIA refers to the Amazon Rain Forest, which covers parts of Bolivia, Brazil, Colombia, Ecuador, French Guiana, Guyana, Peru, Suriname and Venezuela.

THE CONGO FORESTS OF CENTRAL AFRICA, which spread over parts of Angola, Cameroon, Central African Republic, Democratic Republic of the Congo, Equatorial Guinea, Gabon and the Republic of Congo.

THE CHACO, which is an area in South America that includes northern Argentina, southeastern Bolivia, northwestern Paraguay and a tiny portion of Brazil.

THE SERENGETI, located in Kenya and Tanzania, is famous for its wildlife and especially for the overland migration of animals like wildebeests and zebras. Parts of the Serengeti are national parks and game reserves.

The Serengeti

KIMBERLEY, a remote region in the northwest of Australia.

THE SUNDARBANS, a mangrove forest and group of forested islands in Bangladesh and India. The Sundarbans are home to more than 250 species of birds. Endangered species such as the Bengal tiger, estuarine crocodile and Indian python can be found there.

THE SUDD, a large swamp in Sudan. The White Nile runs through the wetlands of the Sudd.

THE MOJAVE DESERT, which is the dry, arid region of the United States. Mostly found in Southern California, it also includes parts of Arizona, Nevada and Utah.

PATAGONIA, the southernmost region of South America. It lies mostly in Argentina and partly in southern Chile.

THE ARCTIC TUNDRA, found in Canada, Finland, Greenland, Iceland, Norway, Russia, Sweden and in the U.S. state of Alaska.

Food and Nutrition

Nutrition Basics

Food provides the human body with the nutrients it needs to grow, repair itself, and stay fit and healthy. These nutrients include proteins, carbohydrates, fats, vitamins and minerals.

Carbohydrates

Carbohydrates are the body's main source of fuel. Your body breaks down carbohydrates into glucose (blood sugar), which travels through your bloodstream and supplies your cells with energy. Simple carbohydrates, which are found in fruits, soda, candy and table sugar, are digested quickly. Complex carbohydrates (**fiber** and **starches**), which are found in rice, bread, whole grains, pasta and vegetables, take longer for the body to digest.

WHAT IS FIBER?

Fiber is a kind of carbohydrate that the body can't digest. Because it helps food and waste move through your body, fiber is necessary for staying healthy. It also helps to lower your risk for heart disease and diabetes. Some great sources of fiber are whole-grain cereals and breads, beans, fruits and vegetables.

Proteins

Proteins, found in fish, meat, poultry, eggs, nuts, dairy products and legumes (such as peanuts, lentils and beans) keep us strong. They help the body build new cells and repair damaged cell tissues. Most Americans eat much more protein than they actually need. Excess protein is often stored in our bodies as fat.

Fats

Not only do fats help your body grow, they also help protect your internal organs and your skin. But they should be eaten only in small quantities. There are different types of fats, and some are better than others. **Saturated fats** are considered "bad" fats, as they increase your risk for diseases. Saturated fats are most often found in foods that come from animals, including meat, cheese and butter. **Monounsaturated fats** and **polyunsaturated fats** are considered "good" fats. They lower your risk for disease. These fats are found in olive, safflower and canola oils, among others. They are also found in fish and nuts.

WHAT ARE TRANS FATS?

Trans fats are the worst types of fats you can put into your body. They are unsaturated fats that have been treated with chemicals to make them stay solid at room temperature. Because of the way they are prepared, they last longer than other fats. Many fast-food restaurants and commercial bakeries use them in their products, though some cities now ban them from using trans fats. Trans fats can be found in margarine and some cookies, potato chips, doughnuts and other snack foods, and will increase your risk for heart disease.

Vitamins and Minerals

Vitamins and minerals are micronutrients that help regulate body processes.

VITAMIN A, found in milk, many greens, carrots and egg yolks, benefits your skin and eyes.

VITAMIN C, found in many fruits and vegetables, is good for skin, teeth and gums.

VITAMIN D, found in fish, eggs, milk, yogurt and cheese, helps promote strong bones and teeth and regulates cell growth.

VITAMIN E, found in spinach, nuts, olives and almonds, has great **antioxidant** properties, and it lowers your risk for heart disease.

MINERALS such as potassium, iron, calcium and magnesium are necessary for healthy bones, blood and muscle. Minerals are found naturally in many foods. For example, milk, yogurt and leafy greens like spinach and broccoli are good sources of calcium, and red meat is a food high in iron. Minerals are sometimes added to foods to make them more nutritious. For example, you may see calcium-fortified orange juice at the grocery store.

WHAT ARE ANTIOXIDANTS? Antioxidants are substances in foods that prevent or repair damage to your cells.

Calories

Calories measure how much energy we get from food. You can tell how many calories a food has by looking at the nutrition facts label. Girls ages 9 through 13 need between 1,600 and 2,200 calories a day, while boys of the same age need between 1,800 and 2,600. Eating too many calories can lead to weight gain.

Guess what? *Turn off the television! Step away from the computer! You burn only about one calorie a minute sitting in front of the boob tube or your Mac.*

EAT SMART, STAY FIT

Here are some simple ways to help yourself be as healthy as you can be.

- Eat plenty of fruits, vegetables and whole grains.
- Drink plenty of water daily.
- Keep your meal portions moderate.
- Avoid eating too many fried foods and sugary sweets.
- Exercise regularly—play baseball, go for a swim or just run around with your dog.

Organic Food

The term *organic* usually refers to food that has been processed or cultivated without the use of any chemicals such as fertilizers, pesticides or artificial additives. Organic farmers believe that these materials are harmful to the environment and bad for the consumer. Organic foods are more expensive to produce and therefore cost more. Many people believe that organic food is safer to eat and more nutritious than food exposed to chemicals—and even swear it tastes better!

Local Fare

going green

A locavore is a person who eats food that has been produced locally, usually within an area of 100 miles (161 km). Local food is fresher and less damaging to the environment (transporting food long distances means more carbon emissions, which contribute to global warming). When you buy from a nearby farmer, you are also helping your community.

Guess what? *The average food item travels 1,500 miles (2,414 km) before it reaches the consumer!*

Food and Nutrition

93

The Food Pyramid

Since 2-year-olds and 80-year-olds don't have the same dietary requirements, the U.S. Department of Agriculture has introduced 12 different versions of the food pyramid. Depending on your age, gender, height, weight and how often you exercise, your dietary needs will be different.

| GRAINS | VEGETABLES | FRUITS | MILK | MEAT & BEANS |

OILS are not a food group, but you need some for good health. Get your oils from fish, nuts and liquid oils such as corn oil, soybean oil and canola oil.

Based on the new food pyramid, here are the recommended food amounts for a 9-year-old girl and an 11-year-old boy of average height and weight, who both exercise 30 to 60 minutes per day.

	9-YEAR-OLD GIRL	11-YEAR-OLD BOY
GRAINS	5 ounces	6 ounces
VEGETABLES	2 cups	2½ cups
FRUITS	1½ cups	2 cups
MILK	3 cups	3 cups
MEAT AND BEANS	5 ounces	5½ ounces

TOP 5 Most Popular Lunch-Box Foods

What did you bring for lunch? If you said a sandwich, chips and an apple, we're not surprised. A recent survey of Americans' eating habits shows that those three items went to school more often than any other foods. The researchers looked into kids' lunch boxes 10,019 times. Here are the lunchtime favorites they found.

1. Fruit		29%
2. Chips		28%
3. Peanut butter and jelly sandwich		26%
4. Cookies		16%
5. Crackers		11%

Source: The NPD Group/
National Eating Trends (Net)

SUPERFOODS TO THE RESCUE!

Whether you include them in your main meals, snack on them or sip them, there are some foods that provide amazing health benefits. These are known as superfoods.

BLUEBERRIES Chock-full of vitamin C, potassium and antioxidants, blueberries are great for your heart and circulation, and they will help lower your risk for heart disease and cancer. Put some in your cereal or yogurt!

SOYBEANS Packed with protein, B vitamins, iron and calcium, soybeans are a nutritional powerhouse. Eat soy in the form of tofu, edamame and soy milk—and you'll decrease your risk for certain cancers, heart disease and kidney disease.

WALNUTS Walnuts have a lot of antioxidants and disease-fighting omega-3 fatty acids, which means that they lower heart disease risk and might help improve memory.

AVOCADOS Packed with potassium and vitamins A, E, B and C, avocados are also rich in antioxidants. They are excellent for your heart and especially good for your skin. Add some slices to a turkey sandwich or make some guacamole.

DARK CHOCOLATE Eat chocolate with 60% or higher cocoa content—the darker it is, the better it is for you. Packed with polyphenols (a type of antioxidant), dark chocolate helps your heart, gives you energy, lowers blood pressure and may improve memory. Just remember that chocolate often has a high fat and sugar content and can be bad for your teeth.

guess what? *Goji berries—cherrylike berries that have been used as medicine in Tibet for 2,000 years—are thought to boost your circulation, protect your liver, improve your vision and help you live longer!*

Rainbow Eating

Take a walk through your supermarket and see how many different-colored foods you can find. Did you know that the pigments that make those foods so colorful are often also what make them so good for you? Some scientists believe that the more vibrantly colored a food is, the better it is for you.

EAT RED (AND PINK)
• Strawberries, red grapes and raspberries are packed with anthocyanins—antioxidants that keep hearts healthy and protect cells.

• Strawberries, raspberries, tomatoes and red peppers are great sources of vitamin C.

• Red tomatoes, pink grapefruits and watermelons have lycopene, an antioxidant that may reduce your risk for cancer.

EAT ORANGE
• Sweet potatoes, pumpkins, cantaloupe and carrots all contain beta-carotene, which is converted to vitamin A in the body. Vitamin A has been associated with a lower risk for lung cancer.

EAT GREEN
• Leafy greens like spinach, broccoli and kale are great sources of folate, a B vitamin that protects your heart. Also try asparagus and kiwi fruits.

EAT BLUE (AND PURPLE)
• Blueberries, blackberries and eggplant all contain antioxidants known as anthocyanins, which give them their rich colors and also help your brain stay healthy. Concord grapes are another food in this group.

Food and Nutrition

Games

TOP 5 Video Game Consoles of 2008

CONSOLE	UNITS SOLD
1. Wii	10,151,000
2. Nintendo DS	9,951,000
3. Microsoft Xbox 360	4,735,400
4. PSP	3,829,600
5. Sony PlayStation 3	3,544,900

Source: NPD group

TOP 5 Best-selling Video Games of 2008

VIDEO GAME	GAMES SOLD
1. *Wii Play*	5.28 million
2. *Madden NFL '09*	5.25 million
3. *Grand Theft Auto IV*	5.22 million
4. *Mario Kart Wii*	5 million
5. *Call of Duty: World at War*	4.63 million

Source: NPD group

guess what? *The familiar thumb-stick control on current game consoles like the Xbox and PlayStation evolved from larger joystick controllers that were used with home video games since the 1970s. But before joysticks were ever used for video games—before video games even existed—the earliest joysticks were used for flying planes!*

The First Home Video Game Console

Way back in 1972—before Wii, before PlayStation, even before Atari—the Magnavox Odyssey was the first home video game console. It came with handheld controllers for games like soccer and volleyball, and consumers could buy a plastic gun that pointed at the screen for the shooting gallery game. Of course there was also a table tennis game, which looked a lot like the more famous *Pong* video game, but *Pong* came out later the same year. Ralph Baer, the mastermind behind the Odyssey, also created the popular electronic game Simon.

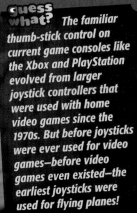

TOP 10 Best-selling PC Games of 2008

1. *World of Warcraft: Wrath of the Lich King*
2. *Spore*
3. *World of Warcraft: Battle Chest*
4. *Age of Conan: Hyborian Adventures*
5. *Warhammer Online: Age of Reckoning*
6. *Call Of Duty 4: Modern Warfare*
7. *The Sims 2: Double Deluxe*
8. *World of Warcraft: Wrath of the Lich King Collector's Edition*
9. *Fallout 3*
10. *World of Warcraft: Burning Crusade*

Source: NPD group

ATARI JOYSTICK

MADDEN NFL '08

Madden NFL '08 was voted Favorite Video Game by the Nickelodeon Kids' Choice Awards in 2008. With some of the most realistic football ever seen in a video game, *Madden NFL '08* beat out three music-related games—*Dance Dance Revolution, Guitar Hero* and *High School Musical: Sing It!*—to win. *Madden NFL '08* lets you switch between players, see the skills of your opponents on the screen and use all sorts of new, realistic moves, such as low-hitting tackles.

Kongregate, Webby Award Winner

Kongregate.com is a Web site for playing video games and meeting friends who play. Kongregate has more than 12,000 games to choose from, with themes that include sports, music, action/adventure, puzzles and games, and more. The games are all the products of independent creators and are free. With thousands of players online at any one time, there are always plenty of people to play with or to chat with about games. Also, if you ever want to make your own video game, you can put it up on Kongregate for others around the world to play!

Fun with Wii

With its wireless remote, the Nintendo Wii (pronounced "we") is one of the coolest new video game consoles out there. The handheld motion-sensitive controller can sense every move you make—up, down, sideways, forward and back—and it can tell how quickly you are moving. This lets players experience video games in new and fun ways. You can swing your arm to hit a tennis ball or move your hand like you're steering a car. With an add-on Nunchuk controller, you can also do two-handed moves.

An even newer addition to the system is the *Wii Fit,* which brings video games to a whole new place—the gym! The "balance board" controller looks like a scale, and it actually measures how much weight you put on each foot. By doing this, *Wii Fit* lets you use the movement of your body to play games or exercise, or to do both at the same time! Ride a snowboard, walk a tightrope or

Play That Funky Music

Many video games combine music and gaming, and *Guitar Hero* is both one of the first and one of the most popular. To play, you use a guitar-shaped game controller and follow the colored bars on the screen as they move toward you. Five colored buttons on the "neck" of the guitar are used together with the "strum" button to play along with songs by bands such as the Rolling Stones and Weezer. Being a real *Guitar Hero* expert is all about rhythm. If you can hit the correct button and strum at just the right time, you'll score big!

Rock Band also uses guitar-shaped game controllers, but adds a drum kit controller and a microphone so you can play the game with an entire "band" at the same time. With the drum kit, you have to hit the color-coded drums in time with the colored bars on the screen. With the microphone, you have to sing in time and in tune. Each member of the band follows his or her own part of the song on the screen like in *Guitar Hero.* You can either cooperate with your bandmates for a joint score or compete against each other to see who

Games

Classic Board Games

MONOPOLY® The object of Monopoly is to make money—and to make your opponents go broke! Each square on the board is a different "property." If you have enough money, you can buy a property and charge rent when others land there. The game ends when all but one player have gone bankrupt. The original game used street names from Atlantic City, New Jersey, but now different versions feature such locations as Las Vegas, Nevada, and London, England. The recent "world" edition features places from all around the globe and even uses electronic bank cards instead of pretend money.

SCRABBLE® Your school vocabulary words come in handy in Scrabble, a game in which you form words from groups of letters. You earn more points for playing rarely used letters like *x* and for placing words on double- and triple-score boxes. After all the letters are used up, the player with the highest score wins.

CHECKERS One of the oldest games in the world, checkers can be played with almost anything. People have used coins or even rocks as game pieces. Today, most people simply use a checker set and board. Two players set up 12 pieces each on a 64-square board and advance toward each other diagonally, capturing their opponent's pieces by jumping over them. The winner is the one who captures all the other's checkers.

TRIVIAL PURSUIT™ Trivial Pursuit came out in the 1980s and became a big hit almost immediately. Players work their way around the board by correctly answering trivia questions that come from six different categories, including history and entertainment. The hugely popular game has inspired many versions, including ones dedicated to *Star Wars* and the 1980s.

Guess what? *Unlike the average board game, Twister® uses people as the playing pieces. Contestants spin a dial that tells them to move a hand or foot to a particular color on the Twister mat. Players reach for unoccupied dots and try not to fall down or touch the mat with their knees or elbows. The last remaining player wins.*

What Is Sudoku?

Sudoku is a number puzzle game that will test your wits. It starts with a nine-by-nine grid of 81 boxes. Some of these boxes come with numbers in them, while the rest are empty. To play, you try to fill in the empty boxes so that each row, each column and every three-by-three square includes all of the numbers 1 through 9 (without repeating!). Depending on which boxes are filled at the start, Sudoku puzzles can be quick and easy or very, very hard—but always addictive!

The first Sudoku puzzles appeared in a 1979 puzzle magazine from New York, but the name Sudoku wasn't used until a Japanese magazine published the puzzles in 1984. The *London Times* newspaper began a regular puzzle in 2004, which set off an international craze!

THE HIGHEST PLACE ON EARTH
Mount Everest in Nepal, the world's tallest mountain, stands 29,035 feet (8,850 m) above sea level.

THE LOWEST PLACE ON EARTH
Deep in the Pacific Ocean is the Mariana Trench, which is 35,827 feet (10,920 m) below sea level.

THE BIGGEST OCEAN
The Pacific Ocean covers about 1/3 of Earth's surface. It stretches from the Bering Sea in the Arctic to Antarctica's Ross Sea.

THE SMALLEST OCEAN
The Arctic Ocean is just 1/10 the size of the Pacific.

THE LONGEST RIVER
The Nile runs for 4,145 miles (6,654 km).

THE WETTEST PLACE ON EARTH
Lloro, Colombia, averages 523.6 inches (13 m) of rainfall a year.

THE COLDEST PLACE ON EARTH
Vostok, Antarctica, reached a low of −129°F (−89°C) on July 21, 1983.

THE SHORTEST RIVER
The Roe River in Wisconsin is just 200 feet (61 m) long.

THE LARGEST RAIN FOREST
The Amazon in South America covers parts of Brazil, Bolivia, Ecuador, Peru, Colombia, Venezuela, Suriname, French Guiana and Guyana.

THE DRIEST PLACE ON EARTH
Arica, Chile, gets just .03 inches (.9 cm) of rainfall a year.

THE TALLEST TREE
A coast redwood in Redwood National Park, California, stands at 378.1 feet (115.5 m).

THE HIGHEST WATERFALL
Angel Falls (*Salto Angel*) in Venezuela's Canaima National Park has a 3,287-foot (1,002-m) drop.

THE HOTTEST PLACE ON EARTH
On September 13, 1922, the temperature reached 136°F (57.8°C) in El Azizia, Libya.

THE DEEPEST CANYON IN THE UNITED STATES
Carved by the Snake River, Hells Canyon on the border of Idaho and Oregon is more than 8,000 feet (2,438 m) deep.

THE LARGEST FRESH-WATER LAKE
Lake Baikal, in southern Russia, has the largest volume of water. Lake Superior, on the United States–Canadian border, has the largest surface area.

THE LARGEST SALT-WATER LAKE
The landlocked Caspian Sea has a greater volume of water than any other lake, including all freshwater lakes.

THE LARGEST VOLCANO
At about 50,000 feet (15,240 m) above its base, Mauna Loa in Hawaii is actually taller than Mount Everest. But most of the volcano is under the sea.

Geography

101

OUR CHANGING EARTH

The North American and Eurasian plates meet in Thingvellir, Iceland.

Soon after Earth formed billions of years ago, its rocky crust hardened. The crust is not a solid piece, however. It's broken into seven major plates (the African, North American, South American, Eurasian, Australian, Antarctic and Pacific plates) and several minor ones (including the Arabian, Nazca or Andean, and Philippine plates). These plates all move across, under or over one another. The breakup and movement of different plates is called continental drift. There are three kinds of drift: divergent, convergent and lateral.

DIVERGENT movements occur when plates pull apart from one another. When two plates diverge, pieces from each plate sink toward the Earth's core, forming a valley, or rift. Magma, which is liquid rock, weighs less than solid rock and flows upward. The magma fills in the base in the rift and forms new crust. The Rift Valley in East Africa is a result of divergence.

CONVERGENT movements occur when plates crash into one another. When two plates converge, they push against each other, forming mountains and deep trenches. The folding and collapsing of convergent plates causes broken rock to sink deep below Earth's outer crust into the magma below. The hot magma melts the rock, which then spews upward as volcanic eruptions. The collision between the South American and the Nazca plates formed the **Andes Mountains.**

The Andes

The movement of plates can lead to cracks on Earth's surface, like this one in Utah.

LATERAL (also called transforming) movements occur when plates move alongside one another in different directions. The movement wears down the sides of each plate and creates narrow gullies. This sideswiping motion causes earthquakes along the gullies. The San Andreas Fault in California is one of the world's best-known meeting places of laterally moving plates.

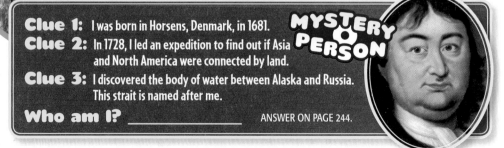

Clue 1: I was born in Horsens, Denmark, in 1681.

Clue 2: In 1728, I led an expedition to find out if Asia and North America were connected by land.

Clue 3: I discovered the body of water between Alaska and Russia. This strait is named after me.

MYSTERY PERSON

Who am I? _____

ANSWER ON PAGE 244.

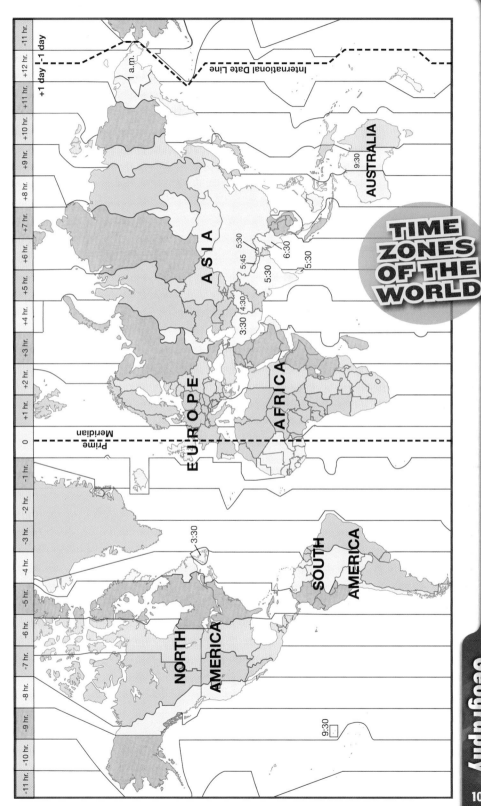

TIME ZONES OF THE WORLD

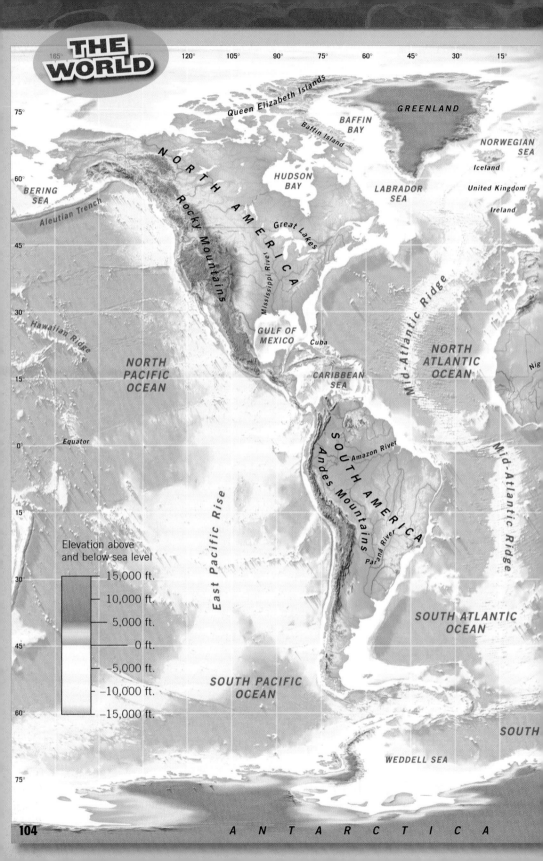

120°   105°   90°   75°   60°   45°   30°   15°

75°

Queen Elizabeth Islands

GREENLAND

BAFFIN
BAY

Baffin Island

NORWEGIAN
SEA

Iceland

60°

BERING
SEA

HUDSON
BAY

LABRADOR
SEA

United Kingdom

Ireland

Aleutian Trench

N O R T H   A M E R I C A

Rocky Mountains

45°

Great Lakes

Mississippi River

Mid-Atlantic Ridge

30°

Hawaiian Ridge

GULF OF
MEXICO

Cuba

NORTH
ATLANTIC
OCEAN

Nig

15°

NORTH
PACIFIC
OCEAN

CARIBBEAN
SEA

Mid-Atlantic Ridge

Equator

0°

S O U T H   A M E R I C A

Amazon River

Andes Mountains

15°

East Pacific Rise

Paraná River

Elevation above
and below sea level

15,000 ft.

10,000 ft.

5,000 ft.

0 ft.

−5,000 ft.

−10,000 ft.

−15,000 ft.

SOUTH ATLANTIC
OCEAN

30°

45°

SOUTH PACIFIC
OCEAN

SOUTH

60°

WEDDELL SEA

75°

A N T A R C T I C A

15°   30°   45°   60°   75°   90°   105°   120°   135°   150°   165°

75°

EUROPE

Ural Mts.

ob River

S i b e r i a

A S I A

Lena River

Sea of
Okhotsk

60°

Baltic
Sea

Alps

Black
Sea

Caspian
Sea

Aral
Sea

Gobi

Huang River

Honshu

Kuril-Kamchatka
Trench

45°

Mediterranean Sea

Euphrates R.

Persian
Gulf

Indus River

Himalayas

Mt.
Everest

Ganges R.

Chang River

Japan Trench

NORTH
PACIFIC
OCEAN

30°

Sahara

Nile River

Red Sea

ARABIAN
SEA

BAY OF
BENGAL

Mekong R.

South
China
Sea

15°

A F R I C A

Congo River

Borneo

New Guinea

Equator   0°

Sumatra

Java

Java Trench

Central Indian Ridge

INDIAN
OCEAN

Ninety East Ridge

Great Barrier Reef

15°

Kalahari
Desert

Madagascar

AUSTRALIA

30°

Southwest Indian Ridge

North
Island

South
Island

45°

N OCEAN

Maps always show a
distorted view of the
Earth because they
are not curved in
three dimensions.

AFRICA

ATLANTIC OCEAN

BLACK SEA

MEDITERRANEAN SEA

RED SEA

EUROPE

PORTUGAL
SPAIN
FRANCE
SWITZERLAND
ITALY
AUSTRIA
SLOVENIA
CROATIA
BOSNIA AND HERZEGOVINA
MONTENEGRO
HUNGARY
ROMANIA
BULGARIA
MACEDONIA
KOSOVO
SERBIA
ALBANIA
GREECE
MOLDOVA
TURKEY
GEORGIA
ARMENIA
AZERBAIJAN
CYPRUS
LEBANON
ISRAEL
JORDAN
SYRIA
IRAQ
IRAN
KUWAIT
BAHRAIN
QATAR
SAUDI ARABIA
YEMEN

Corsica
Sardinia
Majorca
Sicily
MALTA
Crete

Oran
Algiers
Constantine
Tunis
TUNISIA
Qafsah
Tripoli
Banghazi

MOROCCO
Tangier
Casablanca
Rabat
Fès
Marrakech
Erfoud

Canary Is.
Madeira Islands

Laayoune (El Aaiún)
WESTERN SAHARA

Nouakchott
MAURITANIA

Dakar
SENEGAL
Banjul
THE GAMBIA
Bissau
GUINEA-BISSAU
Conakry
GUINEA
Freetown
SIERRA LEONE
Monrovia
LIBERIA

Bamako
MALI
Timbuktu

ALGERIA

S A H A R A

LIBYA

EGYPT
Alexandria
Cairo
Suez
Luxor
Aswan
Al Jawf

Nile River

SUDAN
Port Sudan
Khartoum

ERITREA
Asmara

DJIBOUTI
Djibouti

ETHIOPIA
Addis Ababa
Harer
Gore
Juba

SOMALIA
Hargeysa
Mogadishu

UGANDA
Kampala

KENYA

CHAD
N'Djamena

NIGER
Agadez
Zinder

NIGERIA
Kano
Abuja
Ibadan
Lagos

CENTRAL AFRICAN REPUBLIC
Bangui

Congo River

OF THE CONGO

CAMEROON
Yaoundé
Douala

EQUATORIAL GUINEA
Malabo
Libreville
SÃO TOMÉ

Benue River
Niger River

BURKINA FASO
Ouagadougou
Gaoua

BENIN
TOGO
Lomé
Porto-Novo

GHANA
Accra

CÔTE D'IVOIRE
Yamoussoukro
Abidjan

Niamey

106

INDIAN
OCEAN

Antananarivo ✪

MADAGASCAR

Moroni ✪
COMOROS

Mombasa •
• Dar es Salaam
Zanzibar •

Cidade
de Nacala •

Kigoma •

Bukavu • Lake
Bujumbura ✪ BURUNDI Tanganyika
RWANDA

DEMOCRATIC
REPUBLIC OF
THE CONGO

Kinshasa ✪
Brazzaville ✪
Pointe-Noire •

(EQUATORIAL GUINEA)

TANZANIA

Lake
Nyasa

MALAWI
Lilongwe ✪
Blantyre •

Lubumbashi •
Kitwe •
Kananga •
Luanda ✪

ZAMBIA
Lusaka ✪

Harare ✪
ZIMBABWE

MOZAMBIQUE

Beira •

Mozambique Channel

Maputo ✪
Durban •

Pretoria ✪
Mbabane ✪ SWAZILAND
Johannesburg •
Maseru ✪ LESOTHO

Gaborone ✪
BOTSWANA

SOUTH
AFRICA

Port Elizabeth •

ANGOLA

Lubango •

Namibe •

NAMIBIA
Windhoek ✪

Walvis Bay •

Cape Town •

ATLANTIC
OCEAN

0 mi.   500 mi.   1,000 mi.

0 km   500 km   1,000 km

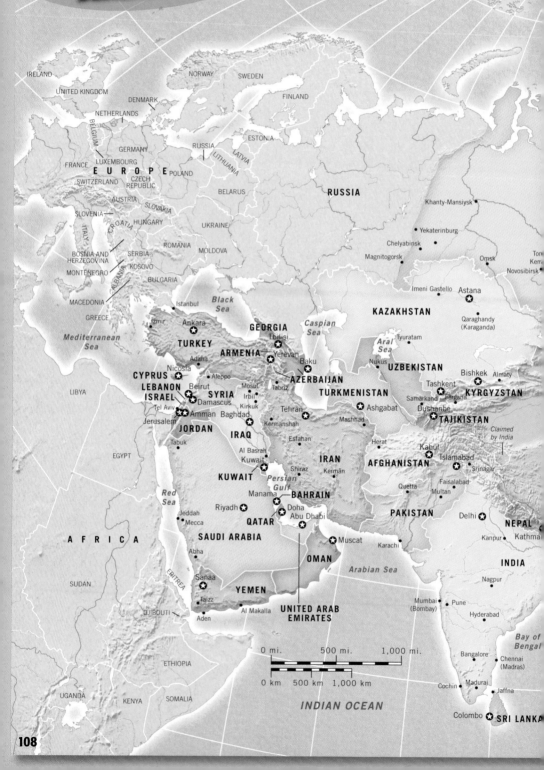

MIDDLE EAST AND ASIA

IRELAND
UNITED KINGDOM
NORWAY
SWEDEN
FINLAND
DENMARK
NETHERLANDS
BELGIUM
GERMANY
LUXEMBOURG
FRANCE
SWITZERLAND
EUROPE
POLAND
CZECH REPUBLIC
AUSTRIA
SLOVAKIA
SLOVENIA
HUNGARY
ITALY
CROATIA
ROMANIA
BOSNIA AND HERZEGOVINA
SERBIA
MONTENEGRO
ALBANIA
KOSOVO
BULGARIA
MACEDONIA
GREECE

RUSSIA
ESTONIA
LATVIA
LITHUANIA
BELARUS
UKRAINE
MOLDOVA

RUSSIA
Khanty-Mansiysk
Yekaterinburg
Chelyabinsk
Magnitogorsk
Omsk
Tom
Kem
Novosibirsk

Imeni Gastello
Astana
KAZAKHSTAN
Qaraghandy
(Karaganda)

Mediterranean Sea
Black Sea
Istanbul
Izmir
Ankara
TURKEY
Adana
GEORGIA
Tbilisi
ARMENIA
Yerevan
Caspian Sea
Baku
Tyuratam

Aral Sea
Nukus
UZBEKISTAN
Bishkek
Almaty
Tashkent
KYRGYZSTAN

CYPRUS
Nicosia
LEBANON
Beirut
ISRAEL
Tel Aviv
Jerusalem
Aleppo
SYRIA
Damascus
Mosul
Irbil
Kirkuk
Amman
Baghdad
JORDAN
Tabuk
IRAQ
Tabriz
AZERBAIJAN
TURKMENISTAN
Ashgabat
Samarkand
Dushanbe
Fergana
TAJIKISTAN
Claimed by India

LIBYA

Tehran
Kermanshah
Esfahan
Mashhad
Herat
Kabul
Islamabad
Srinagar
AFGHANISTAN
IRAN
Shiraz
Kerman
Quetta
Faisalabad
Multan
Delhi
NEPAL
Kanpur
Kathma

EGYPT

Al Basrah
Kuwait
KUWAIT
Persian Gulf
Manama
BAHRAIN
PAKISTAN
Karachi
INDIA
Nagpur

Red Sea
Jeddah
Mecca
Riyadh
Doha
Abu Dhabi
QATAR
Muscat
SAUDI ARABIA
Abha
OMAN
Arabian Sea
UNITED ARAB EMIRATES
Mumbai (Bombay)
Pune
Hyderabad

AFRICA
SUDAN
ERITREA
Sanaa
Taizz
Al Makalla
YEMEN
Aden
DJIBOUTI

Bay of Bengal

0 mi.   500 mi.   1,000 mi.

0 km   500 km 1,000 km

ETHIOPIA
UGANDA
KENYA
SOMALIA
INDIAN OCEAN
Bangalore
Chennai (Madras)
Cochin
Madurai
Jaffna
Colombo
SRI LANKA

ARCTIC OCEAN

Cherskiy

Bering
Sea

Tiksi

Noril'sk

Verkhoyansk

RUSSIA

Magadan

Kamchatka
Peninsula

Yakutsk

Petropavlovsk-
Kamchatskiy

Sea of
Okhotsk

S I B E R I A

Krasnoyarsk

Novokuznetsk

Khabarovsk

Irkutsk

Sakhalin

Sapporo

Harbin

Ulaanbaatar

Changchun

Vladivostok

Gobi

MONGOLIA

Shenyang

JAPAN

Ürümqi

Hohhot

Jinxi

N. KOREA

P'yongyang

Tokyo

Beijing

Seoul

Nagoya

Kyoto
Kobe

Tianjin

Osaka

PACIFIC
OCEAN

Taiyuan

Jinan

S. KOREA

Taegu
Pusan

Hiroshima

Lanzhou

Qingdao

Fukuoka

Xi'an

Nagasaki

CHINA

Hefei

Shanghai

Chengdu

Wuhan

Chongqing

Naha

Lhasa

Fuzhou

Taipei

Thimphu

Xiamen

BHUTAN

TAIWAN

BANGLADESH

Liuzhou

Kao-hsiung

Dhaka

Guangzhou

Calcutta

Mandalay

Chittagong

Nanning

Macao

Hong Kong

Hanoi

MYANMAR
(BURMA)

Luzon

LAOS

Baguio

Chiang Mai

Vientiane

Quezon City

Rangoon

Da Nang

Manila

THAILAND

PHILIPPINES

Bangkok

VIETNAM

Cebu

CAMBODIA

Phnom
Penh

Ho Chi Minh City

Davao

Phuket

Songkhla

Borneo

AUSTRALIA AND THE PACIFIC ISLANDS

JAPAN

CHINA

TAIWAN

ASIA

PHILIPPINE
SEA

LAOS

VIETNAM

PHILIPPINES

THAILAND

CAMBODIA

NORTHERN
MARIANA
ISLANDS (U.S.)
Saipan ★

Wake

Agana ★ Guam
(U.S.)

Yap Islands

Caroline Islands

Koror
⊛

MICRONESIA

Palikir ⊛

PALAU

Bandar Seri Begawan

Manado

Sorong

Jayapura

PAPUA NEW GUINEA

BRUNEI

Kota Kinabalu

Ipoh

M A L A Y S I A

Kuching

Palu

Irian
Jaya

Wewak

Kuala Lumpur

SINGAPORE

Pontianak

Samarinda

Celebes

New Guinea

Medan

Borneo

Pakanbaru

Banjarmasin

Honiara
Guadalcanal
⊛

Palembang

I N D O N E S I A

Ujungpandang

Sumatra

Jakarta
⊛

Surabaya

Port Moresby
⊛

Java

Semarang

Denpasar (Bali)

Kupang

EAST TIMOR

Timor

CORAL
SEA

West Island

Ashmore and Cartier Islands
(Australia)

Timor Sea

Darwin

Gulf of
Carpentaria

Great Barrier Reef

Coral Sea Islands (Australia)

Derby

Cairns

INDIAN OCEAN

Townsville

Mackay

Alice Springs

Rockhampton

Gladstone

A U S T R A L I A

Brisbane

Tropic of Capricorn

Geraldton

Broken Hill

Lord Howe
Island
(Australia)

Kalgoorlie

Sydney

Perth

Whyalla

Canberra
⊛

Bunbury

Esperance

Adelaide

Melbourne

TASMAN
SEA

Hobart

Tasmania

Tropic of Cancer

Honolulu
Hilo

Hawaii
(U.S.)

Johnston Atoll (U.S.)

MARSHALL ISLANDS

Majuro

PACIFIC OCEAN

Tarawa

Kingman Reef (U.S.)
Palmyra Atoll (U.S.)

Howland Island (U.S.)

Baker Island (U.S.)

Line Islands

ren
trict
RU

*Gilbert
Islands*

K I R I B A T I

Jarvis
Island
(U.S.)

Equator

Phoenix Islands

**SOLOMON
ISLANDS**

Funafuti

TUVALU

TOKELAU (N.Z.)

Mata-Utu

SAMOA

Marquesas
Islands

**WALLIS AND
FUTUNA**
(FR.)

Apia

Pago
Pago

COOK ISLANDS
(N.Z.)

VANUATU

Port-Vila

Suva

TONGA

**AMERICAN
SAMOA**

Alofi

Papeete

Society
Islands

Tahiti

Tuamotu Archipelago

Noumea

FIJI

Nuku'alofa

NIUE
(N.Z.)

Avarua

FRENCH POLYNESIA (France)

**NEW
CALEDONIA**
(France)

Kermadec Islands
(N.Z.)

Norfork Island
Kingston
ustralia)

Adamstown

**PITCAIRN
ISLANDS**
(U.K.)

International Date Line

NEW ZEALAND

Auckland

Hastings

Wellington

Christchurch

Chatham Islands

Dunedin
Invercargill

Stewart Island

0 mi.   500 mi.   1,000 mi.

0 km   1,000 km

EUROPE

ICELAND
Reykjavik

Arctic Circle

FAROE ISLANDS
(Denmark)
Tórshavn

SHETLAND ISLANDS

ORKNEY
ISLANDS

HEBRIDES

Trondheim

NORWAY
Bergen
Oslo
Stavanger

Gävle

0 mi.   300 mi.   600 mi.

0 km   300 km   600 km

SWEDEN
Göteborg

Aberdeen
Glasgow
Edinburgh
Belfast
Dublin
IRELAND
Liverpool
Leeds
Manchester
Sheffield
Birmingham
London

UNITED
KINGDOM

NORTH
SEA

DENMARK
Ålborg
Copenhagen
Malmö

NETHERLANDS
Amsterdam
The Hague
Rotterdam

Hamburg
Bremen

Berlin

GERMANY

Poznan

Gd

GUERNSEY (U.K.)
JERSEY (U.K.)
Calais
Lille
Le Havre
Antwerp
Brussels
BELGIUM
LUXEMBOURG
Paris
Luxembourg

Essen
Dusseldorf
Cologne
Bonn
Frankfurt

Wroclaw

Prague
CZECH
REPUBLIC
Brno

ATLANTIC OCEAN

Nantes

FRANCE

Dijon

Strasbourg
Stuttgart

Munich

Bratislava

Vienna

B

LIECHTENSTEIN
Vaduz
Zürich
Bern
Geneva
SWITZERLAND
Lyon

AUSTRIA

HUNGARY

BAY OF
BISCAY

Bordeaux

Toulouse

Bilbao

Turin
Milan

Genoa

Ljubljana
SLOVENIA
Trieste

Zagreb
CROATIA

Porto

PORTUGAL

Madrid

SPAIN

Lisbon

Seville

Faro

Málaga
Gibraltar

Andorra
la Vella
Barcelona

Valencia

Majorca
Palma

ANDORRA

Marseille

Corsica

MONACO
Bastia

Florence

Vatican
City

Rome

ITALY

SAN
MARINO

Sarajevo

BOSNIA AND
HERZEGOVINA

MONTENEGRO

Podgorica

K

Bari

ADRIATIC SEA

Tira

Kor

AL

MEDITERRANEAN SEA

Sardinia

Cagliari

Naples

Kerkira

Palermo
Messina

Sicily

MOROCCO

ALGERIA

TUNISIA

Valletta

MALTA

A F R I C A

112

Murmansk

Pechora

A S I A

Oulu

Arkhangel'sk

FINLAND

R U S S I A

Tampere

Izhevsk

Turku   Helsinki

St. Petersburg

Kazan

Tallinn

Nizhniy Novgorod

ESTONIA

Samara

Riga   **LATVIA**

Moscow

LITHUANIA

Smolensk

Vilnius

Lipetsk   Saratov

Minsk

KAZAKHSTAN

Homyel'

BELARUS

Voronezh

Brest

Kiev   Kharkiv

Volgograd

L'viv   Derazhnya

Voroshilovgrad

UKRAINE

Gorlovka

Makeyevka

Zhdanov   Rostov

Chisinau

Iasi

Odessa   Mykolaiva

Groznyy

MOLDOVA

Kerch'

Arad

Simferopol'

ROMANIA

Sevastopol'

Craiova   Bucharest

Constanta

BLACK SEA

Nis

Varna

Sofia

BULGARIA

MACEDONIA

Skopje

Istanbul

Thessaloniki

T U R K E Y

Volos

GREECE

Izmir

Athens

IRAN

SYRIA

Crete

CYPRUS

IRAQ

LEBANON

Greenland Sea

Tasiilaq (Ammas...

St. John's

Saint-Pierre

GREENLAND
(Denmark)

Narsarssuak

*Island of
Newfoundland*

Charlottetown

*Labrador
Sea*

Happy Valley
Goose Bay

Nuuk (Godthab)

Quebéc

Davis Strait

Iqaluit

CANADA

Baffin Bay

Chisasibi
(Fort George)

Qaanaaq (Thule)

Baffin Island

Moosonee

Alert

Queen Elizabeth Islands

*HUDSON
BAY*

Kayjujitoq (Resolute)

Arctic Circle

Churchill

Winnipeg

**ARCTIC
OCEAN**

Victoria Island

Yellowknife

Banks Island

Echo Bay

Saskatoon

Regina

*Beaufort
Sea*

Bismarck

Edmonton

Prudhoe Bay

Inuvik

Calgary

Helena

Barrow

Whitehorse

Vancouver

Boise

Alaska (U.S.)

Fairbanks

Juneau

Victoria

Seattle

Olympia

Portland

RUSSIA

Nome

Anchorage

Valdez

Salem

Sacramento

Carson City

Bethel

Kodiak

San Francisco

*Bering
Sea*

Aleutian Islands

114

ATLANTIC
OCEAN

BERMUDA (U.K.)
★ Hamilton

1,000 mi.

500 mi.
1,000 km

500 km
0 mi.
0 km

VIRGIN
ISLANDS
(U.S., U.K.)

SAINT MAARTEN/
SAINT MARTIN
(Neth. Antilles)/(Guad.)

ANGUILLA
(U.K.)

SAINT
BARTHELEMY
(Guad.)

ANTIGUA AND
BARBUDA

DOMINICA

MARTINIQUE (Fr.)

GUADELOUPE (Fr.)

SAINT KITTS AND NEVIS

MONTSERRAT (U.K.)

SAINT LUCIA

SAINT VINCENT AND
THE GRENADINES

BARBADOS

GRENADA

TRINIDAD
AND
TOBAGO

GUYANA

NETHERLANDS ANTILLES (Neth.)

ARUBA (Neth.)

VENEZUELA

COLOMBIA

SOUTH AMERICA

San Juan
PUERTO
RICO (U.S.)

TURKS AND
CAICOS ISLANDS
(U.K.)

★ Grand
Turk

DOMINICAN
REPUBLIC

Santiago

Santo
Domingo

HAITI
Port-au-
Prince

BAHAMAS

Freeport

Nassau

Miami

Jacksonville

Savannah

Columbia

Raleigh

Richmond

Norfolk

Charleston

Frankfort

Nashville

Atlanta

Tallahassee

Montgomery

Birmingham

New
Orleans

Baton
Rouge

Jackson

Memphis

Little Rock

Dallas

Austin

Houston

San Antonio

GULF OF
MEXICO

Tampico

Veracruz

Merida

Cancun

CUBA

Havana

Camagüey

Guantánamo
Bay

Guantánamo

Montego
Bay

Kingston

JAMAICA

CARIBBEAN SEA

CAYMAN ISLANDS (U.K.)
★ George Town

HONDURAS

BELIZE
Belize City

Belmopan

Tegucigalpa

NICARAGUA

Managua

COSTA RICA

San José

PANAMA

Panama City

GUATEMALA

Guatemala City

San Salvador
EL SALVADOR

PACIFIC
OCEAN

Acapulco

Oaxaca

Puebla

Mexico City

MEXICO

Veracruz

León

Guadalajara

Monterrey

Mazatlán

Puerto Vallarta

Gulf of California

La Paz

Tropic of Cancer

Hermosillo

Phoenix

Ciudad Juárez

El Paso

Santa Fe

Denver

Cheyenne

Salt Lake City

San Diego

Tijuana

Los Angeles

UNITED STATES

Oklahoma City

Kansas City

Topeka

Jefferson City

Lincoln

Omaha

Des Moines

Madison

Milwaukee

Chicago

Springfield

Saint Louis

Detroit

Toledo

Cleveland

Pittsburgh

Cincinnati

Indianapolis

Louisville

Columbus

Frankfort

Toronto

Buffalo

Albany

Montpelier

Concord

Augusta

Boston

Providence

Hartford

New York

Philadelphia

Dover

Washington, DC

Baltimore

Harrisburg

Ottawa

ATLANTIC
OCEAN

SOUTH AMERICA

ATLANTIC OCEAN

CARIBBEAN SEA

Countries and Regions

DOMINICAN REPUBLIC

Puerto Rico (U.S.)

ANTIGUA AND BARBUDA

GUADELOUPE

SAINT KITTS AND NEVIS

DOMINICA

SAINT LUCIA

BARBADOS

SAINT VINCENT AND THE GRENADINES

GRENADA

TRINIDAD AND TOBAGO

CUBA

JAMAICA

HAITI

BELIZE

HONDURAS

NICARAGUA

COSTA RICA

PANAMA

Aruba

VENEZUELA

GUYANA

SURINAME

FRENCH GUIANA

COLOMBIA

ECUADOR

PERU

BRAZIL

BOLIVIA

Cities and places

Fortaleza

Natal

Recife

Maceió

Salvador

Parnaíba

São Luís

Brasília

Belém

Cayenne

Paramaribo

Georgetown

Macapá

Santarém

Manaus

Porto Velho

Riberalta

Ciudad Guayana

Caracas

Maracaibo

Bogotá

Medellín

Cali

Barranquilla

Cartagena

Cobija

La Paz

Cochabamba

Cusco

Arequipa

Lima

Trujillo

Piura

Iquitos

Cruzeiro do Sul

Benjamin Constant

Esmeraldas

Quito

Guayaquil

Physical features

São Francisco River

Tocantins River

Araguaia River

Xingu River

Amazon River

Negro River

Madeira River

Orinoco River

Magdalena River

Putumayo River

Marañón River

Ucayali River

AMAZON BASIN

Selvas

Andes Mts.

Lake Maracaibo

Lake Titicaca

Equator

116

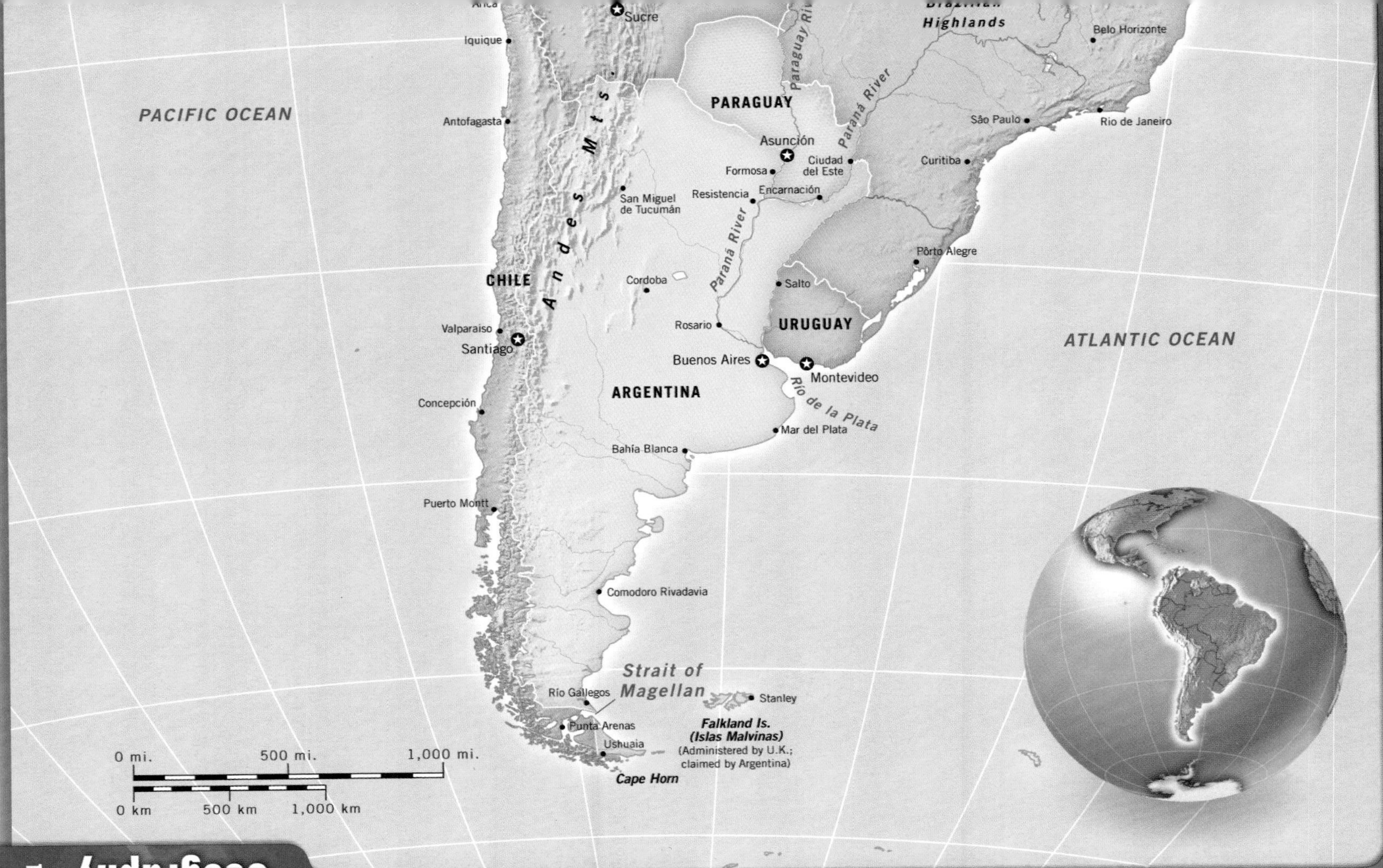

ATLANTIC OCEAN

Belo Horizonte

Rio de Janeiro

Brazilian
Highlands

São Paulo

Curitiba

Porto Alegre

Paraná River

Paraguay River

PARAGUAY

Asunción

Ciudad
del Este

Encarnación

Formosa

Resistencia

Salto

URUGUAY

Montevideo

Río de la Plata

Paraná River

Mar del Plata

Sucre

San Miguel
de Tucumán

Rosario

Buenos Aires

Córdoba

ARGENTINA

Bahía Blanca

Andes Mts.

Comodoro Rivadavia

Strait of
Magellan

Stanley

Falkland Is.
(Islas Malvinas)
(Administered by U.K.;
claimed by Argentina)

Iquique

Antofagasta

CHILE

Valparaíso

Santiago

Concepción

Puerto Montt

Río Gallegos

Punta Arenas

Ushuaia

Cape Horn

PACIFIC OCEAN

1,000 mi.

500 mi.

1,000 km

0 mi.

500 km

0 km

1,000 km

Government and Law

THE CONSTITUTION OF THE UNITED STATES

The signing of the U.S. Constitution

The U.S. Constitution is an extremely important legal document. It has been used as a basis for many other constitutions around the world.

In May 1787, a convention was held in Philadelphia to create a new set of rules by which the young nation of the United States would govern itself. George Washington was unanimously voted to preside over the gathering of 55 representatives of 12 states (Rhode Island refused to take part). James Madison, of Virginia, who later became the fourth President of the United States, was chiefly responsible for the success of the convention. Madison is now known as the Father of the Constitution.

Many writers contributed to the Constitution, which made the process especially challenging. Some leaders (Federalists) wanted to have a strong central government, while others (Anti-Federalists) wanted the strongest powers to remain with the states. There were many angry debates and arguments, but on September 17, 1787, the Constitution of the United States was approved unanimously by the convention. By July 1788, it was ratified by three-quarters of the states, and, on March 4, 1789, it took its place as the supreme law of the land.

The Constitution begins with a passage called the Preamble, which states the document's purpose:

"We the people of the United States, in order to form a more perfect union, establish justice, insure domestic tranquility, provide for the common defense, promote the general welfare, and secure the blessings of liberty to ourselves and our posterity, do ordain and establish this Constitution for the United States of America."

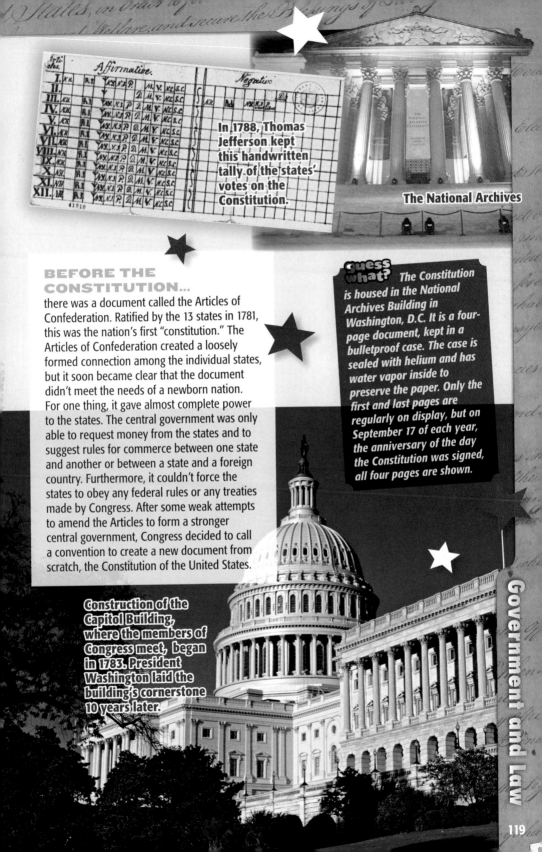

In 1788, Thomas Jefferson kept this handwritten tally of the states' votes on the Constitution.

The National Archives

BEFORE THE CONSTITUTION...

there was a document called the Articles of Confederation. Ratified by the 13 states in 1781, this was the nation's first "constitution." The Articles of Confederation created a loosely formed connection among the individual states, but it soon became clear that the document didn't meet the needs of a newborn nation. For one thing, it gave almost complete power to the states. The central government was only able to request money from the states and to suggest rules for commerce between one state and another or between a state and a foreign country. Furthermore, it couldn't force the states to obey any federal rules or any treaties made by Congress. After some weak attempts to amend the Articles to form a stronger central government, Congress decided to call a convention to create a new document from scratch, the Constitution of the United States.

guess what? The Constitution is housed in the National Archives Building in Washington, D.C. It is a four-page document, kept in a bulletproof case. The case is sealed with helium and has water vapor inside to preserve the paper. Only the first and last pages are regularly on display, but on September 17 of each year, the anniversary of the day the Constitution was signed, all four pages are shown.

Construction of the Capitol Building, where the members of Congress meet, began in 1783. President Washington laid the building's cornerstone 10 years later.

Government and Law

THE BILL OF RIGHTS

The Bill of Rights was added to the Constitution after some states refused to sign the document. Some people worried that the federal government would become too powerful and would take too many rights away from the states. James Madison and Thomas Jefferson put those fears to rest by writing a group of 10 amendments, or changes, to the Constitution. These amendments made it clear that individuals had certain personal freedoms that couldn't be taken away by the government. This document was ratified by three-fourths of the states in 1791 and is considered a part of the Constitution.

THOMAS JEFFERSON

JAMES MADISON

AMENDMENT I provides for freedom of religion, speech and the press. It also guarantees the right to assemble peacefully and to petition the government to hear and resolve any citizen's complaints.

AMENDMENT II guarantees citizens the right to own and use firearms to defend their country.

AMENDMENT III states that in peacetime a soldier cannot stay in a citizen's home without the owner's consent. In wartime, any such arrangement must be made according to the law.

AMENDMENT IV protects citizens, their belongings and their homes from being searched without a reasonable cause and prior legal consent.

AMENDMENT V says that no person can be tried for a nonmilitary peacetime crime without having the crime first determined by a grand jury. It also states that people can't be tried twice for the same crime or forced to testify against themselves. Citizens can't have their possessions or property taken away without a trial, and private property can't be taken by the government for public use without fair payment to the owner.

AMENDMENT VI guarantees citizens the right to a speedy, public trial by jury. If accused, a person has the right to know what he or she is accused of, to be confronted by witnesses to the crime and to have an attorney and witnesses on behalf of his or her defense.

AMENDMENT VII states that the outcome of a trial can be determined by a jury and that any further appeal process must be done according to the law.

AMENDMENT VIII guarantees that reasonable amounts be set for fines and bail, which is a sum of money provided by a prisoner so that he or she may leave prison while awaiting trial. This amendment also prohibits cruel and unusual punishment for convicted criminals.

AMENDMENT IX declares that citizens have rights other than those stated in the Constitution.

AMENDMENT X guarantees that any powers not assigned to the federal government as provided in the Constitution belong to the states and the people.

CIVIL RIGHTS LAWS IN AMERICA

WOMAN SUFFRAGE HEADQUARTERS.
MEN OF OHIO!
GIVE THE WOMEN A SQUARE DEAL
Vote For Amendment No. 23 On September 3 – 1912.

COME IN AND LEARN WHY WOMEN OUGHT to Vote.

Civil rights are the rights that people have guaranteeing fair treatment, without regard to race, gender, age, marital status, physical or mental abilities or disabilities, or other characteristic. Many important civil rights laws have been written into the U.S. Constitution in the form of amendments or issued as Acts of Congress. Here are some important amendments and laws that protect American citizens against discrimination.

THE THIRTEENTH AMENDMENT abolished slavery, but it did not give African Americans equal rights. It was passed in 1865.

THE FOURTEENTH AMENDMENT, passed in 1868, declared that the states could not pass laws that denied voting rights to citizens of the United States, including African Americans.

THE NINETEENTH AMENDMENT extended the right to vote to women in 1920.

THE EQUAL PAY ACT OF 1963 maintained that men and women should be paid the same for equal work.

THE CIVIL RIGHTS ACT OF 1964 made it illegal for states and businesses to discriminate on the basis of "race, color, religion or national origin." This act aimed to prohibit discrimination in housing and in access to public spaces, including classrooms, making school segregation illegal.

THE AGE DISCRIMINATION IN EMPLOYMENT ACT OF 1967 prohibited employment discrimination against people between the ages of 40 and 65. In 1986, the law was amended to extend to people over the age of 65.

THE 26TH AMENDMENT, which passed in 1971, extended voting rights to people 18 years old. The voting age was lowered during the Vietnam War because young people demanded it, saying that if they were old enough to fight and die for their country, they were old enough to choose its leaders.

THE AMERICANS WITH DISABILITIES ACT, signed in 1990, prohibits discrimination by employers against people with disabilities. It requires that all nongovernment buildings constructed or renovated after 1992 and government buildings erected or renovated after 1993 be accessible to people with disabilities.

Ideas of freedom are still evolving. Today, lawmakers throughout the states and in federal government debate whether marriage laws that discriminate against nontraditional couples should be allowed. Some advocates for children say that kids should have the same rights as adults. As ideas change, laws change. And as laws change, people's ideas about justice change too.

Government and Law

THE BRANCHES

The Constitution divides the basic structure of the U.S. government into three branches: the legislative, executive and judicial branches. The purpose of this structure is to provide a separation of powers among three equally important sectors—one that makes laws, another that carries out those laws and a third that determines whether those laws are constitutional. In the process of carrying out their responsibilities, the three branches ensure that no single branch becomes too powerful. This system of checks and balances has served the United States well since its birth and has been a model of democracy for other nations in the world.

CHECKS AND BALANCES

EXECUTIVE

- Appoints Supreme Court Justices
- Can grant pardons

- Can veto bills presented by the legislature
- Can call emergency sessions of the legislature

- Can impeach the President
- Can override presidential vetoes
- Has the power to declare war, enact taxes and allocate funds

- Interprets laws and presidential actions

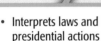

- Can approve judicial appointments
- Can initiate constitutional amendments
- Can establish jurisdiction of the courts

JUDICIAL

LEGISLATIVE

- Interprets the laws of the land
- Decides constitutional issues

THE LEGISLATIVE BRANCH

The legislative branch was the first of the three branches of government to be created in the Constitution. The founders did this on purpose, because they wanted to set up a government that represented and was accountable to the people of the United States. The legislature is a **bicameral** structure, which means that it has two chambers: the **House of Representatives** and the **Senate.**

The membership of the House of Representatives is based on state population. In contrast, the Senate gives every state equal representation. In this way, the large states are not able to dominate political affairs. In general, the Senate determines many national and foreign policies, and the House is in charge of finding ways to carry out these policies in an effective, financially responsible manner. Both chambers have the power to hold hearings to gather information on the bills they are considering and to investigate wrongdoings relating to any issues they are responsible for. Every bill must be approved by both chambers to become a law.

The political party with the most members in either chamber is called the majority party. The other is called the minority party. In each chamber, each party selects a **leader,** who coordinates party strategy and schedules when bills are introduced, and a **whip,** who tries to get party members to vote the same way for each bill considered.

THE HOUSE OF REPRESENTATIVES

This chamber includes 435 representatives chosen based on the population of each state, with a minimum of one representative for each state. The larger a state's population, the more representatives it has. For example, California has 53 representatives, and Montana has one. Representatives are elected to two-year terms. They must be at least 25 years old, a U.S. citizen for at least seven years and live in the state they represent. The **Speaker of the House** presides over the sessions. The House of Representatives has the following special powers and responsibilities:

- create bills that allow the government to collect taxes

- create bills that empower the government to spend money

- elect the President in the event that no one candidate receives a majority of electoral votes

- vote to impeach the President, Vice President or other elected official, which means to formally charge a public official with wrongdoing

guess what? *The District of Columbia and U.S. territories (Guam, American Samoa, U.S. Virgin Islands, Northern Mariana Islands and Puerto Rico) have one delegate each in the House of Representatives. In this way, they can participate in debates and vote in committee meetings. On rare occasions, these delegates can vote with the rest of the House, but only if their votes wouldn't change the outcome. This is to allow an official record of their stance on an issue.*

The House of Representatives votes to impeach President Andrew Johnson.

THE SENATE

This chamber includes 100 senators, two for each state. Senators are elected to six-year terms, with one-third of the Senate being elected every even-numbered year. They must be at least 30 years old, a U.S. citizen for at least nine years and live in the state they represent. The Vice President (or president pro tempore, in the Vice President's absence) presides over the sessions. The Senate has the following special powers and responsibilities:

- ratify, or approve, treaties made by the President. (This requires a two-thirds vote of all senators.)

- accept or reject (by majority vote of all senators) the President's appointments of Supreme Court justices and federal judges, ambassadors, Cabinet secretaries and other high-level executive-branch officials

- hold trials of officials impeached by the House of Representatives and convict or acquit them. (A two-thirds vote of all senators is needed for conviction.)

Hillary Clinton testifies in front of a Senate committee before she can become the U.S. Secretary of State.

Government and Law

THE EXECUTIVE BRANCH

When George Washington was inaugurated President of the United States on April 30, 1789, it was the beginning of the executive branch of the U.S. government as outlined in Article II of the Constitution. The President, Vice President and Cabinet make up this branch.

Barack Obama

THE PRESIDENT

The President serves a term of four years, with a maximum of two terms. A President must be a native-born U.S. citizen, at least 35 years old and have lived in the United States for at least 14 years. The President has the following powers and responsibilities:

- carry out the laws of the land
- appoint U.S. ambassadors, Supreme Court justices, federal judges and Cabinet secretaries (who then must be approved by the Senate)
- give the annual State of the Union address to Congress
- receive foreign ambassadors, thus recognizing their governments
- propose treaties with other nations
- serve as commander in chief of the armed forces; send troops overseas (but needs congressional approval to declare war)
- call both houses of Congress to meet in a special session
- approve or veto bills passed by Congress
- grant pardons for federal crimes

Joe Biden

THE VICE PRESIDENT

Under Article I of the Constitution, the Vice President presides over the Senate and votes only to break a tie. Article XXV allows the Vice President to assume the office of President under certain conditions. The Vice President must meet the same age and residential qualifications as the President.

guess what? Ken Salazar, secretary of the interior, is one of eight siblings. He grew up on a ranch in a remote area of Colorado, without electricity or running water.

THE CABINET

Since 1789, Presidents have designated certain responsibilities to members of their Cabinet, called secretaries, who oversee separate executive departments. The first Cabinet consisted of four secretaries: foreign affairs, treasury, war and the attorney general. Today the Presidential Cabinet consists of 15 secretaries. Here are the Cabinet departments in the order of their creation.

DEPARTMENT	SECRETARY	WEB SITE
State	Hillary Clinton	state.gov
Treasury	Timothy Geithner	treasury.gov
Interior	Ken Salazar	doi.gov
Agriculture	Tom Vilsack	usda.gov
Justice (Attorney General)	Eric Holder Jr.	usdoj.gov
Commerce	Gary F. Locke	commerce.gov
Labor	Hilda Solis	dol.gov
Defense	Robert Gates	defenselink.mil
Housing and Urban Development	Shaun Donovan	hud.gov
Transportation	Ray LaHood	dot.gov
Energy	Steven Chu	energy.gov
Education	Arne Duncan	ed.gov
Health and Human Services	(not available)	hhs.gov
Veterans Affairs	Ret. Gen. Eric K. Shinseki	va.gov
Homeland Security	Janet Napolitano	dhs.gov

guess what? Secretary of homeland security Janet Napolitano has climbed Mount Kilimanjaro.

THE JUDICIAL BRANCH

Supreme Court Justices (clockwise, from top left): Stephen Breyer, Clarence Thomas, Ruth Bader Ginsburg, Samuel Alito Jr., David Souter, Antonin Scalia, Chief Justice John Roberts, John Paul Stevens, Anthony Kennedy.

On February 1, 1790, the Supreme Court held its first session. As part of the checks and balances and the separation of powers built into the nation's governmental structure, the main task of the judicial branch, and of the Supreme Court in particular, is to see that the Constitution and the laws formed under its provisions are preserved and followed. Because they have the power to declare as unconstitutional any law or practice that doesn't comply with the laws of the land and they can interpret the way an established law must be carried out, the Supreme Court and federal courts play an equally powerful role along with the legislative and executive branches in the administration of the government.

Supreme Court justices and federal judges are appointed by the President and confirmed by the Senate. They serve for life or until they decide to resign or retire. The Supreme Court consists of eight associate justices and a chief justice. All decisions are made by a majority vote of the justices.

MYSTERY PERSON

Clue 1: I was born February 1, 1878, in Tennessee, but later moved to Arkansas.

Clue 2: After my husband, Thaddeus, died, I was appointed to fill his seat in the U.S. Senate.

Clue 3: On January 12, 1932, I became the first woman to be elected to the Senate.

Who am I? _____

ANSWER ON PAGE 244.

All About Voting

WHO CAN VOTE?
Citizens of the United States and its territories who are age 18 or over. In some states, a person with a criminal record is barred from voting.

HOW DO YOU REGISTER TO VOTE?
The process of voter registration differs somewhat from state to state. In some states, a voter can register right up until Election Day, but in other states, registration must be completed weeks in advance. No matter where you are, registering is easy. Citizens can sign up online by going to rockthevote.com. They may also register by phone or in person at various locations throughout their state. In some states, photo identification is required. Other states require only a statement of residency.

DOES EVERY VOTE COUNT? Yes!
Though Presidents are chosen by the delegates that make up the Electoral College (see page 161), the allotment of delegates is based on every vote.

In local elections, sometimes a single vote can have an obvious effect on the outcome. In 2008 in Minnesota, a protracted recount between senatorial candidates took place. In some recounts, the difference between the two candidates was as few as two votes! The final tally showed a difference of just 225 votes.

guess what? *In 1960, 63.1% of eligible voters cast their ballots in the presidential election. In 1996, only 49.1% of people who could vote did so. In 2008, however, 56.8% made it to the polls—many of whom were first-time voters.*

Government and Law

125

History

BUDDHA

3500–5000 B.C. Sumer, located in what is now Iraq, becomes the earliest known civilization. Among other advancements, Sumerians develop a written alphabet.

3500–2600 B.C. People settle in the Indus River Valley in what is now India and Pakistan.

2600 B.C. Minoan civilization begins on the island of Crete in the Mediterranean Sea.

2560 B.C. APPROX. The Egyptian king Khufu finishes building the Great Pyramid at Giza. The Great Sphinx is completed soon after by his son Khaefre.

CONFUCIUS

2000 B.C. Babylonians develop a system of mathematics. • The Kingdom of Kush in Africa becomes a major center of trade and learning.

1792 B.C. Hammurabi becomes the ruler of Babylonia. He creates the first set of laws, now known as Hammurabi's Code.

1600–1050 B.C. APPROX. The Shang dynasty is the first Chinese dynasty to leave written records.

JULIUS CAESAR

1200 B.C. The Trojan War is fought between the Greeks and Trojans.

ALEXANDER THE GREAT

TEOTIHUACÁN

814 B.C. The city of Carthage, now located in Tunisia, is founded by the Phoenicians.

753 B.C. According to the legend, Rome is founded by Romulus.

563 B.C. Siddhartha Gautama, who becomes the Buddha, or Enlightened One, is born. He will become the founder of the Buddhist religion.

551 B.C. Chinese philosopher Confucius is born. His teachings on honesty, humanity and how people should treat one another are the foundations of Confucianism.

510 B.C. Democracy is established in Athens, Greece.

431 B.C. The Peloponnesian War breaks out between Sparta and Athens. In 404 B.C., Sparta finally wins the war and takes over Athens.

334 B.C. Alexander the Great invades Persia. He eventually conquers lands from Greece to India, even crossing into North Africa.

100 B.C. The great city of Teotihuacán flourishes in Mexico.

58 B.C. Julius Caesar leaves Rome for Gaul (France) and spends nine years conquering much of Central Europe. He is murdered in 44 B.C.

27 B.C. Octavian becomes the first Roman emperor, ushering in a long period of peace. He is also known by the title Augustus.

RUINS OF POMPEII

CIRCA A.D. 1 Jesus Christ is born. He is crucified by the Romans around 30 A.D.

66 Jews rebel against Roman rule. The revolution is quashed by the Romans, who destroy Jerusalem in 70 A.D. and force many Jews into slavery.

79 Mount Vesuvius erupts, destroying the city of Pompeii.

122 Hadrian's Wall is built across northern England for protection from the barbarian tribes to the north.

250 APPROX. The classic period of Mayan civilization begins and lasts until about 900. The Maya erect impressive stone buildings and temples.

CHARLEMAGNE

330 Constantine the Great chooses Byzantium as the capital of the Roman Empire, and the city becomes known as Constantinople.

476 The Roman Empire collapses.

CONSTANTINE

622 Muhammad, the founder of Islam, flees from Mecca to Medina in what is called the Hegira. After the death of Muhammad in 632, Muslims conquer much of North Africa and the Middle East. In 711, Muslims conquer Spain.

800 Charlemagne is crowned the first Holy Roman Emperor by Pope Leo III.

960 The Song dynasty begins in China. This dynasty is known for its advances in art, poetry and philosophy.

HADRIAN'S WALL

During the rule of the emperor Hadrian, the Roman Empire built fortifications in what is now northern England to prevent raids from the Pictish people to the north. The most famous of these partitions is known as Hadrian's Wall. Beginning in 122, troops used stone and turf to create the barrier, along with small forts and guard posts spread out along the wall. At the time, many boundaries were simply based on naturally occurring geographical features such as mountains or lakes. Hadrian's Wall, which was probably 13 to 15 feet (4 to 4.6 m) tall, was an early and important man-made marker of the boundary of Roman Britain. Although it was initially built to thwart invaders, the forts also ended up serving as trading posts. Much of the wall is still standing, and many visitors walk along the 73 miles (117 m) of stone wall that remain.

History

ANASAZI CLIFF DWELLINGS

CIRCA 1000—1300 During the classic period of their culture, Anasazi Indians build homes and other structures into the sides of cliffs in what is now the southwestern United States.

1066 At the Battle of Hastings, the Norman king, William the Conqueror, invades England and defeats English King Harold II.

1095 Pope Urban II delivers a speech urging Christians to capture the Holy Land from the Muslims. The fighting between 1096 and 1291 is known as the Crusades.

MACHU PICCHU

1200 APPROX. The Inca Empire begins, and elaborate stone structures are eventually built in Cuzco and Machu Picchu, Peru. The Incas flourish until Francisco Pizarro, a Spaniard, conquers them in 1533.

1206 A warrior named Temujin is proclaimed Genghis Khan. He expands his empire so that it includes most of Asia.

1215 A group of barons in England force King John to sign the Magna Carta, a document limiting the power of the king.

1271—95 Marco Polo, a Venetian merchant, travels throughout Asia. His book, *Il Milione* (*The Million*), is a major European source of information about Asia.

GENGHIS KHAN

1273 The Habsburg dynasty begins in Eastern Europe. It will remain a powerful force in the region until World War I.

DA GAMA

1325 Aztecs begin building Tenochtitlán on the site of modern Mexico City.

1337 The Hundred Years' War starts between the English and French. France finally wins in 1453.

1347 The Black Death, or bubonic plague, breaks out in Europe. It spreads quickly, killing more than one-third of Europe's population.

1368 The Ming dynasty is founded in China by Buddhist monk Zhu Yuanzhang (or Chu Yuan-Chang).

1433 Portuguese explorer Gil Eannes sails past Cape Bojador in western Africa, which was thought to be the end of the world.

1453 Constantinople falls to the Ottoman Turks, ending the Byzantine Empire.

1455 Johannes Gutenberg invents the printing press. The Gutenberg Bible is the first book printed on the press.

1478 The Spanish Inquisition begins.

1487—88 Bartholomeu Dias of Portugal leads the first European expedition around the Cape of Good Hope at the southern tip of Africa, opening up a sea route to Asia.

1492 Christopher Columbus leaves Spain, hoping to sail to the West Indies. Instead, he and his crew land in the Bahamas and visit Cuba, Hispaniola (which is now Haiti and the Dominican Republic) and other small islands.

1497—99 Vasco da Gama leads the first European expedition to India by sea via the Cape of Good Hope.

WORLD HISTORY 1500—1899

MAGELLAN

MAYFLOWER LANDING

1517 Martin Luther protests the abuses of the Catholic Church, which leads to a religious split and the rise of the Protestant faith.

1519 While exploring Mexico, Spanish adventurer Hernán Cortés conquers the Aztec Empire.

1519—22 Ferdinand Magellan's expedition circumnavigates, or sails around, the globe.

1532—33 Francisco Pizarro conquers the Inca Empire in South America.

1543 Copernicus releases his theory that the sun, not Earth, is the center of the universe.

1547 Ivan the Terrible becomes the first tsar, or ruler, of Russia.

1588 The English defeat the Spanish Armada, or fleet of warships, when Spain attempts to invade England.

1618 The Thirty Years' War breaks out between European Protestants and Catholics.

1620 English pilgrims aboard the *Mayflower* land at Plymouth Rock.

1632 The astronomer Galileo, the first person to use a telescope to look into space, confirms Copernicus's theory that Earth revolves around the sun.

1642 The English Civil War, sometimes called the Puritan Revolution, begins in Britain.

1688 The Glorious Revolution, or Bloodless Revolution, takes place in England. James II is removed from the throne, and William and Mary become the heads of the country.

1721 Peter the Great becomes emperor of Russia.

1789 An angry mob storms the Bastille, a prison in Paris, setting off the French Revolution.

BOXER REBELLION

1819 Simón Bolívar crosses the Andes to launch a surprise attack against the Spanish, liberating New Granada (now Colombia, Venezuela, Panama and Ecuador) from Spain.

1824 Mexico becomes independent from Spain.

1848 This is known as the year of revolutions in Europe, as there is upheaval in France, Italy, Germany, Hungary and elsewhere.

1845 A blight ruins the potato crop in Ireland. More than one million Irish starve to death, and another million leave for America to escape the famine.

1859 Charles Darwin writes *On the Origin of Species.*

DARWIN

1871 A group of independent states unify, creating the German Empire.

1876 Alexander Graham Bell invents the telephone.

1884 Representatives of 14 European countries meet at the Berlin West Africa Conference and divide Africa into areas of control.

1892 The diesel engine is invented by Parisian Rudolf Diesel.

1893 New Zealand becomes the first country to extend to women the right to vote. • The Columbian Exposition, also known as the Chicago World's Fair, is held.

1894 The Sino-Japanese War breaks out between China and Japan, who are fighting for control of Korea. An 1895 treaty declares Korea independent.

1898 The Spanish-American War begins.

1899 During the Boxer Rebellion, the Chinese fight against Christian and foreign influences in their country. American, Japanese and European forces help stop the fighting by 1901.

WORLD HISTORY 1900–2008

1904 Japan declares war on Russia, beginning the Russo-Japanese War. The countries clash over influence in Manchuria and Korea. Japan wins the conflict and becomes a world power.

THE RUSSO-JAPANESE WAR

1909 Robert Peary is credited as the first to reach the North Pole, though new evidence suggests he might have been as much as 30 to 60 miles (48 to 97 km) away.

PEARY

1911 Roald Amundsen, the first man to travel the Northwest Passage, reaches the South Pole.

1914 Austro-Hungarian Archduke Franz Ferdinand is assassinated, setting off a chain of events that starts World War I.

ATOMIC BOMB

1917 The United States enters World War I.
• The Russian Revolution begins. The tsarist government is overthrown and, in 1922, the Soviet Union is formed.

1918 A flu epidemic spreads quickly around the world, killing more than 20 million people.

1919 The Treaty of Versailles ends World War I.

1927 Philo Farnsworth invents the television.

1928 Alexander Fleming discovers penicillin accidentally after leaving a dish of staphylococcus bacteria uncovered and finding mold.

HITLER

1929 The U.S. stock market collapses, beginning the Great Depression.

APARTHEID

1933 Adolf Hitler becomes chancellor of Germany.
• Frequency modulation, or FM, radio is developed by Edwin Armstrong.

1936 The Spanish Civil War breaks out.

1939 World War II begins when Germany invades Poland. Britain responds by declaring war on Germany. The United States declares neutrality.

1941 The Japanese launch a surprise attack on the United States, bombing U.S. ships docked in Hawaii's Pearl Harbor. In response, the U.S. declares war on Japan, and both Germany and Italy declare war on the U.S.

1945 Germany surrenders on May 7, ending the war in Europe. In August, the United States drops two atomic bombs in Japan, on the cities of Hiroshima and Nagasaki. Japan surrenders, ending World War II.

1947 India and Pakistan become free of British colonial rule.

1948 Israel becomes a nation.

1949 Following China's Civil War, Mao Zedong sets up the Communist People's Republic of China.
• South Africa enacts apartheid laws, which make discrimination against nonwhite people part of public policy.

1950 North Korean Communist forces invade South Korea, beginning the Korean War. American forces support South Korea. China backs North Korea. The war ends three years later.
• Frank McNamara develops the first credit card, the Diners' Club. It is not made out of plastic but paper stock.

1952 The hydrogen bomb is developed by Edward Teller and a team at Los Alamos, New Mexico.

1953 Edmund Hillary and Tenzing Norgay climb to the top of Mount Everest.

1955 Jonas Salk's polio vaccine is introduced.

NET BLANKES
WHITES ONLY

1963 U.S. President John F. Kennedy is assassinated. Lyndon B. Johnson is inaugurated.

1964 The United States begins sending troops to Vietnam to aid South Vietnam in its civil war with North Vietnam.

VIETNAM WAR

1967 The Six-Day War breaks out between Israel and neighboring Arab nations Egypt, Syria and Jordan. Israel seizes the Golan Heights, the Gaza Strip, the Sinai Peninsula and part of the West Bank of the Jordan River.

1973 The Paris Peace Accords end the Vietnam War. North Vietnam later violates the terms of the treaty and, in 1975, takes control of Saigon, the capital of South Vietnam.
• Egypt and Syria conduct a surprise attack on Israel, beginning the Yom Kippur War.

1978 U.S. President Jimmy Carter, Israeli President Menachem Begin and Egyptian President Anwar Sadat sign the Camp David Accords in an attempt to achieve peace in the Middle East.

1979 Religious leader Ayatollah Khomeini returns to Iran and declares it an Islamic republic.

1981 NASA develops the first reusable spacecraft, the Space Shuttle. The Space Shuttle *Columbia* is the first to fly.

1989 The Chinese army crushes a demonstration in Tiananmen Square in Beijing, killing hundreds or thousands of students and protestors.
• The Berlin Wall is torn down and the city of Berlin, Germany, is reunified.

THE CARTERS

1990 Apartheid ends in South Africa. Four years later, Nelson Mandela is elected president in the country's first free, multiracial elections.
• The Persian Gulf War begins when Iraq invades Kuwait.

TSUNAMI DAMAGE

THE FALL OF THE BERLIN WALL

1991 The Soviet Union dissolves. Croatia, Slovenia and Macedonia declare independence from Yugoslavia. The next year, Bosnia and Herzegovina also declares independence, but war breaks out and does not end until 1995.
• Tim Berners-Lee develops the World Wide Web.

1994 Conflict between the Hutu majority and the Tutsi minority in the African nation Rwanda leads to a bloody civil war and genocide, which is the systematic killing of a racial or ethnic group.

1999 Honda releases the two-door Insight, the first hybrid car mass marketed in the United States. A year later, the Toyota Prius, the first hybrid four-door sedan, is released.

2001 After the September 11th terrorist attacks in New York City and Washington, D.C., the U.S. declares an international war on terror, attacking the Taliban government in Afghanistan and searching for Osama Bin Laden and Al Qaeda.

2003 With the aid of Britain and other allies, the United States invades Iraq. Though the government falls quickly, resistance and fighting continue. In 2006, Saddam Hussein is executed for crimes against humanity.
• War in the Darfur region of Sudan begins, leading to a humanitarian crisis.

2004 An interim government is inaugurated in Iraq.
• A powerful tsunami kills nearly 300,000 people in Indonesia, Sri Lanka, India, Thailand and other Asian countries.

2006 Montenegro becomes independent from Serbia.

2008 Kosovo declares its independence from Serbia.
• Global economic crisis leads to loss of jobs, homes and credit and a downturn in trade worldwide.

U.S. HISTORY

POCAHONTAS AND SMITH

1524 Giovanni da Verrazano is the first European to reach New York Harbor.

1540 In search of gold, Francisco Vásquez de Coronado travels north from Mexico. One of his lieutenants is the first European to spot the Grand Canyon.

JEFFERSON

1541 Spaniard Hernando de Soto crosses the Mississippi River.

1579 Sir Francis Drake of England explores California's coastline.

1607 English settlers found Jamestown in Virginia. The colony's leader, John Smith, is captured by Indians. According to legend, he is saved by Pocahontas.

1609–11 Henry Hudson visits the Chesapeake, Delaware and New York bays and becomes the first European to sail up the Hudson River.

1620 Pilgrims land at Plymouth, Massachusetts.

1626 Dutchman Peter Minuit buys the island of Manhattan from the Canarsie Indians.

1692 Accusations of witchcraft lead to the Salem Witch Trials and executions of 20 people.

1770 Tensions between British soldiers and colonists erupt in the Boston Massacre, when British troops kill five men.

1773 Colonists protest a tax on tea by dressing up as Indians, boarding three ships, and dumping tea into Boston Harbor. Known as the Boston Tea Party, the protest angers the British, who pass other harsh laws.

1775 Paul Revere warns the colonists that the British are coming. The Battle of Lexington and Concord is the first fight of the American Revolution. The English surrender at Yorktown, Virginia, in 1781.

REVERE

1776 Drafted by Thomas Jefferson, the Declaration of Independence is signed and the United States is formed.

1787 The U.S. Constitution is written and submitted to the states for ratification. By the end of the year, Delaware, Pennsylvania and New Jersey have accepted it.

1789 George Washington becomes the first President of the United States.

1791 The Bill of Rights, written mostly by James Madison, becomes part of the Constitution.

1803 Thomas Jefferson buys the Louisiana Territory from France.

1804–06 Meriwether Lewis and William Clark explore the Louisiana Territory. They travel from St. Louis up the Missouri River, then past the Rockies on horseback, reaching the Pacific Ocean in November 1805.

WAR OF 1812

1812 The War of 1812 breaks out between the United States and Britain because of trade and border disputes, as well as disagreements about the freedom of the seas. Signed in 1814, the Treaty of Ghent ends the war.

1823 President Monroe issues the Monroe Doctrine, warning that the Americas are not open to colonization.

1836 Texas declares independence from Mexico. In response, the Mexican Army attacks and kills the 189 Texans defending the Alamo.

1838 In what is known as the Trail of Tears, European settlers force 16,000 Cherokee Indians to leave their land in Georgia and relocate to a reservation in Oklahoma. Roughly a quarter of the Cherokees die.

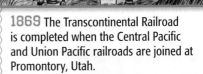
GOLD RUSH

1846 The Mexican-American War begins. At the end of the fighting in 1848, Mexico cedes California and New Mexico (which includes present-day Arizona, Utah and Nevada) to the United States. In return, the U.S. agrees to pay Mexico $15 million.

1848 John Sutter strikes gold in California, kicking off the California gold rush.

1860 Tensions between the North and the South over slavery, taxes and representation reach a boiling point, and South Carolina secedes from the United States.

1861 Mississippi, Florida, Alabama, Georgia, Louisiana and Texas secede from the Union, and the Confederate government is formed. The first shots of the American Civil War are fired at Fort Sumter in Charleston Harbor in South Carolina. Virginia, Arkansas, Tennessee and North Carolina also secede from the Union.

A GLIDER MADE BY THE WRIGHT BROTHERS

1862 The Homestead Act promises 160 acres of land to anyone who remains on the land for five years. This law encourages settlers to move west.

1863 President Lincoln issues the Emancipation Proclamation, which frees all slaves in the Confederate states. The Battle of Gettysburg is fought. It is the bloodiest battle of the Civil War.

LINCOLN AND THE EMANCIPATION PROCLAMATION

1865 General Robert E. Lee of the Confederacy surrenders to Union General Ulysses S. Grant at Appomattox Court House in Virginia, ending the Civil War.
• President Lincoln is assassinated at Ford's Theater by John Wilkes Booth, and Andrew Johnson becomes President.
• The Thirteenth Amendment, which puts an end to slavery, is ratified.

1867 The United States buys Alaska from Russia for $7.2 million.

A FAMILY DURING THE GREAT DEPRESSION

1869 The Transcontinental Railroad is completed when the Central Pacific and Union Pacific railroads are joined at Promontory, Utah.

1890 The Battle of Wounded Knee is the last major defeat for Native American tribes.

1898 The Spanish-American War is fought. At the end of the war, Cuba is independent, and Puerto Rico, Guam and the Philippines become territories of the United States.

1903 Wilbur and Orville Wright complete their first airplane flight at Kitty Hawk, North Carolina.

1908 Henry Ford, founder of the Ford Motor Company, builds the Model T and sells it for $950, making automobiles much more affordable.

1917 The United States enters World War I.

1920 With the passage of the Nineteenth Amendment, women get the right to vote.

1929 The U.S. stock market crashes, and the Great Depression begins.

1941 In a surprise attack, Japan bombs the U.S. fleet at Pearl Harbor in Hawaii. The United States declares war on Japan. Germany and Italy declare war on the U.S.

1945 Germany surrenders on May 7, ending the war in Europe. In August, the United States drops two atomic bombs in Japan, on the cities of Hiroshima and Nagasaki. Japan surrenders, ending World War II.

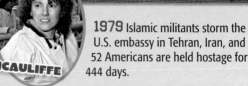

1946 The first bank-issued credit card was developed by John Biggins for the Flatbush National Bank of Brooklyn in New York City.

MCAULIFFE

1979 Islamic militants storm the U.S. embassy in Tehran, Iran, and 52 Americans are held hostage for 444 days.

1950 Communist North Korean forces invade South Korea. American forces enter the Korean War to defend South Korea. Little land changes hands during three years of fighting.

1986 The *Challenger* space shuttle explodes, killing seven crew members, including teacher Christa McAuliffe.

1954 In *Brown v. Board of Education of Topeka, Kansas,* the U.S. Supreme Court declares that segregated schools are unconstitutional.

1991 After Iraq invades Kuwait, the United States begins bombing raids. The first Persian Gulf War ends quickly as Iraqi forces are driven from Kuwait.

1955 Rosa Parks is arrested for refusing to give up her bus seat to a white person, leading to a boycott of the entire bus system in Montgomery, Alabama.

GORE

1999 President Bill Clinton is acquitted of impeachment charges.

2000 In the extremely close election between Democrat Al Gore and Republican George W. Bush, allegations of voter fraud lead to an election recount. The U.S. Supreme Court determines the outcome, and Bush is declared the winner.

1963 Martin Luther King Jr. delivers his famous "I have a dream" speech to a crowd of more than 250,000 participants in Washington, D.C.
• President John F. Kennedy is assassinated.

1965 Malcolm X is killed.
• A race riot in the Watts section of Los Angeles, California, is one of the worst in history.
• President Johnson authorizes air raids over North Vietnam.

MALCOLM X

2001 On September 11, two passenger planes are highjacked and flown into the World Trade Center in New York, causing the buildings to collapse. Another plane is flown into the Pentagon near Washington, D.C. A fourth hijacked plane is crashed into a field in Pennsylvania by the passengers onboard. The United States and Britain respond by attacking the Taliban government in Afghanistan. The U.S. government declares the War on Terror.

1968 James Earl Ray shoots and kills Martin Luther King Jr. in Memphis, Tennessee. Riots break out across the country.

1973 The Vietnam War ends when peace accords are signed. Two years later, North Vietnam takes over Saigon, the capital of South Vietnam.

THE WORLD TRADE CENTER AFTER THE SEPTEMBER 11TH ATTACKS

1974 Due to his involvement in the Watergate scandal, President Nixon resigns. Gerald Ford becomes President.

NIXON

2003 The space shuttle *Columbia* breaks apart during reentry into Earth's atmosphere, killing all seven crew members.
• Along with its allies, Britain and other countries, the United States goes to war in Iraq. Saddam Hussein's government falls quickly, but resistance and fighting continue.

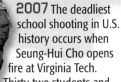
COLUMBIA'S CREW

2005 Hurricane Katrina hits the Gulf Coast, destroying parts of Mississippi and Louisiana and areas along the coast of the southeastern United States. The levee system in New Orleans, Louisiana, cannot withstand the hurricane, and 80% of the city is flooded.

OBAMA

2007 The deadliest school shooting in U.S. history occurs when Seung-Hui Cho opens fire at Virginia Tech. Thirty-two students and teachers are killed and many others are wounded in the rampage.

2009 Barack Obama is inaugurated on January 20, becoming America's first African-American President. He quickly signs a $787 billion economic stimulus bill to combat the severe economic downturn that began in 2008.

TFK GAME

DIGGING UP THE PAST

The grid map shows some items that archaeologists uncovered at Jamestown, Virginia. Find the jug with a handle. Its location on the map is A2. Use the grid to complete the activity below.

1. Put one finger on the B and one finger on the 2. Slide your fingers together? What is in block B2? Circle it.

2. Find a piece of jewelry. Letter _____ Number _____

3. In which block is the small statue? Letter _____ Number _____

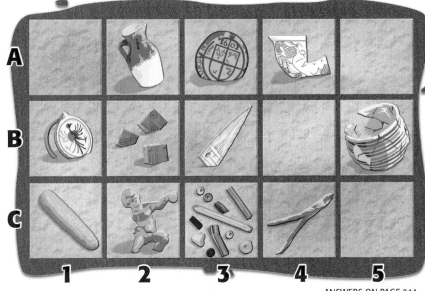

ANSWERS ON PAGE 244.

Take It From Nature

The pudgy boxfish may not look speedy, but it swims through the water with ease. That's why car designers copied it.

"We were surprised when this clumsy-looking fish became our model," says Thomas Weber. He works for a car company in Germany. The car his company made is fast. Just like the boxfish, it can turn, back up and stop easily.

NATURE'S BEST

Nature inspires many new inventions. Scientist Janine Benyus named this science *biomimicry* (bye-oh-*mih*-mick-ree). *Bio* means "life." *Mimicry* means "copying." Benyus works with companies that want to use nature's best ideas when they invent new things. The inventions have copied rats, butterflies, whales, plants and even termites.

In Zimbabwe, a country in southern Africa, engineers designed energy-efficient buildings modeled on termite mounds. The buildings use vents to keep the air flowing and the temperature cool. A company in Atlanta, Georgia, developed a self-cleaning paint modeled on the lotus leaf. When the paint dries, it becomes bumpy, just like the lotus leaf. Rain droplets form on the bumps and roll off, carrying dirt along with them.

Only the best-designed living things have survived. We owe Mother Nature a debt for all this hard work, Benyus says. She thinks companies should use part of

These images show how engineers used the boxfish as inspiration for a new car.

their profits from their special inventions to protect the Earth. "It's a way of saying thank you for these incredible ideas that are now helping us," Benyus says.

WHAT'S NEXT?

For scientists and inventors, ideas for brilliant new designs are all around. Take a walk outside. Watch a squirrel race up a tree. Look at the veins of a leaf. Such small details may help inventors solve big problems in the future.

Coolest Inventions of 2008

TIME reporting by Jeremy Caplan, Laura Fitzpatrick,
Sean Gregory, Lev Grossman, Jeffrey Kluger, Richard
Lacayo, Lisa McLaughlin, Bryan Walsh

**A towering skyscraper that doesn't cast a
shadow. A camera that lets the blind take
photos. Inventors break new ground every
day as they develop ways to improve our
lives and bring more fun to our world.
Check out some of 2008's most innovative
gadgets and products. Which ones could
make your life easier?**

Towering Triangle

For 31 years, city officials have banned the construction of tall buildings in Paris, France. But designers got approval to build a 50-story shadowless skyscraper. The team that created the "Bird's Nest" Olympic stadium in Beijing, China, came up with the design concept for **Le Projet Triangle**. They are working on a glass-and-steel pyramid that won't cast shadows on surrounding streets.

A Helping Hand

Scientists are giving this mechanical hand a big thumbs-up. The **iLimb,** by Touch Bionics, is the first bionic hand people can buy. Artificial hands are often hooklike, limiting movements to simple open-and-close gestures. But each of the iLimb's plastic fingers has a tiny motor. Users can grasp a variety of objects, from thin library cards to big coffee mugs. Now that deserves a high five!

What a Face!

Meet **Nexi.** It is the first of a new class of robots from scientists at the Massachusetts Institute of Technology. Nexi is designed to interact with humans. The robot can pick up objects weighing up to 10 pounds (5 kg). It can also make many facial expressions, showing emotions such as sadness and surprise. Nexi is also able to roll on wheels. You go, Nexi!

Inventions

137

A Touching Sight

The **Touch Sight** camera makes it possible for the visually impaired to take pictures. The photographer holds the camera up to his or her forehead. A screen on the back of the camera makes a raised image of what the lens sees. The user can then touch the image on the screen. The image can be saved and shared.

Just Charge It!

going green

Three environmentally friendly electric cars are leading the way to the future. The **Chevy Volt** has an electric motor that lets it run up to 40 miles (64 km) on just one charge. The speedy battery-powered **Tesla Roadster** sports car uses the same kind of battery that laptop computers use. It can travel at a top speed of 125 miles (201 km) per hour. The **Aptera,** whose name means "wingless flight" in Greek, can go from zero to 60 miles per hour (96 km) in fewer than 10 seconds.

Aptera

Chevy Volt

Tesla Roadster

Return to the Moon

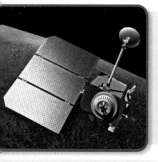

The United States is headed back to the moon, and its new spacecraft couldn't be cooler. In April 2009, NASA plans to launch the **Lunar Reconnaissance** (re-*con*-eh-sense) **Orbiter.** It will be the space agency's first unmanned moon mission in 11 years. The craft will study gravity and temperature and create 3-D lunar maps. It will also look for signs of water ice, an important resource for any future moon base.

Clean Cement

going green

A street in Segrate, Italy, is paved with cement that breaks down smog. Italian inventors spent 10 years developing the smog-eating cement, **TX Active.** They say it has cut some pollutants by as much as 60%. Buildings made with TX Active stay cleaner too.

Cool Bike

If you like motorcycles but don't want to get wet when it rains, try the **MonoTracer.** The vehicle combines the excitement of riding a motorcycle with the comforts of car travel. It even has air-conditioning. When the MonoTracer leans into corners, a small wheel pops out to keep it steady. Good luck getting one, though. Only 100 of the sleek superbikes will be built each year. Production began in 2009.

Still Growing?

Most fresh food comes stamped with a date when its freshness might expire. But designer Agata Jaworska thinks food should be purchased while it's still growing. She created **Gropak**, packaging in which produce can keep growing during shipping. This means that some fruits and vegetables could be harvested fresh at the market.

Second Skin

Ready to run? Nike's **Zoom Victory** track spike is made with a paper-thin surface that hugs feet like a second skin. Narrow threads of Vectran run from the laces to the bottom of the shoe. NASA uses superstrong Vectran to sew balloons onto the lunar rover, which cushion its landing. The streamlined shoe weighs just 3.5 ounces (99 g).

Save Energy! going green

Why waste energy? Power is all around us, if we just know how to use it. Max Donelan, a scientist at Simon Fraser University, in Canada, has invented a device that collects the energy people make while walking. The 3.5-pound (1.6-kg) device wraps around the wearer's knee. A walker with a **Bionic Energy Harvester** on one knee could generate enough power to charge five cell phones.

A Red-Planet Rover

The last two rovers NASA sent to Mars are still going strong after nearly five years. The next one, the **Mars Science Laboratory,** which launches in 2011, is even tougher. The 9-foot (3-m) craft will carry 176 pounds (80 kg) of instruments. One of the tools will be used to detect permafrost, or permanently frozen soil.

MYSTERY PERSON

Clue 1: I was born in Galesburg, Illinois, in 1859.

Clue 2: I designed an engineering marvel for a world's fair held in Chicago, Illinois. It debuted in 1893.

Clue 3: Replicas of my invention, which is named after me, still spin in amusement parks.

Who am I? _____ ANSWER ON PAGE 244.

Language

A Language Art

Jessica Bucknam shouts "tiao!" (tee-ow) and her fourth-grade students jump. "Dun!" (doo-wen) she commands, and they crouch. They giggle as the commands keep coming in Mandarin Chinese. Most of the kids have studied Chinese since they were in kindergarten.

They are part of a Chinese-immersion program at Woodstock Elementary School, in Portland, Oregon. Bucknam, who is from China, introduces her students to approximately 150 new Chinese characters each year. Students read stories, sing songs and learn math and science, all in Chinese.

Half of the 340 students at the K-5 school are enrolled in the program. They can continue studying Chinese in middle and high school. The goal: to speak like natives.

About 24,000 American students are currently learning Chinese. Most are in high school. But the number of younger students is growing in response to China's emergence as a global superpower. In some instances, the U.S. government is even helping to pay for language instruction. In 2006, the Defense Department gave Oregon schools $700,000 for classes like Bucknam's.

"China has become a strong partner of the United States," says Mary Patterson, Woodstock's principal. "Children who learn Chinese at a young age will have more opportunities for jobs in the future."

WANT TO LEARN CHINESE?
You have to memorize 3,500 characters to really know this 6,000-year-old language.

Contestants wait for their turns to spell.

ONE SERIOUS SPELLER

Sameer Mishra

A record 288 kids participated in the 81st annual Scripps National Spelling Bee, held in Washington, D.C., on May 29–30, 2008. The winner, 13-year-old Sameer Mishra from Lafayette, Indiana, received a trophy and more than $40,000 in cash and prizes. Sameer loves to read and is a member of his school's book club. His sister, Shruti, a three-time competitor, is his spelling coach. He correctly spelled words including "macédoine," "basenji" and "hyphaeresis." He won with the word "guerdon." Here are the winning words since 1990.

Year	Word	Year	Word
2008	guerdon	1998	chiaroscurist
2007	serrefine	1997	euonym
2006	Ursprache	1996	vivisepulture
2005	appoggiatura	1995	xanthosis
2004	autochthonous	1994	antediluvian
2003	pococurante	1993	kamikaze
2002	prospicience	1992	lyceum
2001	succedaneum	1991	antipyretic
2000	démarche	1990	fibranne
1999	logorrhea		

TOP 5 Languages Spoken in the U.S.

1. English (only)	215,423,557 people
2. Spanish	28,101,052 people
3. Chinese	2,022,143 people
4. French	1,643,838 people
5. German	1,382,613 people

Source: U.S. Census Bureau

The Newest Words in the Dictionary

Edamame

To stay on top of important trends and advances in technology, dictionaries add new words every year. Here are a few of the 2008 additions to the Merriam-Webster dictionary.

FANBOY: a boy who is a huge fan, or an enthusiastic devotee, of something like comics, movies or a particular musical group

EDAMAME: immature green soybeans, usually in the pod

KITEBOARDING: the sport of riding on a small surfboard propelled across water by a large kite; the rider is harnessed to the kite

PESCATARIAN: vegetarian whose diet includes fish

SUPERCROSS: motorcycle race held in a stadium on a dirt track having hairpin turns and high jumps

Pescatarian

EASILY CONFUSED WORDS

WORDS	MEANING/USAGE	EXAMPLE
affect	to have an influence on	*Your grades can affect your future.*
effect	the result of a cause	*Studying has a good effect on grades.*
all together	refers to a group	*Six students sat all together on the bench.*
altogether	entirely	*We're altogether happy about winning.*
beside	next to	*Please sit beside me.*
besides	also	*Besides, I like you.*
capital	the city in which the government works	*Washington, D.C., is the capital of the United States.*
Capitol	the building in which lawmakers of government meet	*The Senate meets in the Capitol.*
farther	more distant	*We traveled farther than you did.*
further	to a greater extent	*We need to study further in order to understand this problem.*
laid	past-tense of lay	*I laid the blanket on the lawn.*
lay	past-tense of lie	*I lay down and took a nap.*
lightening	to make brighter or to reduce in weight	*They were lightening the load by removing things from their bags.*
lightning	an electrical charge in the sky	*The lightning lit up the sky.*
passed	past-tense of pass	*He passed the store on his way home.*
past	an earlier time	*He liked reading about the past.*

the Capitol

Language

Going green

When you are writing for pleasure or printing assignments for school, keep in mind that paper makes up a large percentage of our trash. How can you cut back? Write on both sides when you can, use scrap paper whenever possible, always recycle and think twice before hitting Print when you are on the computer.

WORDS ABOUT WORDS

ANTONYM a word that has the opposite meaning of another word.

EXAMPLES: enormous/tiny   always/never
hottest/coldest   strong/weak

SYNONYM a word with a similar, or the same, meaning as another

EXAMPLES: beautiful/gorgeous   hop/jump
fast/quick   cry/weep

METAPHOR a figure of speech comparing two things without using the words 'like' or 'as'

EXAMPLES: "Julie's so sweet. She is a ray of sunshine."
"He can eat anything—his stomach is a bottomless pit."

SIMILE a figure of speech comparing two things using the words 'like' or 'as'

EXAMPLES: "After lunch, she fell asleep and slept **like** a baby."
"Be as quiet **as** a mouse and you won't disturb anyone."

HOMOGRAPH a word that is spelled the same as another but has a different meaning. They may be pronounced the same or differently.

EXAMPLES: "I feel **well** enough today to help dig the **well**."
"He **dove** behind a tree when he saw the **dove**."

HOMOPHONE a word that sounds the same as another but has a different meaning. They may be spelled the same or differently.

EXAMPLES: "I will **write** the letter **right** now."
"When the **two** puppies ran **to** the house, the boys ran **too**."

ALLITERATION more than two words in a row that begin with the same consonant

EXAMPLES: "The silly snakes slithered toward Sally."
"Tim tickled her teeny, tiny toe."

HYPERBOLE an exaggeration

EXAMPLES: "I almost died laughing."
"I have a mountain of homework to do!"

PALINDROME a word or sentence that is the same when read forwards and backwards

WORD EXAMPLES: mom, dad, pop, eye, nun, civic, kayak, radar, racecar
LONGER EXAMPLES: Never odd or even.
Madam, I'm Adam.
Too bad I hid a boot.

KAYAK—SAME WORD READ FORWARDS OR BACKWARDS!

Say "Hi" Like a Local

ARABIC Al salaam a'alaykum
(Ahl sah LAHM ah ah LAY koom)

BENGALI Ei Je (EYE jay)

CHINESE Ni hao (Nee HOW)

FRENCH Bonjour (Bohn ZHOR)

HINDUSTANI Namaste (Nah MAH stay)

JAPANESE Konichiwa (Kon I shee wa)

MALAY-INDONESIAN Selamat pagi
(Se LA mat PA gee)

PORTUGUESE Bon dia (Bohn DEE ah)

RUSSIAN Zdravstvuite (ZDRAST vet yah)

SPANISH Hola (OH la)

1.	Chinese (Mandarin)	1,075,000,000
2.	English	514,000,000
3.	Hindustani	496,000,000
4.	Spanish	425,000,000
5.	Russian	275,000,000
6.	Arabic	256,000,000
7.	Bengali	215,000,000
8.	Portuguese	194,000,000
9.	Malay-Indonesian	176,000,000
10.	French	129,000,000

Source: *Ethnologue*

TFK GAME

FEEL THE WORDS

At age 15, Louis Braille began to develop a system of writing that blind people could read. The system is based on the alphabet. Each letter is made of raised dots within a six-dot group. Use the chart to finish the saying below. Poke the point of your pencil into the dots. Then touch the other side of the page. That's how Braille feels.

a b c d e f g h i
j k l m n o p q r
s t u v w x y z

for the

ANSWER ON PAGE 244.

Clue 1: I was born in Feeding Hills, Massachusetts, on April 14, 1866.

Clue 2: An illness left me nearly blind at age 5. This made me want to help other people who had disabilities.

Clue 3: I taught Helen Keller, who was deaf and blind, how to read, write and speak. Under my care, brilliant Helen connected with the world.

Helen Keller

Who am I? _____

MYSTERY PERSON

ANSWER ON PAGE 244.

Language

Math and Money

3.141592

WHAT IS MATHEMATICS?

Mathematics is the study of figures and numbers. It deals with shapes, sizes, amounts and patterns. There are many branches of mathematics, including arithmetic (addition, subtraction, multiplication and division), algebra, geometry and statistics.

COMMON FORMULAS

To find the AREA of a TRIANGLE:
Multiply the base of the triangle by the height of the triangle. Divide by 2.

area = ½ (base x height)

EXAMPLE:

area = ½ (6 x 8) or 24 square units

8

6

To find the AREA of a RECTANGLE:
Multiply the base of the rectangle by its height.

area = base x height

EXAMPLE:

area = 6 x 3 or 18 square units

3

6

To find the AREA of a SQUARE:
Multiply the length of one side of the square by itself.

area = side x side

EXAMPLE:

area = 4 x 4 or 16 square units

4

The radius of a circle is the length between the center of the circle and any point on the perimeter of the circle.

To find the AREA of a CIRCLE:
Multiply the radius by itself. Then multiply the product by 3.14 (which is also known as **pi** or π):

**area = radius x radius x 3.14
(or area = πr^2)**

EXAMPLE:

**area = 5 x 5 x 3.14 or
78.5 square units**

5

The diameter of a circle is the length of a straight line beginning on the perimeter of the circle, passing through the center and ending on the perimeter of the circle. The diameter is twice as long as the radius.

10

The circumference of a circle is the distance around the entire circle.

To find the CIRCUMFERENCE of a CIRCLE:
Multiply the diameter by 3.14.

**circumference = diameter x 3.14 or
(circumference = diameter x π)**

EXAMPLE:

circumference = 10 x 3.14 or 31.4

Easy as Pi?

The number 3.14, used in some common mathematical formulas (above right), is π rounded to two decimal places. Pronounced "pi," π is a Greek letter. The actual value of π continues for trillions of digits. Here are the first 50 digits after the decimal point:

3.14159265358979323846264338327950288419716939937510

MULTIPLICATION TABLE

	1	2	3	4	5	6	7	8	9	10	11	12
1	1	2	3	4	5	6	7	8	9	10	11	12
2	2	4	6	8	10	12	14	16	18	20	22	24
3	3	6	9	12	15	18	21	24	27	30	33	36
4	4	8	12	16	20	24	28	32	36	40	44	48
5	5	10	15	20	25	30	35	40	45	50	55	60
6	6	12	18	24	30	36	42	48	54	60	66	72
7	7	14	21	28	35	42	49	56	63	70	77	84
8	8	16	24	32	40	48	56	64	72	80	88	96
9	9	18	27	36	45	54	63	72	81	90	99	108
10	10	20	30	40	50	60	70	80	90	100	110	120
11	11	22	33	44	55	66	77	88	99	110	121	132
12	12	24	36	48	60	72	84	96	108	120	132	144

COMMON METRIC CONVERSIONS

LENGTH

MULTIPLY	BY	TO FIND
centimeters	.3937	inches
feet	.3048	meters
inches	2.54	centimeters
kilometers	.6214	miles
meters	3.2808	feet
meters	1.0936	yards
miles	1.6093	kilometers
yards	.9144	meters

WEIGHT

grams	.0353	ounces
kilograms	2.2046	pounds
ounces	28.3495	grams
pounds	.4536	kilograms

AREA

square kilometers	.3861	square miles
square meters	1.196	square yards
square miles	2.59	square kilometers
square yards	.8361	square meters

VOLUME

gallons	3.7843	liters
liters	1.0567	quarts
liters	.2642	gallons
quarts	.946	liters

12-INCH RULER OR 30.5-CM RULER?

1.5 KILOGRAMS OR 3.25 POUNDS OF APPLES?

1 GALLON OR 3.7843 LITERS OF MILK?

Math and Money

145

EVERYDAY MATH

Ever wonder why you have to memorize multiplication tables or slave over long-division problems? Here are just a few practical ways your hard work can come in handy.

USE MATH SKILLS TO UNDERSTAND SPORTS STATS

HOW MUCH IS AN 18% TIP?

- Mixing a double-size batch of brownies
- Calculating a tip at a restaurant
- Making sure you have enough money for the tax on a purchase
- Figuring how long a car trip will take
- Determining and predicting athletes' statistics
- Finding the best shopping bargain based on price and quantity
- Buying enough snacks and party favors for a celebration
- Figuring out when to call a family member in a different time zone
- Counting your change at the store
- Evenly dividing snacks among friends

There are also countless jobs that make regular use of arithmetic, algebra, geometry, calculus, statistics and more. Here are just a few: bicycle designer, farmer, musical-instrument maker, architect, accountant, carpenter, geologist, computer programmer, doctor, meteorologist and, of course, math teacher.

How to Round Numbers

A number can be rounded to any place value. Here's how to round a number to the nearest 10.

If a number ends with a 1, 2, 3 or 4, round it down to the nearest number that ends in 0. EXAMPLES:

22 should be rounded down to 20.
54 should be rounded down to 50.
631 should be rounded down to 630.

If a number ends with a 5, 6, 7, 8 or 9, round it up to the nearest number that ends in 0. EXAMPLES:

9 should be rounded up to 10.
87 should be rounded up to 90.
516 should be rounded up to 520.

Here's how to round a number to the nearest 100.

If the last two digits of a number are 00 through 49, round it down to the nearest number that ends in 00. EXAMPLES:

122 should be rounded down to 100.
746 should be rounded down to 700.
1,314 should be rounded down to 1,300.

If the last two digits in a number end in 50 through 99, round it up to the nearest number that ends in 00. EXAMPLES:

189 should be rounded up to 200.
656 should be rounded up to 700.
3,791 should be rounded up to 3,800.

How to Average Numbers

Averages are used to get a sense of a group of numbers. You find the average by adding up the numbers in the group, then dividing the sum by the number of numbers in the group. For example, if you have three numbers, add them up and divide the sum by 3:

10+11+12=33 and 33/3=11
The average of 10, 11 and 12 is 11.

If you have 5 numbers, add them up and divide the sum by 5:

31+34+29+30+21=145 and 145/5=29.
The average of 31, 34, 29, 30 and 21 is 29.

WHAT IS ECONOMICS?

Economics is the study of how people and businesses exchange money, goods and services in a community. **Goods** are physical items that you can buy, like clothing, video games, books and cars. **Services** are jobs that are done for you, like getting your teeth cleaned or your hair cut. Babysitters, plumbers and gardeners are just a few of the people who provide services. **Economists** study all of the factors that affect the economy. They are interested in such problems as how rising prices for gasoline will affect how many cars are sold this year—or what kind of cars will sell.

CLOTHES AND OTHER ITEMS ARE GOODS.

Throughout the world, there are different kinds of economic systems. Some societies have a **traditional economy,** where people make their own goods and don't use money. Instead, they may trade for things they don't have. In a **command economy,** the government controls the prices and the production of goods and services.

The United States has a **market economy,** where the prices are determined by the **law of supply and demand.** Supply is how much of an item or service is available for purchase. Demand is how much of that item or service people want. Both supply and demand influence how many products a company will create, what kinds of products they will work on for the future and how much they will charge for an item. For example, both the quantity of computers available and the number of people who want to buy a computer will effect the price of the machines. The same goes for services. If there are 10 hairdressers on one street, they must compete for customers and keep their prices low. On the other hand, imagine that there is only one pet store in an entire town full of pet lovers. Without any competition, this store might charge more for its animals and pet food.

A HAIRCUTTER PROVIDES A SERVICE.

$1 International Shopping Spree

- **United States:** 1/3 of a Starbucks tall latte
- **Philippines:** 4/5 of a Big Mac
- **Bangladesh:** 7 bars of soap
- **India:** 2 to 3 pieces of bamboo for building
- **Kenya:** 8 cups of milk

Source: World Resources Institute, wri.org

Math and Money

Handling your own money is one of the first steps toward becoming an adult. Whether you have an allowance or a job, it is important to budget. When you create a **budget**, you estimate how much money you will be earning and list how much money you can spend and save. Without a budget, you might go broke!

A bank account helps you keep track of your money while storing it safely. You can add money to your account by making a **deposit** and take money out with a **withdrawal.**

With a **savings account**, you can collect interest. Interest is a small percentage of money that the bank pays you in exchange for letting it hold on to your money. If you put $100 in the bank, after a year you might have $103! It doesn't sound like much, but it can add up over time. Another option is a **checking account**, which allows you to write checks or use a debit card to pay for purchases or bills instead of using cash.

Using a **credit card** allows you to buy things now and pay later, but be careful—you will be charged interest for using credit, so you may end up paying a lot more than you bargained for!

Investing 101

When you invest, you buy something with the expectation that it will become more valuable over time—you may hope to sell it for more money than you originally paid. A house, an antique car or a famous painting can be investments, but you can also invest in stocks, bonds and mutual funds.

A stock is a share in the ownership of a corporation, which is a type of large company. When you buy a stock, you actually become part owner of that company. If the company does well, the value of your stock goes up. But if the company does poorly, the value of your stock goes down. If you sell your stock when the company is doing well, you may make a significant profit, which means you get the difference between the stock's price at the time you purchased it and the price at the time you sell it. For example, if you bought one share of a particular stock for $10 and sell it a month later for $15, you make $5. Imagine if you owned 100 or 1,000 shares of that stock! Also, if the company makes a profit itself in business, you may be given a dividend, which is a portion of the company's profit.

A bond, like a stock, is an investment with a corporation or a large public organization, such as a school or a hospital. Unlike a stock, a bond does not give you a stake in the ownership of the company. Instead, it is like you are letting the company borrow your money and then pay it back later with interest. A bond normally lasts for a fixed length of time, usually anywhere from 5 to 30 years. For example, you might buy a bond for $100. If this bond pays 10% per year for a period of 10 years, you will receive $10 each year for 10 years. Then, when the bond reaches maturity, you will get your original $100 investment back too. Bonds are seen as a safe investment because they rarely go down in value.

A mutual fund is a company that makes investments for you. Investors trust that the mutual fund will invest their money wisely, whether in stocks, bonds or other specialized investments. A mutual fund can spread a large amount of money from many investors evenly across many different kinds of investments. In this way, the fund managers can balance out the profits from some investments with losses in others.

53-

Former Treasury Secretary Henry Paulson and Bureau of Engraving and Printing Director Larry Felix inspect new $20 bills as they come off the press.

How Money Is Made

The Bureau of Engraving and Printing goes through a painstaking 65-step process to make our paper money. First, the pictures and writing are carefully engraved by hand into pieces of steel. Plastic imprints are then made of the steel engravings and are put together to create a template for making 32 bills at the same time. After several steps, a printing plate made from this template is put on a rotary printing press that can print 8,000 sheets in an hour. That's a lot of sheets—and a lot of money!

Coins are made by first stamping blank disks out of a coiled sheet of metal that is 1,500 feet (457 meters) long. The blanks are cleaned, shined and milled to create the raised (and sometimes grooved) edge of the coin. Then the coins are put through a press, which imprints the words and pictures onto them. After inspection, they are counted, bagged and sent out to Federal Reserve Banks, which pass them on to local banks.

Stumping Counterfeiters

Counterfeiters are criminals who make fake money or products. The Bureau of Engraving and Printing uses a couple of tricks to make it hard for counterfeiters to print phony copies of U.S. currency.

- On the lower right corner of a $20 bill, the number 20 changes color from copper to green as you tilt the bill.

- When you hold a new bill up to the light, on the far right you can see a faint picture of the same face on the center of the bill. This is called a watermark.

- There is also a "security thread" on every bill. This is a thin strip woven right into the paper, running from top to bottom next to the picture on the front of a bill. Looking closely at this thread, you can see the amount of the bill, a small American flag and the letters "USA."

To keep ahead of counterfeiters, the U.S. government changes the way our money looks every seven to 10 years.

Movies and TV

FROM TFK MAGAZINE

WALL-E Wins an Oscar!

THE TALE OF A FUTURISTIC ROBOT WINS THE ACADEMY AWARD FOR BEST ANIMATED FEATURE

By Vickie An

A tiny trash-compacting robot beat out a kung-fu-fighting panda and a heroic TV super dog to win Hollywood's biggest honor. *WALL-E* took home the Oscar for Best Animated Feature on February 22, 2009, at the 81st annual Academy Awards. The event took place at the Kodak Theatre in Los Angeles, California. It was hosted by actor Hugh Jackman, of *X-Men* and *Happy Feet*.

Disney/Pixar's robot love story was up against DreamWorks's *Kung Fu Panda* and Disney's *Bolt*. Director Andrew Stanton accepted the award. "It's been such an inspiration to spend time with a character who so tenaciously struggles to find the beauty in everything that he sees," said Stanton in his speech.

This is Disney/Pixar's fourth triumph since 2001, when the Best Animated Feature category was introduced. The studios' past winners include *Ratatouille*, the superhero flick *The Incredibles* and the heartwarming fish tale *Finding Nemo*. *WALL-E* was nominated for five categories in all.

THE LITTLE MOVIE THAT COULD

Slumdog Millionaire was the major winner on Oscar night 2009. The movie follows two orphaned brothers on their journey to escape the slums, or poor areas, of Mumbai, India. The rags-to-riches story struck Oscar gold, taking home eight of the 10 awards for which it was nominated. The wins included two of the night's most prized awards: Best Director and Best Picture.

Accepting the directing Oscar, a delighted Danny Boyle jumped up and down on stage. He had promised his children that if he ever won an Academy Award he would bounce around in the "spirit of Tigger from *Winnie the Pooh*." Overjoyed cast and crew members joined producer Christian Colson on stage as he accepted the Best Picture award. "We had passion and we had belief, and our film shows if you have those two things, truly anything is possible," Colson said.

Top 8 Movies of 2008

RANK	TITLE	MONEY MADE	OPENING DATE
1.	The Dark Knight	$530,540,885	7/18/2008
2.	Iron Man	$318,313,199	5/2/2008
3.	Indiana Jones and the Kingdom of the Crystal Skull	$317,023,851	5/22/2008
4.	Hancock	$227,946,274	7/2/2008
5.	WALL-E	$223,704,223	6/27/2008
6.	Kung Fu Panda	$215,434,591	6/6/2008
7.	Madagascar: Escape 2 Africa	$165,653,852	11/7/2008
8.	Dr. Seuss' Horton Hears a Who	$154,529,439	3/14/2008

Source: The Nielsen Company/*The Hollywood Reporter*
Note: Data from January 1–December 7, 2008, in the United States and Canada only.

And the Oscar Goes To…

On February 22, 2009, the top names in Hollywood gathered for the Academy Awards. Here are the night's big winners.

BEST PICTURE: *Slumdog Millionaire*

BEST DIRECTOR: Danny Boyle, *Slumdog Millionaire*

Kate Winslet, Sean Penn, Penelope Cruz

BEST ANIMATED FEATURE: *WALL-E*

BEST FEATURE DOCUMENTARY: *Man on Wire*

BEST ACTOR: Sean Penn, *Milk*

BEST ACTRESS: Kate Winslet, *The Reader*

BEST SUPPORTING ACTRESS: Penelope Cruz, *Vicky Cristina Barcelona*

BEST SUPPORTING ACTOR: Heath Ledger, *The Dark Knight*

BEST ORIGINAL SONG: "Jai Ho" from *Slumdog Millionaire*

BEST ORIGINAL SCORE: *Slumdog Millionaire*

BEST ORIGINAL SCREENPLAY: *Milk* by Dustin Lance Black

BEST ADAPTED SCREENPLAY: *Slumdog Millionaire* by Simon Beaufoy

BEST VISUAL EFFECTS: *The Curious Case of Benjamin Button*

BEST FILM EDITING: Chris Dickens, *Slumdog Millionaire*

BEST CINEMATOGRAPHY: Anthony Dod Mantle, *Slumdog Millionaire*

BEST COSTUME DESIGN: Michael O'Connor, *The Duchess*

BEST MAKEUP: Greg Cannom, *The Curious Case of Benjamin Button*

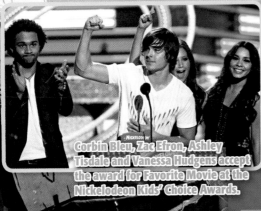

Corbin Bleu, Zac Efron, Ashley Tisdale and Vanessa Hudgens accept the award for Favorite Movie at the Nickelodeon Kids' Choice Awards.

Nickelodeon Kids' Choice Awards

SATURDAY, MARCH 28, 2009

MOVIES

Favorite Movie: *High School Musical 3: Senior Year*

Favorite Female Movie Star: Vanessa Hudgens in *High School Musical 3: Senior Year*

Favorite Male Movie Star: Will Smith in *Hancock*

Favorite Animated Movie: *Madagascar: Escape 2 Africa*

Favorite Voice from an Animated Movie: Jack Black in *Kung Fu Panda*

TELEVISION

Favorite Reality Show: *American Idol*

Favorite TV Show: *iCarly*

Favorite TV Actress: Selena Gomez in *Wizards of Waverly Place*

Favorite TV Actor: Dylan Sprouse in *The Suite Life of Zack and Cody*

Favorite Cartoon: *SpongeBob SquarePants*

TOP 5 DVD Sales

RANK TITLE	RELEASE DATE
1. *Iron Man*	9/30/08
2. *I Am Legend*	3/18/08
3. *Alvin and the Chipmunks*	4/1/08
4. *Enchanted*	3/18/08
5. *National Treasure 2: Book of Secrets*	5/20/08

Source: The Nielsen Company

Movies and TV

GOLDEN GLOBES

The 65th Annual Golden Globe Awards took place on January 11, 2009, at the Beverly Hilton in Beverly Hills, California. Members of the Hollywood Foreign Press Association vote on the winners of these film and television awards.

Alec Baldwin

Anna Paquin

BEST MOTION PICTURE–DRAMA: *Slumdog Millionaire*

BEST MOTION PICTURE–MUSICAL OR COMEDY: *Vicky Cristina Barcelona*

BEST DIRECTOR–MOTION PICTURE: Danny Boyle, *Slumdog Millionaire*

BEST ACTRESS–DRAMA: Kate Winslet, *Revolutionary Road*

BEST ACTOR–DRAMA: Mickey Rourke, *The Wrestler*

BEST ACTRESS–MUSICAL OR COMEDY: Sally Hawkins, *Happy-Go-Lucky*

BEST ACTOR–MUSICAL OR COMEDY: Colin Farrell, *In Bruges*

BEST SUPPORTING ACTRESS: Kate Winslet, *The Reader*

BEST SUPPORTING ACTOR: Heath Ledger, *The Dark Knight*

The Dark Knight

BEST ANIMATED FEATURE FILM: *WALL-E*

BEST FOREIGN LANGUAGE FILM: *Waltz with Bashir* (Israel)

BEST SCREENPLAY: *Slumdog Millionaire* by Simon Beaufoy

BEST TELEVISION SERIES–DRAMA: *Mad Men*

BEST ACTRESS IN A TV SERIES–DRAMA: Anna Paquin, *True Blood*

BEST ACTOR IN A TV SERIES–DRAMA: Gabriel Byrne, *In Treatment*

BEST TELEVISION SERIES–MUSICAL OR COMEDY: *30 Rock*

BEST ACTRESS IN A TV–MUSICAL OR COMEDY: Tina Fey, *30 Rock*

BEST ACTOR IN A TV SERIES–MUSICAL OR COMEDY: Alec Baldwin, *30 Rock*

CECIL B. DEMILLE AWARD: Steven Spielberg

THE CECIL B. DEMILLE AWARD

Every year, the Hollywood Foreign Press Association gives out an award to recognize "outstanding contributions to the entertainment field." This honor, the Cecil B. DeMille Award, is named after an important filmmaker who produced and directed more than 70 films in his lifetime. The award's first recipient was DeMille himself.

The recipient of the 2008 Cecil B. DeMille Award was Steven Spielberg, best known for directing such movies as *Indiana Jones and the Kingdom of the Crystal Skull*, *War of the Worlds*, *A.I.: Artificial Intelligence*, *Jurassic Park*, *E.T.: The Extra-Terrestrial*, *Raiders of the Lost Ark* and *Jaws*. Other recent Cecil B. DeMille winners include Warren Beatty (2007), Anthony Hopkins (2006), Robin Williams (2005), Michael Douglas (2004), Gene Hackman (2003), Harrison Ford (2002), Al Pacino (2001) and Barbra Streisand (2000).

Steven Spielberg and Karen Allen on the set of *Indiana Jones and the Kingdom of the Crystal Skull*

A LITTLE MOVIE MUSIC

Movies are also recognized during the Grammy Awards. In 2009, the film *Juno* won an award for Best Compilation Sound Track. The Grammy for Best Score Sound Track went to *The Dark Knight*.

TEEN CHOICE AWARDS

MOVIES

AUGUST 4, 2008

BREAKOUT MALE: Drake Bell, *Superhero Movie*
BREAKOUT FEMALE: Ellen Page, *Juno*
VILLAIN: Johnny Depp, *Sweeney Todd*
ACTRESS, HORROR/THRILLER: Jessica Alba, *The Eye*
ACTOR, HORROR/THRILLER: Will Smith, *I Am Legend*
ACTRESS, COMEDY: Ellen Page, *Juno*
ACTOR, COMEDY: Ashton Kutcher, *What Happens in Vegas*
ACTRESS, ACTION/ADVENTURE: Rachel Bilson, *Jumper*
ACTOR, ACTION/ADVENTURE: Shia LaBeouf, *Indiana Jones and the Kingdom of the Crystal Skull*
ACTRESS, DRAMA: Keira Knightley, *Atonement*
ACTOR, DRAMA: Channing Tatum, *Stop-Loss*
HORROR/THRILLER: *I Am Legend*
COMEDY: *Juno*
ROMANTIC COMEDY: *What Happens in Vegas*
CHICK FLICK: *27 Dresses*
DRAMA: *Step Up 2: The Streets*
ACTION-ADVENTURE: *Chronicles of Narnia: Prince Caspian*

Will Smith

Channing Tatum

Prince Caspian

TV

BREAKOUT MALE: Chace Crawford, *Gossip Girl*
BREAKOUT FEMALE: Blake Lively, *Gossip Girl*
BREAKOUT SHOW: *Gossip Girl*
DRAMA: *Gossip Girl*
COMEDY: *Hannah Montana*
ACTION/ADVENTURE: *Heroes*
ANIMATED SHOW: *Family Guy*
ACTRESS, DRAMA: Blake Lively, *Gossip Girl*
ACTOR, DRAMA: Chad Michael Murray, *One Tree Hill*
ACTRESS, COMEDY: Miley Cyrus, *Hannah Montana*
ACTOR, COMEDY: Steve Carell, *The Office*
ACTRESS, ACTION/ADVENTURE: Hayden Panettiere, *Heroes*
ACTOR, ACTION/ADVENTURE: Milo Ventimiglia, *Heroes*
FEMALE, REALITY/VARIETY: Lauren Conrad, *The Hills*
MALE, REALITY/VARIETY: David Cook, *American Idol*
VILLAIN: Ed Westwick, *Gossip Girl*
PERSONALITY: Tyra Banks
GAME SHOW: *Deal or No Deal*
CELEBRITY/REALITY: *The Hills*
REALITY MUSIC COMPETITION: *American Idol*
REALITY DANCE: *America's Best Dance Crew*

Hayden Panettiere

Miley Cyrus

guess what? *Walt Disney released his first feature-length animated film in 1937. It was Snow White and the Seven Dwarfs. He worked on that film for three years. As the head of his own film company, he oversaw the creation of many beloved films, including Pinocchio (1940), Fantasia (1940), Dumbo (1941), Bambi (1942), Cinderella (1950), Alice in Wonderland (1951) and Mary Poppins (1964).*

Movies and TV

153

BLOCKBUSTER BUDGETS

Movies sure can be expensive. Not just the tickets, but the making of the movie itself. For example, *Spider-Man 3* cost $250 million to make!

Why so much? Well, famous actors are paid a lot for what they do, as are well-known directors, writers and producers. For example, Tobey Maguire received more than $15 million to act in *Spider-Man 3*. Working with live actors can be pricey, but that doesn't mean that animated movies are cheap. In fact, both *Iron Man* and the Oscar-winning feature *WALL-E* had estimated budgets of at least $180 million. *Slumdog Millionaire* is considered a low-budget film because it cost just $15 million to make.

Camera equipment and other technology add a lot to a film's price tag. For example, if a filmmaker wants to use 35mm film—as in *Pirates of the Caribbean: Dead Man's Chest*—a single movie camera can cost around $75,000. Of course, you could just rent one for the bargain price of $700 a day—though that doesn't even include the film!

All the people listed in the credits at the end of a movie are also getting paid to do important work behind the scenes—building the set, designing and making costumes, preparing lighting and effects, setting up stunts, and more. Then, after the movie is shot, there is still a lot of work to be done: editing scenes together, creating music and sound effects, and, in many cases, using special computer programs to create amazing visual effects such as those in The Chronicles of Narnia series.

There is also the less glamorous side of things, like paying for hotels and travel expenses, getting food for everyone—even paying accountants to keep track of where all the money is going. Finally, somebody has to clean up and do the laundry on the set—and it's not Tobey Maguire!

TOP 10 Highest-Grossing Movies in the U.S.

RANK	MOVIE TITLE	YEAR RELEASED	USA BOX OFFICE TOTAL
1.	*Titanic*	1997	$600,779,824
2.	*The Dark Knight*	2008	$533,184,219
3.	*Star Wars*	1977	$460,935,665
4.	*Shrek 2*	2004	$436,471,036
5.	*E.T.: The Extra-Terrestrial*	1982	$434,949,459
6.	*Star Wars: Episode 1: The Phantom Menace*	1999	$431,065,444
7.	*Pirates of the Caribbean: Dead Man's Chest*	2006	$423,032,628
8.	*Spider-Man*	2002	$403,706,375
9.	*Star Wars: Episode 3: Revenge of the Sith*	2005	$380,262,555
10.	*The Lord of the Rings: Return of the King*	2003	$377,019,252

COOL MOVIE TECHNOLOGY: 3-D

In the 1950s, people flocked to theaters to watch early 3-D (three-dimensional) movies like *Creature from the Black Lagoon*. Up until then, most movies were only 2-D–they had height and width, but appeared on a flat screen and had no depth. 3-D movies tricked the audience into seeing depth by showing two slightly different pictures–one for your left eye and one for your right. Special red-and-blue glasses made sure that each eye saw only what it was supposed to, and your brain would think you were seeing in 3-D. This was exciting, but it used two projectors and didn't always work so well. Sometimes the jittery picture would

give people headaches or make them feel ill.

In the early 1980s, 3-D returned for a short time, but now new technology promises to make the experience better than ever. Digital projectors and special new glasses are used for realistic 3-D movies that won't give you a headache. Some of the biggest names in the music business have recently released 3-D movie versions of their concerts. *Hannah Montana and Miley Cyrus: The Best of Both Worlds Concert* in digital 3-D came out in February 2008, and *Jonas Brothers: The 3D Concert Experience* came out in February 2009. *Avatar, Shrek Goes Fourth, Harry Potter and The Half-Blood Prince* and the computer-animated *Monsters vs. Aliens* are just a few of the movies in 2009 and 2010 to feature the up-to-date technology. Some day television, video games and even surfing the Internet might all be in 3-D!

guess what? The 3-D movie, *Coraline*, released in February 2009 and based on the book by Neil Gaiman, had a budget of between $70 million and $100 million.

MYSTERY PERSON

Clue 1: I was born near Beaver City, Utah, on August 19, 1906.

Clue 2: I invented television. At the age of 21, I produced the first electronic television image–a straight line.

Clue 3: I later became a harsh critic of TV and wouldn't even let my children watch it.

Who am I? _____

ANSWER ON PAGE 244.

Music

And the Grammy Went To...

MUSIC'S BIGGEST STARS SHINE AT THE 51ST ANNUAL GRAMMY AWARDS

By Andrea Delbanco

Recording artists from around the world took the stage on Sunday, February 8, 2009, at the Staples Center in Los Angeles, California, to celebrate the music industry. Each year, Grammy Awards are given by the music industry's Recording Academy to outstanding performers and their music in 110 categories. The 2009 awards cover music released from October 1, 2007, to September 30, 2008. Artists of all styles and ages won awards at the electrifying ceremony.

THREE ACTS STOLE THE SHOW

Robert Plant and Alison Krauss won five awards, including Album of the Year and Record of the Year. Krauss has won 26 awards, the most ever for a female artist in Grammy history.

Rapper Lil Wayne took home four awards, including Best Rap Album and Best Rap Performance by a Duo or Group. He entered the awards with eight nominations, the most of any artist.

Another top winner at music's biggest party was British rock group Coldplay, who took home three awards, including Song of the Year for "Viva La Vida."

Coldplay

Jennifer Hudson

Miley Cyrus and Taylor Swift

OTHER GRAMMY GREATS

The three-and-a-half-hour show was packed with all-star performances. Irish rock band U2 kicked off the night with "Get on Your Boots." Coldplay and the rapper Jay-Z paired up for a performance. Taylor Swift and Miley Cyrus sang a duet version of Swift's song "Fifteen." The Jonas Brothers sang their song "Burning Up" with Stevie Wonder.

Former American Idol contestant Jennifer Hudson won Best R&B Album. "I first would like to thank God, who has brought me through," she said, while accepting the award for her self-titled album. "I would like to thank my family in heaven and those who are with me today." That night, Hudson sang her song "You Pulled Me Through" to an emotional audience.

Alison Krauss and Robert Plant

Grammy Awards

RECORD OF THE YEAR: *Please Read the Letter,* Robert Plant and Alison Krauss

SONG OF THE YEAR: "Viva La Vida," Coldplay

BEST NEW ARTIST: Adele

BEST FEMALE POP VOCAL PERFORMANCE: "Chasing Pavements," Adele

BEST POP PERFORMANCE BY A DUO OR GROUP WITH VOCALS: "Viva La Vida," Coldplay

Lil Wayne

BEST POP VOCAL ALBUM: *Rockferry,* Duffy

BEST SOLO ROCK VOCAL PERFORMANCE: "Gravity," John Mayer

BEST ROCK SONG: "Girls in Their Summer Clothes," Bruce Springsteen

BEST ROCK ABLUM: *Viva La Vida or Death and All His Friends,* Coldplay

BEST ALTERNATIVE MUSIC ALBUM: *In Rainbows,* Radiohead

BEST FEMALE R&B VOCAL PERFORMANCE: "Superwoman," Alicia Keys

BEST MALE R&B VOCAL PERFORMANCE: "Miss Independent," Ne-Yo

BEST R&B SONG: "Miss Independent," Ne-Yo

BEST R&B ALBUM: *Jennifer Hudson,* Jennifer Hudson

BEST CONTEMPORARY R&B ALBUM: *Growing Pains,* Mary J. Blige

BEST RAP SOLO PERFORMANCE: "A Milli," Lil Wayne

B.B. King

BEST RAP SONG: "Lollipop," Lil Wayne, featuring Static Major

BEST FEMALE COUNTRY VOCAL PERFORMANCE: "Last Name," Carrie Underwood

BEST MALE COUNTRY VOCAL PERFORMANCE: "Letter to Me," Brad Paisley

BEST COUNTRY SONG: "Stay," Sugarland

BEST COUNTRY ALBUM: *Troubadour,* George Strait

BEST LATIN POP ALBUM: *La Vida… Es Un Ratico,* Juanes

BEST TRADITIONAL BLUES ALBUM: *One Kind Favor,* B.B. King

Carrie Underwood

BEST MUSICAL ALBUM FOR CHILDREN: *Here Come the 123s,* They Might Be Giants

BEST MUSICAL SHOW ALBUM: *In the Heights*

Music

2008 American Music Awards

NOVEMBER 23, 2008

ARTIST OF THE YEAR: Chris Brown

T-MOBILE BREAKTHROUGH ARTIST AWARD: Jonas Brothers

FAVORITE MALE ARTIST, POP OR ROCK: Chris Brown

FAVORITE FEMALE ARTIST, POP OR ROCK: Rihanna

FAVORITE BAND, DUO OR GROUP, POP OR ROCK: Daughtry

FAVORITE ALBUM, POP OR ROCK: *As I Am,* Alicia Keys

FAVORITE BAND, DUO OR GROUP, COUNTRY: Rascal Flatts

FAVORITE MALE ARTIST, COUNTRY: Brad Paisley

FAVORITE FEMALE ARTIST, COUNTRY: Taylor Swift

FAVORITE ALBUM, COUNTRY: *Carnival Ride,* Carrie Underwood

FAVORITE ARTIST, ADULT CONTEMPORARY: Jordin Sparks

FAVORITE BAND, DUO OR GROUP, RAP/HIP-HOP: Three 6 Mafia

FAVORITE MALE ARTIST, RAP/HIP-HOP: Kanye West

FAVORITE ALBUM, RAP/HIP-HOP: *Graduation,* Kanye West

FAVORITE ARTIST, LATIN: Enrique Iglesias

FAVORITE ARTIST, ALTERNATIVE ROCK: Linkin Park

FAVORITE ALBUM, SOUND TRACK: *Alvin and the Chipmunks*

Rihanna

Brad Paisley

Alicia Keys

Kanye West

TOP 5 High School Musicals

What are the favorite musicals being performed by high school students?

1. *Disney's Beauty and the Beast*
2. *Little Shop of Horrors*
3. *Guys and Dolls*
4. *Seussical: The Musical* (tie)
4. *Thoroughly Modern Millie* (tie)

Source: Educational Theatre Association

2009 Nickelodeon Kids' Choice Awards

Favorite Song: "Single Ladies (Put a Ring on It)," Beyoncé
Favorite Male Singer: Jesse McCartney
Favorite Female Singer: Miley Cyrus
Favorite Music Group: Jonas Brothers

Jesse McCartney

2008 MTV Video Music Awards

SEPTEMBER 7, 2008

VIDEO OF THE YEAR: "Piece of Me," Britney Spears

BEST MALE VIDEO: "With You," Chris Brown

BEST FEMALE VIDEO: "Piece of Me," Britney Spears

BEST DANCING IN A VIDEO: "When I Grow Up," Pussycat Dolls

BEST ROCK VIDEO: "Shadow of the Day," Linkin Park

BEST HIP-HOP VIDEO: "Lollipop," Lil Wayne

BEST NEW ARTIST: "Ready, Set, Go!," Tokio Hotel

BEST POP VIDEO: "Piece of Me," Britney Spears

BEST ART DIRECTION: "Run," Gnarls Barkley

BEST CHOREOGRAPHY: "Run," Gnarls Barkley

Linkin Park

Britney Spears

Tokio Hotel

Teen Choice Awards

AUGUST 4, 2008

BREAKOUT GROUP: Jonas Brothers

BREAKOUT ARTIST: Taylor Swift

FEMALE ARTIST: Miley Cyrus

MALE ARTIST: Chris Brown

SINGLE: "When You Look Me in the Eyes," Jonas Brothers

RAP ARTIST: Kanye West

ROCK TRACK: "Crushcrushcrush," Paramore

ROCK GROUP: Paramore

R&B TRACK: "Forever," Chris Brown

R&B ARTIST: Chris Brown

LOVE SONG: "When You Look Me in the Eyes," Jonas Brothers

HOOK UP: "No Air," Jordin Sparks and Chris Brown

Miley Cyrus

Kevin, Nick and Joe Jonas

Music

Presidents

The Road to the White House

Before the disputed election of 2000, many Americans forgot that our Presidents are not chosen by majority vote. Instead, members of the electoral college cast the final votes. Here's how the election process works in the United States.

START

THIS WAY

1.
Candidates announce that they are running for President.

To be eligible, a person must be a natural-born U.S. citizen and at least 35 years of age. He or she must have been a U.S. resident for at least 14 years.

Senator John McCain and Governor Sarah Palin

2.
Let the campaigns begin!

The first part of a presidential run is known as the **nomination campaign.** This is when several Democratic candidates and several Republican candidates compete against one another for votes within their party. Candidates crisscross the country giving speeches, raising money and trying to win the trust of the voters. They are also fighting for the support of the delegates. Delegates are members of the Democratic and Republican parties who attend the national party conventions in the summer before each presidential election. By pledging their support for a candidate, they choose which candidate gets nominated by each party.

Hillary Clinton and Barack Obama debate.

4.
Each party holds a national nominating convention.

In the summer of a presidential election year, both parties gather their members for a **national convention.** Thousands of members of each party flock to the conventions, where they attempt to whip up excitement for the party and the upcoming election. The delegates from each party cast their ballots for their nominee. With rousing speeches, the nominee from each party is formally announced. Each nominee also introduces his or her running mate, who will become Vice President if he or she is elected. In 2008, the Democratic National Convention was held in Denver, Colorado. The Republicans held their convention in Minneapolis, Minnesota.

THIS WAY

3.
Primary elections and caucuses take place.

To help decide which candidate from each party will win that party's nomination, states hold gatherings to hear from potential voters. Some states hold **primary elections.** These are similar to the general election except people may vote only for candidates or delegates from their own political party.

Some states hold a **caucus,** at which party leaders and citizens get together, discuss the issues, debate the candidates and then cast their votes. Caucuses vary from state to state and are different for both political parties.

THIS WAY

guess what? *When it comes to presidential campaigns, Iowa is known as "first in the nation." That is because its caucus is the first to take place in the nominating process for both presidential candidates.*

5.
The nominees campaign and campaign . . . and campaign.

During this part of the process, the nominees from both major parties compete against one another for votes all around the country. Representatives from third parties (such as the Independence Party, the Green Party or the Libertarian Party) try to get voters to rally behind them as well.

THIS WAY

Jimmy Carter campaigns in 1976.

6.
Citizens vote in the general election.

Every election year, votes are cast on the Tuesday following the first Monday in November.

7.
The Electoral College votes for President.

The **Electoral College** came about as a compromise. When the Constitution was being written in 1787, some of the founding fathers wanted Congress to be in charge of electing the President. Others felt that the citizens should be allowed to elect their leader by popular vote. So our early leaders put the Electoral College in place. With this system, a group of electors from each state actually choose the President.

When voters cast their ballots for a candidate on election day, it is as if they are voting for the group of electors rather than a particular candidate. Each state has a number of electors equal to the number of its senators and representatives. Washington, D.C., also has three electors. Usually, all of the electors vote for the party that won the most votes in their state. Maine and Nebraska divide their electoral votes among the candidates. To win the presidency, a candidate must receive at least 270 of the 538 possible electoral votes. If this majority is not reached, the House of Representatives chooses the President.

Lyndon B. Johnson casts his ballot in 1964.

THIS WAY

8.
The new President takes the oath of office.

On January 20, the country's new leader is inaugurated. He or she states the presidential oath:

"I do solemnly swear (or affirm) that I will faithfully execute the office of President of the United States, and will to the best of my ability, preserve, protect and defend the Constitution of the United States."

Bill Clinton's 1993 inauguration

FINISH

The Presidents in Order

George Washington (served 1789-1797)

Born: February 22, 1732, in Virginia Died: December 14, 1799
Political Party: None (first term), Federalist (second term)
Vice President: John Adams First Lady: Martha Dandridge Custis

 George Washington is the only U.S. President who never lived in the White House.

John Adams (served 1797-1801)

Born: October 30, 1735, in Massachusetts Died: July 4, 1826
Political Party: Federalist
Vice President: Thomas Jefferson First Lady: Abigail Smith

 *When John Adams moved into the White House, most of the rooms had no windows, and the staircase to the second floor was not yet built.*

Thomas Jefferson (served 1801-1809)

Born: April 13, 1743, in Virginia Died: July 4, 1826
Political Party: Democratic-Republican
Vice Presidents: Aaron Burr, George Clinton
First Lady: Martha Wayles Skelton

Thomas Jefferson was the principal author of the Declaration of Independence. He and John Adams both died on July 4, 1826, the 50th anniversary of the signing of that document.

James Madison (served 1809-1817)

Born: March 16, 1751, in Virginia Died: June 28, 1836
Political Party: Democratic-Republican
Vice Presidents: George Clinton, Elbridge Gerry
First Lady: Dorothy "Dolley" Payne Todd

 James Madison was President when British soldiers burned the White House on August 24, 1814.

James Monroe (served 1817-1825)

Born: April 28, 1758, in Virginia Died: July 4, 1831
Political Party: Democratic-Republican
Vice President: Daniel D. Tompkins First Lady: Elizabeth "Eliza" Kortright

 As a young man, James Monroe studied law under Thomas Jefferson.

John Quincy Adams (served 1825-1829)

Born: July 11, 1767, in Massachusetts Died: February 23, 1848
Political Party: Democratic-Republican
Vice President: John C. Calhoun First Lady: Louisa Catherine Johnson

 John Quincy Adams liked to swim naked in the Potomac River early every morning. Once a woman reporter followed him there, hid his clothes and refused to give them back until he granted her an interview.

Andrew Jackson (served 1829–1837)

Born: March 15, 1767, in South Carolina **Died:** June 8, 1845
Political Party: Democratic
Vice Presidents: John C. Calhoun, Martin Van Buren
First Lady: Rachel Donelson Robards

 Andrew Jackson was the first President to have indoor plumbing in the White House. The work was completed in 1833.

Martin Van Buren (served 1837–1841)

Born: December 5, 1782, in New York **Died:** July 24, 1862
Political Party: Democratic
Vice President: Richard M. Johnson **First Lady:** Hannah Hoes

 Martin Van Buren spoke Dutch at home, though he was the first American-born president. (Previous Presidents had been born when the United States was still a colony of England.)

William Henry Harrison (served 1841)

Born: February 9, 1773, in Virginia **Died:** April 4, 1841
Political Party: Whig
Vice President: John Tyler **First Lady:** Anna Tuthill Symmes

 Though William Henry Harrison gave the longest inaugural address (one hour 45 minutes), he had the shortest presidency—just 30 days.

John Tyler (served 1841–1845)

Born: March 29, 1790, in Virginia **Died:** January 18, 1862
Political Party: Whig
Vice President: None **First Ladies:** Letitia Christian (d. 1842), Julia Gardiner

 As Harrison's Vice President, John Tyler was elected as a member of the Whig party. After becoming President and vetoing a bill the Whigs favored, he was disowned by his own party. For the rest of his term, he was not a member of any political party—the only President ever to serve without a party's support.

James K. Polk (served 1845–1849)

Born: November 2, 1795, in North Carolina **Died:** June 15, 1849
Political Party: Democratic
Vice President: George M. Dallas **First Lady:** Sarah Childress

 In 1848, James Knox Polk signed a treaty to end a two-year-long war with Mexico. This treaty gave the U.S. control over present-day Arizona, California, Colorado, Nevada, New Mexico, Utah and Wyoming.

Zachary Taylor (served 1849–1850)

Born: November 24, 1784, in Virginia **Died:** July 9, 1850
Political Party: Whig
Vice President: Millard Fillmore **First Lady:** Margaret Mackall Smith

 Zachary Taylor spent 40 years in the army. He kept his old army horse, Whitey, on the White House lawn.

Millard Fillmore (served 1850–1853)

Born: January 7, 1800, in New York **Died:** March 8, 1874
Political Party: Whig
Vice President: None
First Ladies: Abigail Powers (d. 1853), Caroline Carmichael McIntosh

guess what? *Millard Fillmore taught himself to read after he met his wife, a schoolteacher. He grew to love reading and, once in office, he aided his wife in the creation of the White House library.*

Franklin Pierce (served 1853–1857)

Born: November 23, 1804, in New Hampshire **Died:** October 8, 1869
Political Party: Democratic
Vice President: William R. King **First Lady:** Jane Means Appleton

guess what? *Franklin Pierce tried to convince Spain to sell the island of Cuba to the United States.*

James Buchanan (served 1857–1861)

Born: April 23, 1791, in Pennsylvania **Died:** June 1, 1868
Political Party: Democratic
Vice President: John C. Breckinridge
First Lady: None–his niece Harriet Lane acted as White House hostess

guess what? *James Buchanan didn't like being President. After his first term, he refused to run for office again.*

Abraham Lincoln (served 1861–1865)

Born: February 12, 1809, in Kentucky **Died:** April 15, 1865
Political Party: Republican
Vice Presidents: Hannibal Hamlin, Andrew Johnson **First Lady:** Mary Todd

guess what? *According to a poll of historians, Abraham Lincoln was the greatest U.S. President. He presided over the Civil War and signed the Emancipation Proclamation. He was also the first President to have a beard.*

Andrew Johnson (served 1865–1869)

Born: December 29, 1808, in North Carolina **Died:** July 31, 1875
Political Parties: Union, Democratic
Vice President: None **First Lady:** Eliza McCardle

guess what? *Andrew Johnson married younger than any other President—at the age of 18. His bride was just 16.*

Ulysses S. Grant (served 1869–1877)

Born: April 27, 1822, in Ohio **Died:** July 23, 1885
Political Party: Republican
Vice Presidents: Schuyler Colfax, Henry Wilson **First Lady:** Julia Boggs Dent

guess what? *Ulysses was not really the 18th President's first name. His given name was Hiram. Ulysses was his middle name and the S initial didn't stand for anything.*

Rutherford B. Hayes (served 1877–1881)

Born: October 4, 1822, in Ohio **Died:** January 17, 1893
Political Party: Republican
Vice President: William A. Wheeler **First Lady:** Lucy Ware Webb

 Rutherford Birchard Hayes oversaw the first Easter egg roll on the White House lawn.

James A. Garfield (served 1881)

Born: November 19, 1831, in Ohio **Died:** September 19, 1881
Political Party: Republican
Vice President: Chester A. Arthur **First Lady:** Lucretia Rudolph

 James Abram Garfield was the first left-handed President.

Chester A. Arthur (served 1881–1885)

Born: October 5, 1829, in Vermont **Died:** November 18, 1886
Political Party: Republican
Vice President: None **First Lady:** Ellen Lewis Herndon

 Chester Alan Arthur removed 24 carts of old furniture from the White House before moving in and ordering a redecoration.

Grover Cleveland (served 1885–1889)

Born: March 18, 1837, in New Jersey **Died:** June 24, 1908
Political Party: Democratic
Vice President: Thomas A. Hendricks **First Lady:** Frances Folsom

 Grover Cleveland dedicated the Statue of Liberty in New York Harbor on October 28, 1886.

Benjamin Harrison (served 1889–1893)

Born: August 20, 1833, in Ohio **Died:** March 13, 1901
Political Party: Republican
Vice President: Levi P. Morton
First Ladies: Caroline Lavina Scott (d. 1892), Mary Scott Lord Dimmick

 To date, Benjamin Harrison is the only President to be elected from the state of Indiana.

Grover Cleveland (served 1893–1897)

Born: March 18, 1837, in New Jersey **Died:** June 24, 1908
Political Party: Democratic
Vice President: Adlai E. Stevenson **First Lady:** Frances Folsom

 Grover Cleveland is the only President (so far) to be elected to nonconsecutive terms.

William McKinley (served 1897–1901)

Born: January 29, 1843, in Ohio **Died:** September 14, 1901
Political Party: Republican
Vice Presidents: Garret A. Hobart, Theodore Roosevelt **First Lady:** Ida Saxton

Guess what? *William McKinley was the first President to use a telephone while campaigning for office.*

Theodore Roosevelt (served 1901–1909)

Born: October 27, 1858, in New York **Died:** January 6, 1919
Political Party: Republican
Vice President: Charles W. Fairbanks **First Lady:** Edith Kermit Carow

Guess what? *Theodore Roosevelt built the West Wing of the White House as an office for himself and his staff. With his six children and their many pets, he found it too noisy to work in the main house.*

William H. Taft (served 1909–1913)

Born: September 15, 1857, in Ohio **Died:** March 8, 1930
Political Party: Republican
Vice President: James S. Sherman **First Lady:** Helen Herron

Guess what? *Though he was a very big man (weighing more than 300 pounds/136 kg), William Howard Taft was reportedly a great dancer.*

Woodrow Wilson (served 1913–1921)

Born: December 28, 1856, in Virginia **Died:** February 3, 1924
Political Party: Democratic
Vice President: Thomas R. Marshall
First Ladies: Ellen Louise Axson (d. 1914), Edith Bolling Galt

Guess what? *Woodrow Wilson served as President during World War I. During his second term, the 19th Amendment, granting women the vote, became law.*

Warren G. Harding (served 1921–1923)

Born: November 2, 1865, in Ohio **Died:** August 2, 1923
Political Party: Republican
Vice President: Calvin Coolidge **First Lady:** Florence Kling

Guess what? *Warren G. Harding was the first President to support anti-lynching legislation while in office.*

Calvin Coolidge (served 1923–1929)

Born: July 4, 1872, in Vermont **Died:** January 5, 1933
Political Party: Republican
Vice President: Charles G. Dawes **First Lady:** Grace Anna Goodhue

Guess what? *Calvin Coolidge kept a pet raccoon, which he named Rebecca, in the White House. He walked her on a leash around the White House grounds.*

Herbert C. Hoover (served 1929–1933)

Born: August 10, 1874, in Iowa **Died:** October 20, 1964
Political Party: Republican
Vice President: Charles Curtis **First Lady:** Lou Henry

Herbert Hoover loved to fish. Shortly before he died, he even published a book called Fishing for Fun and To Wash Your Soul.

Franklin D. Roosevelt (served 1933–1945)

Born: January 30, 1882, in New York **Died:** April 12, 1945
Political Party: Democratic
Vice Presidents: John Garner, Henry Wallace, Harry S. Truman
First Lady: Anna Eleanor Roosevelt

Franklin Delano Roosevelt was related by blood or marriage to 11 former Presidents.

Harry S Truman (served 1945–1953)

Born: May 8, 1884, in Missouri **Died:** December 26, 1972
Political Party: Democratic
Vice President: Alben W. Barkley
First Lady: Elizabeth "Bess" Virginia Wallace

The S in Harry S Truman is his complete middle name, not an initial.

Dwight D. Eisenhower (served 1953–1961)

Born: October 14, 1890, in Texas **Died:** March 28, 1969
Political Party: Republican
Vice President: Richard M. Nixon **First Lady:** Mamie Geneva Doud

Dwight David Eisenhower was the only President to have served in the army in both World War I and II.

John F. Kennedy (served 1961–1963)

Born: May 29, 1917, in Massachusetts **Died:** November 22, 1963
Political Party: Democratic
Vice President: Lyndon B. Johnson **First Lady:** Jacqueline Lee Bouvier

John Fitzgerald Kennedy established the Peace Corps in 1961.

Lyndon B. Johnson (served 1963–1969)

Born: August 27, 1908, in Texas **Died:** January 22, 1973
Political Party: Democratic
Vice President: Hubert H. Humphrey
First Lady: Claudia Alta "Lady Bird" Taylor

Lyndon Baines Johnson knew Claudia Alta "Lady Bird" Taylor for less than a week before proposing to her. She finally accepted his offer about 10 weeks later.

Presidents

Religion

Five Major Faiths

There are about 20 major religions in the world, five of which have had the greatest influence on global culture: Judaism, Christianity, Islam, Hinduism and Buddhism.

Jesus Christ's last supper

Judaism

Judaism began as a religion in the Middle East nearly 6,000 years ago with its founder, Abraham. Jews believe that there is one god and that God made a covenant, or agreement, with Abraham, appointing him the leader of God's chosen people.

The **Bible** (or Old Testament, as Christians refer to it) is the great book of Judaism, along with the **Talmud,** which includes many laws for daily living. Jewish worship includes readings from the **Torah** (the first five books of the Hebrew Bible). Jews believe the words in the Torah were spoken by God and revealed to Moses at Mount Sinai more than 3,000 years ago. The Torah begins with God's creation of the universe and includes the Ten Commandments.

There are three basic practices in Judaism: Orthodox, Conservative and Reform. Orthodox Judaism is the most traditional, and Reform Judaism is the most modern. Judaism influenced the rise of Christianity and Islam, because all three religions claim Abraham as their ancestor.

A dreidel

Christianity

Christianity is named after Jesus Christ. Christians believe that Jesus's mission as the son of God was to sacrifice his life in payment for the sins of humanity. Jesus, along with his 12 followers, called apostles, preached messages of love and compassion.

Christians believe that Jesus and the apostles performed miracles, and these acts are recorded in the **New Testament** (an addition to the Hebrew **Bible**). Christians believe that after Jesus's death by crucifixion (being nailed to a cross) in Jerusalem, he rose from the dead and went to heaven. They also believe that he will return to Earth on the Day of Judgment.

There are many kinds of Christians, including Roman Catholics, Orthodox and Protestants (including Episcopalians, Presbyterians, Baptists, Methodists, Lutherans and Evangelicals).

guess what? The Bible is the bestselling book in the world. It is also the world's most shoplifted book.

A father and son celebrate the Jewish holiday of Passover.

Christian teens read the Bible.

Muslims pray five times a day.

Buddhism

Although many people think of Buddhism as a religion, it is more of a philosophy, or a way of life. That is because Buddhists don't believe in a specific god. Instead, they follow the teachings of their founder, Siddhartha Gautama (born in India about 563–483 B.C.), known as the Buddha. **Buddha** means "the Awakened One," and Buddhists believe that he "awoke" to the reality of what life is about, which he summed up in **Four Noble Truths.**

1. There is suffering in the world.
2. The cause of suffering is desire.
3. Suffering can be ended.
4. The way to end suffering is by following the **Noble Eightfold Path.** This path involves correct ways to speak, act, work, improve oneself, be aware, concentrate, understand and think.

Like Hindus, many Buddhists believe in reincarnation. There are three main kinds of Buddhism—Theravada, Mahayana, Vajrayana—each following different beliefs, practices and rituals.

A Buddha statue in Nepal

Islam

Islam is another major faith that traces its history back to Abraham. Muslims believe in the same supreme being as Jews and Christians, and they call him Allah. Islam's founder and greatest prophet is Muhammad (570–632), and its great book is the **Qur'an,** or Koran. Muslim devotion includes five practices called the **Great Pillars.**

1. The statement of faith, which is "There is no God but Allah, and Muhammad is his prophet"
2. Praying five times a day
3. Giving to charity
4. Fasting (refraining from eating and drinking) at certain times, including during the daylight hours of the month of Ramadan
5. Making a pilgrimage, or religious trip, to Mecca, Muhammad's birthplace, located in Saudi Arabia

The Blue Mosque in Turkey

guess what? The hamsa hand is popular with both Jewish and Islamic faiths. It is said to ward off the evil eye and offer protection.

A Buddhist monk in Myanmar

Hinduism

The Hindu god Shiva

Regarded as the oldest of the five major faiths, Hinduism began in Asia. Hinduism as a religion appears in many forms. Some Hindus believe in only one god; others believe in many gods and goddesses. The religion's sacred texts include the **Vedas** and **Upanishads.**

In general, Hindus believe that life is a journey of learning and that how a person acts affects his or her destiny. They believe in reincarnation, in which a person's soul returns to Earth in the form of another human being or other creature until that soul learns all its lessons and becomes perfect. Hinduism is the main religion in India and Nepal.

A young Hindu woman

guess what? Cats were highly respected in ancient Egypt because they were thought to embody the cat goddess Bastet. Cats were protected from harm by law. In death, they were mummified and given as offerings to the feline goddess.

Science

Lost and Found

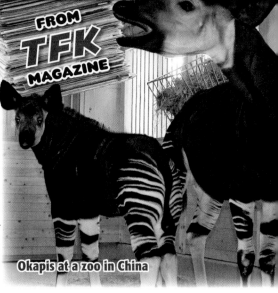

Extinction is final. When a species completely dies out, it is extinct. But when humans declare a species extinct, they are not always right! In September 2008, scientists in central Africa captured photos of **okapis** (oh-*kah*-peez) in the wild. The okapi is related to the giraffe, but has zebra-like stripes on its legs. The images were taken in Virunga National Park in the Democratic Republic of the Congo. Until now, biologists feared that okapis were extinct in the wild, surviving only in zoos and protected areas.

Okapis at a zoo in China

Each year, the International Union for Conservation of Nature (IUCN) releases its Red List, a scorecard of species at risk of extinction. On the 2007 list, 16,306 species were threatened with extinction and 785 were extinct. Climate change, pollution and other factors threaten species daily.

Another species that hopped back into the picture recently is Australia's armoured mistfrog. Scientists reported a sighting of the tiny frog in July 2008. Experts thought it had been wiped out by a deadly fungus infecting frog populations worldwide.

The **western lowland gorilla** also got a good report. A recent survey found 125,000 of the primates in the Republic of the Congo. If confirmed, the new population count would more than double the previous estimate. Experts warn that the gorillas continue to face danger from disease and hunting. Still, says researcher Craig Stanford, "[It's] the kind of good news we rarely find in the conservation of highly endangered animals."

Scientific Fields

Thinking of becoming a scientist? Here are the names of some different types of scientists and what they study.

Geologist

Zoologist

Ecologist

anthropologist	cultures, languages and the physical development of humans
archaeologist	creatures' fossils and bones; ruins of past civilizations
astronomer	history, development and motion of things in the universe
botanist	plants
ecologist	structure and balance of environmental life systems
geneticist	DNA (see page 175), heredity and gene therapy
geologist	Earth's structure; formation and composition of rocks, minerals and volcanoes
meteorologist	climate, weather patterns and predictions
oceanographer	ocean life and currents
physicist	relationship between energy and matter
zoologist	animals

The Five Kingdoms

Every form of life belongs to one of five kingdoms.

MONERA This kingdom consists of one-celled bacteria that don't have a nucleus. Some are able to move, and others can't. Some can make their own food to live on, but others need to feed on things outside themselves.

FUNGI These organisms have more than one cell, and their cells have nuclei. Fungi generally can't move. They must rely on outside sources for their food. This kingdom includes molds, mushrooms and yeast.

mold

PROTISTA The one-celled organisms of this kingdom share the same characteristics as those in the monera kingdom except that they have a nucleus. Examples of protista are amoebas, paramecia and some one-celled algae.

ANIMALS The animal kingdom consists of multicellular organisms that move and rely on outside sources for food. In general, they are the most complex creatures on Earth, with most having the ability to communicate and form social groups. Examples of animals are sponges, jellyfish, insects, amphibians, fish and mammals, including humans. (For more on the animal kingdom, see page 17.)

PLANTS The plant kingdom consists of multicellular organisms that have nuclei and remain in one place. In a process called photosynthesis, plants use sunlight and a chemical called *chlorophyll* to produce their own food. Some plants produce flowers and fruit; others don't. Examples of the plant kingdom are multicellular algae, ferns, mosses, trees, shrubs, wildflowers, fruits and vegetables.

Science

173

Branches of Science

Science is the field of knowledge that systematically studies and organizes information and draws conclusions based on measurable results. Traditionally, scientists have classified their fields into three branches: physical sciences, earth sciences and life sciences. Social sciences, technology and mathematics may also be included. Each branch has many fields of study; some are included here.

PHYSICAL SCIENCES

These sciences study the properties of energy and matter, as well as their relationship to each other. **Physics** seeks to explain how the universe behaves through the workings of matter, energy, force and time. **Chemistry** is the study of chemical elements and how they interact on an atomic level. **Astronomy** is the study of space, its galaxies and all heavenly objects.

EARTH SCIENCES

These sciences focus on the Earth and study its composition and structure. **Geology** is the study of Earth's inner rock formations. **Geography** concerns the study and mapping of Earth's terrain. **Oceanography** focuses on Earth's oceans and their currents and habitats. **Meteorology** is the study of weather. **Paleontology** focuses on the remains of ancient plants and animals.

LIFE SCIENCES

These sciences explore the nature of living things. **Biology** covers the study of how living things evolve, reproduce, thrive and relate to one another. It is further divided into many braches including **botany,** which focuses on plants; **zoology,** which deals with animals; and **microbiology,** which zeroes in on microscopic organisms.

Cells

Cells are the basic building blocks of life. Whether it's a plant, an animal or a fungus, all forms of living organisms are made up of cells, and each cell itself is alive. The simplest forms of life—such as amoebas—are just a single cell.

Most cells have a nucleus, which acts like the brain of the cell. The nucleus controls everything the cell does, and all cells perform some of the same basic functions as every living thing.

A cell dividing

- Cells take in raw materials (eating).
- They get energy from raw materials they take in (digesting).
- They get rid of waste.
- They reproduce, which creates more cells.

Most cells can get only so big before they divide and become two cells. When this happens, the nucleus makes a duplicate copy of all of the information it has about the cell. Then the nucleus splits into two halves, and each goes on to have a cell of its own. Trees, dogs and humans all grow by this kind of cellular division, called mitosis.

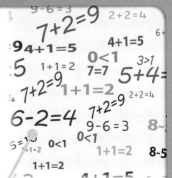

SOCIAL SCIENCES

These sciences investigate how humans behave and live together. **Psychology** explores individual human behavior, and **sociology** analyzes human behavior in groups. **Anthropology** studies human physical traits as well as cultures and languages. **Economics** is the study of how money, goods and businesses affect society. **Law** focuses on the rules of society, and **political science** studies governmental processes and institutions.

TECHNOLOGY

This branch is concerned with the practical application of scientific knowledge. **Engineering** is concerned with the design and construction of objects, machines and systems. **Biotechnology** is the application of biological processes to create medicines and vaccines and to alter food and crops. **Computer science** focuses on meeting industrial needs by creating computers and new software.

MATHEMATICS

This science differs from other branches because it deals with concepts rather than physical evidence. Its focus is on measuring numeric relationships, analyzing data and predicting outcomes. **Arithmetic** uses only numbers to solve problems, while **algebra** uses both numbers and unknown variables in the form of letters. **Geometry** is the study of two- and three-dimensional shapes. **Calculus** involves the computation of problems that contain constantly changing measurements. Nearly all scientists use mathematics in their research.

DNA

Chromosome

DNA stands for deoxyribonucleic acid. It is a large molecule found inside every living cell, usually (but not always) in the nucleus. The combination of chemical patterns in DNA forms a sort of blueprint, or set of instructions, that tells the cell what kind of organism it is part of. It also tells the cell itself what to do.

Since no two people are exactly alike (nope, not even identical twins), the DNA inside each person on the planet is slightly different. That way, we all get a different set of instructions!

DNA is tiny, and scientists must use extremely powerful microscopes to see it. A DNA molecule looks like a long, twisted ladder. Scientists call this shape a double helix. The specific information about our hair, eyes and more is stored in our genes, which are short sections of DNA found in several thread-like packages called chromosomes. Humans have 23 pairs of chromosomes in every cell in their bodies. The chromosomes carry all the details about how we're made.

guess what? *You, your parents and your siblings all have very similar—though not identical—DNA. Your own DNA is found in your skin, fingernails, blood, bones and in every other part of your body. By comparing the DNA found in strands of hair from two different people, scientists can tell if they are related and how!*

Science

175

Minerals and Rocks

Minerals are naturally occurring substances found on Earth. They can be found in dirt or water. Combined together, minerals help to make up rocks. They are solid chemicals that often form into crystals. Some minerals are made from a single element, like gold, copper or nickel, but most are a combination of elements. Gemstones like diamonds, opals and sapphires are minerals that are often cut and polished to be used in fancy jewelry.

Rocks are made up of combinations of minerals and belong to one of three categories: igneous, sedimentary or metamorphic.

Quartz is a mineral that is structured in crystals.

IGNEOUS ROCKS are made from molten magma. This burning hot substance, found deep inside Earth, cools and hardens once it reaches the air. Granite and **basalt** are common igneous rocks.

SEDIMENTARY ROCKS are made from bits of larger rocks, other pieces of earth and even seashells that get washed into riverbeds, lakes and oceans. These particles settle under the water, and more and more pieces of earth are piled on top of them. Over extremely long periods of time, these fragments become cemented together. Limestone and **sandstone** are examples of sedimentary rocks.

METAMORPHIC ROCKS are formed when either igneous or sedimentary rocks are subject to so much heat or pressure underground that they change form. **Marble** and slate are both well-known metamorphic rocks.

guess what? *When volcanoes erupt, magma from inside the Earth pours onto the Earth's surface. Once the magma reaches the surface of the Earth, it is known as lava.*

Botany and Trees

Botany is the study of plants, from moss and ferns to flowers and giant redwood trees. The Greek philosopher Aristotle developed a system for categorizing plants more than 2,000 years ago, and we now know of more than 400,000 different species of plants on Earth. Plants and trees can offer animals shade from the hot sun, provide nutrition for humans and animals, supply people with sturdy building materials or simply be colorful and beautiful (and fun to climb). They also play an important role in our environment.

Many human activities—including breathing, driving cars and creating electricity—add carbon dioxide (CO_2) to the atmosphere. Too much CO_2 in the atmosphere causes global warming, which can have disastrous effects on the environment (see page 85). Plants help to purify our air and keep the planet healthy by using up this harmful CO_2.

Through a process called photosynthesis, plants help to replenish our oxygen supply. Here is how it works.

- Plants absorb carbon dioxide from the air, and water and minerals from the soil.
- They use the energy from sunlight to convert these materials into food for themselves while releasing oxygen into the atmosphere.
- Animals and people use the cleaned oxygen to breathe.

In addition to cleaning up the air we breathe, plants also give us energy. When humans and animals eat plants, their bodies convert the raw materials in the plants into energy for ourselves.

HAVE YOU EVER HEARD OF...?

NIKOLA TESLA (1856–1943), an electrical engineer and inventor, was born in what is now Croatia (at the time, it was part of the Austro-Hungarian Empire) and moved to the United States in 1884. His innovative work in developing high-voltage alternating current (AC) power eventually won out over Thomas Edison's preference, direct current (DC), in a competition for how electricity would be distributed. Present-day power plants and the electricity in our homes are still the result of Tesla's work. Among his other inventions was the Tesla coil, a component used in televisions and radios.

MAX PLANCK (1858–1947) was a German physicist who developed one of the most important scientific ideas of the 20th century. The idea, called quantum theory, challenged long-held beliefs about how atoms work. Quantum theory also helped us to understand semiconductors, which are important for nearly all of the electronics we use today, including radios, computers and navigation systems. Planck was deeply respected by other scientists and was awarded the Nobel Prize for Physics in 1918 for his studies on quantum theory.

LOUIS S.B. LEAKEY (1903–72) was a Kenyan-born anthropologist and archaeologist. His parents were English missionaries who worked with the Kikuyu people of Kenya. After attending the University of Cambridge in England, Leakey returned to Africa, where he led expeditions to the Olduvai Gorge in Tanzania. It was there that he and his team—including his second wife, Mary Douglas Leakey— discovered many important stone tools and fossils that helped to change our understanding of human evolution. His research supported the theory that humans originated in Africa, not in Asia, as others had thought.

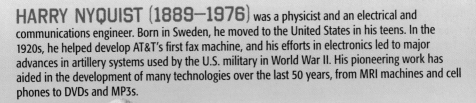

HARRY NYQUIST (1889–1976) was a physicist and an electrical and communications engineer. Born in Sweden, he moved to the United States in his teens. In the 1920s, he helped develop AT&T's first fax machine, and his efforts in electronics led to major advances in artillery systems used by the U.S. military in World War II. His pioneering work has aided in the development of many technologies over the last 50 years, from MRI machines and cell phones to DVDs and MP3s.

JANE GOODALL (1934–) is an ethologist and conservationist who spent decades working with African chimpanzees. She revealed the toolmaking and communication skills of chimps and was the first to discover that chimpanzees eat meat as well as plants. Her work with chimps has also helped scientists understand more about what it means to be human. Today she continues to teach others about saving chimpanzees and protecting the environment.

HOW SCIENCE CAN HELP SOLVE MYSTERIES: THE STORY OF ÖTZI THE ICEMAN

ÖTZI

Have You Ever Wondered...

...why clouds don't fall from the sky?

ANSWER: Is it because they're lighter than air? Nope. If this were the case, they would float up, up and away like helium balloons do when you let go of them. Clouds are actually made up of small droplets of water, and it is wind that keeps them from falling. The kind of wind that keeps clouds in the sky does not blow back and forth. Instead, it blows upward from the ground. These updrafts keep the clouds up, like kites. However, if the droplets of water get too big and heavy, they fall. These falling droplets are, of course, rain.

...where helium balloons end up when you let go of them?

ANSWER: They certainly don't keep going up forever. If they don't pop, they eventually lose all their helium and fall back to Earth. Often, strong winds blow them over the ocean, which can cause a lot of trouble. Birds, sea turtles and even whales mistake them for food and can easily choke trying to swallow them. So hold on to those balloons!

In 1991, hikers high in the Alps (a mountain range in Europe) made a fascinating discovery. Near the border of Italy and Austria, just visible in the Schnalstal glacier, was a frozen body. As it turns out, this was not just any body—it was that of a man who lived roughly 5,300 years ago.

When the Austrian authorities were alerted, they thought it was somebody who had died recently, perhaps a lost hiker. It wasn't until the body had reached the morgue that they realized it was actually a mummy! The glacier that settled over this man shortly after he died kept his body, clothing and belongings preserved for thousands of years.

When Ötzi (named after the Ötztal region, where he was found) was taken to archaeologists in Austria, they began to try to piece together the story of this mystery man. By measuring his bone density, they estimated he was approximately 45 years old when he died. This was actually pretty old in 3,300 B.C., when people didn't live as long as we do now.

He stood 5 feet 3 inches tall (160 cm) and weighed about 110 pounds (50 kg) when alive. Pollen residue and his tooth enamel suggest that he was born about 30 miles (48.3 km) from where he was found and that he probably left that region in his twenties or thirties.

By examining his intestines, the researchers learned what kinds of food he ate, including deer meat, berries, wheat bran and legumes (a kind of plant). They also discovered that he had

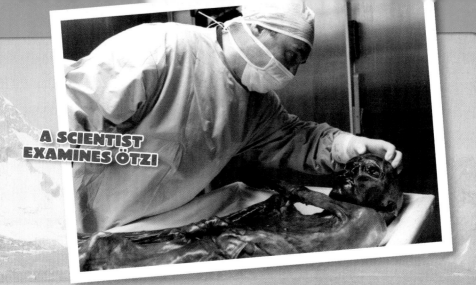

an infection called whipworm. Lines found on his one remaining fingernail revealed he was sick three times in the last six months of his life.

By taking a three-dimensional, or 3-D, CAT scan, researchers were able to make a replica of his skull. From this, a computer system re-created what Ötzi's face may have looked like.

His belongings included a mat made of woven grass, a bearskin hat, a belt with a pouch and leather shoes stuffed with grass to keep his feet warm. At the time of his death, he was carrying a bow and arrows, a knife, a flint for making fire, some berries and fungi that were probably used as medicine.

HOW DID ÖTZI DIE?

Archaeologists teamed up with forensics experts to try to find out what happened to Ötzi. Forensics is the study and scientific analysis of physical evidence, such as the clues found at a crime scene.

Analysis of the ice that surrounded Ötzi revealed a type of pollen that is in the air only during autumn. Investigators also noted a copper ax propped up against a nearby stone, as if it had been carefully placed there by Ötzi. They guessed that Ötzi may have been caught in a snowstorm in late fall and froze to death. However, X-ray and CAT scan results showed that he had several fractured ribs. Austrian archaeologist Konrad Spindler hypothesized (offered an explanation based on the available facts) that while Ötzi was shepherding animals, he was involved in some sort of fight and escaped to the mountains. High in the Alps, exhausted and weakened by his injuries, he then died of hypothermia.

These theories were challenged when scientists found pollen from hop hornbeam (a type of tree in the birch family) in Ötzi's intestines. Since the pollen was revealed to be fresh in his system, it looked like Ötzi must have died during late spring, when hop hornbeam pollen could still be found in the air. This clue disproved the theory that Ötzi had died in autumn. A closer look at the skeleton also suggested that his ribs were broken after he died and not in a fight beforehand.

One of the biggest clues in this mystery came when X-rays in Italy revealed a flint arrowhead lodged in Ötzi's shoulder. They also showed a deep cut on his thumb that appeared to have happened shortly before his death. DNA research then found evidence of blood from four different people on Ötzi's knife, back and arrow. This new information led to many theories—and many questions—about Ötzi's final days. Was he involved in a small battle? Did he carry an injured friend on his back? Did he use the same arrow on two different people? Was he the victim of a ritual sacrifice at the top of the mountain?

The more we learn, the more questions we have, but with new forensic techniques, maybe some day we can answer those too. What we do know is that Ötzi was shot with an arrow shortly before he died. Perhaps he removed the arrow himself or perhaps someone else— maybe even the shooter— turned him onto his stomach to take the arrow out. It was in this position that he lay frozen for thousands of years, leaving the rest a mystery.

ARROWHEAD

Space

Making More Space on the Space Station

THE SPACE SHUTTLE *ENDEAVOUR* DELIVERED ASTRONAUTS AND SUPPLIES TO SPACE

By Suzanne Zimbler

In November 2008, the International Space Station (ISS) got a makeover. The crew of the space shuttle *Endeavour* transported a giant trunk of equipment from the shuttle to the ISS, a giant orbiting space lab in the sky. The astronauts got a helping hand from a robotic crane. The special delivery weighed 14,000 pounds (6,350 kg).

The new gear would make it possible for NASA to double the size of the space station's three-person crew. "We're about to get an extreme home makeover," Commander Mike Fincke told Mission Control before the arrival of the *Endeavour*. The delivery included an extra bathroom and kitchen and two bedrooms as well as an exercise machine, a refrigerator and a water-recycling system.

THE MISSION: A SPACE STATION MAKEOVER

Endeavour and her seven-person crew reached ISS on November 16, 2008, for a 16-day visit and repair mission. An hour before docking, Commander Christopher Ferguson guided the shuttle through a 360-degree backflip while space-station residents took pictures. Ferguson wasn't putting on a show. He was letting them get a good look at the shuttle from all angles to check for damage. Two pieces of debris had been spotted after takeoff, but were not believed to pose any risk. Once the pictures had been taken, Ferguson guided the shuttle to a smooth docking.

Stefanyshyn-Piper at work

ASTRONAUTS AT WORK

The first of four planned space walks took place two days later. Astronauts Heidemarie Stefanyshyn-Piper and Stephen Bowen set out to repair a giant joint that rotates half of the space station's solar panels. The joint had been jammed for more than a year and had not been able to point those panels toward the sun.

Just as Stefanyshyn-Piper began to repair the joint, she accidentally let go of her backpack-size tool bag. She said that the bag slipped from her grip after the grease gun she was using exploded. As she wiped grease from her helmet camera and gloves, the bag—and everything in it—floated away. Stefanyshyn-Piper and Bowen finished the space walk in almost seven hours by sharing tools from Bowen's bag. "Despite my little hiccup, or major hiccup, I think we did a good job out there," Stefanyshyn-Piper said after returning to the station. The astronauts did their delicate work 220 miles (354 km) above Earth.

The bag was one of the largest items ever to be lost by a space walker. But officials were not worried that it would hit the space station or the shuttle—by late that same night, it was already 2.5 miles (4 km) away.

FROM THE UNIVERSE TO YOU

UNIVERSE
▼
GALAXIES
▼
THE MILKY WAY
▼
OUR SOLAR SYSTEM
▼
EARTH
▼
YOU

Guess what?

Right now, you're spinning through space at 67,000 miles per hour (108 km/h) as Earth orbits the sun. You're also traveling at about 1,000 miles per hour (1,609 km/h) as our planet spins on its axis.

WHAT'S IN SPACE?

Our solar system is the space neighborhood that includes one star (the sun) and its eight large planets, a few dwarf planets, about 170 moons and a lot of space junk (such as bits of rocks and ice). The universe consists of billions of stars. Some of these stars have planets orbiting them. Scientists aren't sure if every star has other bodies orbiting it and many stars are simply too far away to observe with today's tools.

The surface of Mars

Our sun and its planets exist in an area of space called the Milky Way Galaxy. The Milky Way is huge. If it were possible to travel at the speed of light (186,282 miles per second/299,792 km per second), it would take 100,000 years to go from one end of the Milky Way to the other. There are other galaxies out there, far beyond the edges of the Milky Way. Together, all the galaxies make up the universe.

THE PLANETS IN OUR SOLAR SYSTEM

When your parents and teachers were growing up, they learned that there were nine planets. However, today, most scientists agree that there are really only eight.

Pluto, once considered a planet, is now classified as a dwarf planet. Some planets are made of liquid and gas, such as Saturn. Others, like Mars, are rocky. Some planets, such as Venus, can be broiling hot. Or, like Neptune, they can be freezing cold.

All planets in our solar system travel in an orbit around the sun. The time it takes to make a complete trip around the sun is its year. Each planet also spins on its axis, turning toward and away from the sun. Each rotation makes that planet's day. How long is a day? How long is a year? It depends which planet you're on.

PLANET	LENGTH OF DAY	LENGTH OF YEAR
Mercury	176 Earth days	88 Earth days
Venus	243 Earth days	225 Earth days
Earth	24 hours	365 1/4 days
Mars	24 hours and 40 minutes	687 Earth days
Jupiter	10 hours	12 Earth years
Saturn	10 hours	29 Earth years
Uranus	18 hours	84 Earth years
Neptune	19 hours	165 Earth years

MOONS

A moon is a natural satellite made of rock or ice that orbits a planet or other solar body. Mercury and Venus have no moons. Mars has two. Neptune has 13. Uranus has 27, and Jupiter has 62! Some moons orbit dwarf planets that are large enough to have a field of gravity to hold them in an orbit. Earth has just one moon, which is about 240,000 miles (386,243 km) away.

Jupiter's moon, Io

Guess what? *Our moon moves about 12 feet (3.7 meters) away from Earth every century. Billions of years ago, it was much closer to Earth. In the distant future, it will be farther away.*

Mars's moon, Phobos

Earth and its moon

THE SOLAR SYSTEM

The sun is at the center of our solar system. It consists mostly of ionized gas and supports life on Earth. Planets rotate around the sun. Early astronomers were able to see the six closest planets to the sun simply by looking up, but Uranus, Neptune and Pluto (which is now considered a dwarf planet) can be seen only by telescope. Mercury, Venus, Earth and Mars are called the terrestrial planets because they have solid, rocky bodies. The outer four planets do not have surfaces because they are made up of gases. Below is a montage of the solar system.

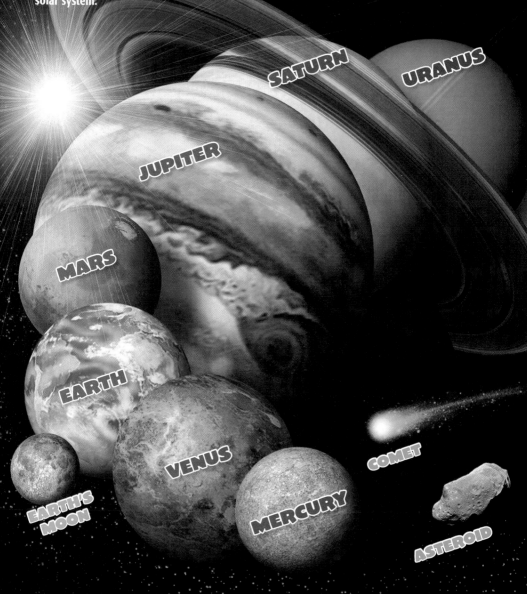

MERCURY

Because it's so close to the sun, Mercury can be seen only within an hour or so of the rising or setting of the sun.

How big is it? **With a diameter of 3,025 miles (4,868.3 km), it is less than half the size of Earth.**

Where is it? **About 36 million miles (57.9 million km) from the sun**

How's the weather? **The average surface temperature is 354°F (179°C).**

Moons: **0** Rings: **0**

VENUS

Venus is similar in size to Earth but has no oceans. It's covered by a layer of thick clouds, which trap heat in its atmosphere.

How big is it? **With a diameter of 7,504 miles (12,077 km), it is a little smaller than Earth.**

Where is it? **About 67.24 million miles (108.2 million km) from the sun**

EARTH

About 70% of Earth is covered with water. Nearly all of Earth's water is found in the oceans, which are salty. Only 3% is drinkable freshwater.

How big is it? **Earth has a diameter of 7,926.2 miles (12,756 km).**

Where is it? **About 92.9 million miles (149.6 million km) from the sun**

How's the weather? **The average surface temperature is 59°F (15°C).**

Moons: **1** Rings: **0**

MARS

Mars is prone to dust storms that engulf the entire planet.

How big is it? **With a diameter of 4,222 miles (6,795 km), it is roughly half as big as Earth.**

Where is it? **About 141.71 million miles (227.9 million km) from the sun**

How's the weather? **The average surface temperature is −82°F (−63°C).**

Moons: **2** Rings: **0**

JUPITER

Jupiter is the solar system's biggest planet. Four of its many moons are planet-size themselves.

How big is it? **At 88,650 miles (142,668 km), its diameter is 11 times bigger than Earth's.**

Where is it? **About 483.9 million miles (778.3 million km) from the sun**

How's the weather? **The average surface temperature is −238°F (−150°C).**

Moons: **62** Rings: **3**

SATURN

Known as the ringed planet, Saturn spins very quickly. It only takes 11 hours for the planet to rotate fully on its axis. Saturn's famous rings are made up of ice and rock.

How big is it? **With a diameter of 74,732 miles (120,270 km), it is 9 1/2 times the size of Earth.**

Where is it? **About 885.9 million miles (1.43 billion km) from the sun**

How's the weather? **The average surface temperature is −285°F (−176°C).**

Moons: **61** Rings: **About 1,000**

URANUS

Uranus was discovered by William Herschel in 1781.

How big is it? **With a diameter of 31,693 miles (51,005 km), it is about four times the size of Earth.**

Where is it? **About 1.78 billion miles (2.87 billion km) from the sun**

How's the weather? **The average surface temperature is −353°F (−214°C).**

Moons: **27** Rings: **13**

NEPTUNE

Neptune was the first planet located by mathematical predictions instead of observation.

How big is it? **With a diameter of 30,707 miles (49,418 km), it is four times bigger than Earth.**

Where is it? **About 2.8 billion miles (4.5 billion km) from the sun**

How's the weather? **The average surface temperature is −373°F (−225°C).**

NEPTUNE

Sports

Regular Season NFL

Peyton Manning

ROOKIES OF THE YEAR

It was an incredible season for rookies of all ages, as multiple first-year quarterbacks and coaches led their teams to amazing turnarounds.

Tony Sparano

The Miami Dolphins had a rough 2007–08 season, finishing with a 1–15 record. But in 2008–09 under first-year coach **TONY SPARANO,** they made a comeback, ending at 11–5 and finishing first in their division.

Led by first-year coach **MIKE SMITH** and rookie quarterback **MATT RYAN,** the Atlanta Falcons (who finished at 4–12 the previous season) went 11–5 in 2008–09. They even made the playoffs as a wild card team.

James Harrison scores a touchdown.

JOHN HARBAUGH, another first-year coach, and rookie Joe Flacco led the Baltimore Ravens to an 11–5 record (they were 5–11 in 2007–08) and the playoffs as a wild card team. Flacco also became the first rookie quarterback in National Football League history to win two playoff games.

THE AGONY OF DEFEAT

The Detroit Lions made history during the 2008–09 season and not in a way they would like to remember. It became the first team ever to finish a season 0–16 and the second team ever to lose all of its games (the 1976 Tampa Bay Buccaneers did this when the season was only 14 games long). Head Coach Rod Marinelli was fired the day after the season ended.

THE LIONS NEED A FEDERAL BAILOUT

2008–09 NFL AWARD WINNERS

MOST VALUABLE PLAYER: Peyton Manning, quarterback, Indianapolis Colts

OFFENSIVE ROOKIE OF THE YEAR: Matt Ryan, quarterback, Atlanta Falcons

DEFENSIVE ROOKIE OF THE YEAR: Jerod Mayo, linebacker, New England Patriots

DEFENSIVE PLAYER OF THE YEAR: James Harrison, linebacker, Pittsburgh Steelers

OFFENSIVE PLAYER OF THE YEAR: Drew Brees, quarterback, New Orleans Saints

COACH OF THE YEAR: Mike Smith, Falcons

COMEBACK PLAYER OF THE YEAR: Chad Pennington, quarterback, Miami Dolphins

TOP 5 Spectator Sports

According to a recent ESPN poll of 27,398 sports fans ages 12 and up, more Americans watch professional football than any other spectator sport. These sports drew the most votes.

1. National Football League	6,439 votes
2. Major League Baseball	3,534
3. College football	2,247
4. National Basketball Association	2,164
5. College basketball	1,123
6. NASCAR auto racing	1,123

Source: ESPN Sports Poll, TNS Sport

Super Bowl XLIII

The 2008–09 Super Bowl was a fierce matchup between the Arizona Cardinals and the Pittsburgh Steelers. The game was held at Raymond James Stadium in Tampa, Florida, before a crowd of 70,774 people, and it did not disappoint. The Steelers scored in the final minute to take the lead 27–23 and win a thrilling Super Bowl XLIII.

The game was full of amazing plays. The first one occurred with a mere 18 seconds left in the first half. Trailing 10–7, the Cardinals had the ball on Pittsburgh's one-yard line, needing only one yard to take the lead going into halftime. However, a pass by Cardinals quarterback Kurt Warner was intercepted by James Harrison (the Defensive Player of the Year) who ran 100 yards the other way for a Steeler touchdown. This 100-yard interception return gave the Steelers a 17–7 lead going into the second half.

The Cardinals refused to give up. They were down 20–7 going into the fourth quarter but a one-yard touchdown pass from Warner to wide receiver Larry Fitzgerald cut the lead to 20–14. The Cardinals defense then tackled the Steelers in their own end zone for a safety, giving the Cards two points and the ball. Warner threw to Fitzgerald again, this time for a 64–yard touchdown, and the Cardinals miraculously led 23–20 with two minutes 37 seconds remaining. The Cardinals had scored 16 unanswered points (all in the fourth quarter) and were on the verge of staging the biggest comeback in Super Bowl history!

But the Steelers fought for a win. Quarterback Ben Roethlisberger and wide receiver Santonio Holmes led them on a 78–yard drive capped by a stunning six–yard touchdown catch by Holmes. Though he had been playing pro football for only three years, Holmes was named the game's Most Valuable Player.

With the win, Roethlisberger became the second-youngest player ever to win two Super Bowl titles (Tom Brady was the first), and the Steelers clinched their sixth Super Bowl championship— the most by any franchise in National Football League history.

Ike Taylor tackles Larry Fitzgerald.

College Football

GATORS REGAIN GLORY

The BCS (Bowl Championship Series) championship game, held in Miami, Florida, on January 8, 2009, featured a battle of Heisman Trophy–winning quarterbacks Sam Bradford and Tim Tebow. Bradford, the 2008 winner, led Oklahoma against 2007 winner Tebow of Florida. With a 24–14 victory, the Gators captured their second national championship in three years.

OTHER 2009 BCS BOWL GAMES

ROSE BOWL (Pasadena, California)
Southern California 38, Penn State 24

SUGAR BOWL (New Orleans, Louisiana)
Utah 31, Alabama 17

ORANGE BOWL (Miami, Florida)
Virginia Tech 20, Cincinnati 7

FIESTA BOWL (Glendale, Arizona)
Texas 24, Ohio State 21

GATOR BOWL (Jacksonville, Florida)
Nebraska 26, Clemson 21

Southern California wins the Rose Bowl.

Baseball

Game 5 is suspended because of rain.

2008 WORLD SERIES

The Philadelphia Phillies beat the Tampa Bay Rays four games to one to capture their first World Series win since 1980 and only their second in team history. After winning their division, the Phillies beat the Milwaukee Brewers in the National League Division Series and the Los Angeles Dodgers in the National League Championship Series to advance to the World Series.

AMAZING RAYS It was an incredible turnaround season for the Rays, who set many franchise records on their path to the World Series. The Rays have been a major league team only since 1998. In that time, they have finished last in their division nine out of 11 times.

In 2008, the Rays managed to win the American League East division crown for the first time. The 2008 season also marked the first time the Rays finished with a winning record, the first time they made the playoffs and the first time they won the American League title.

Jimmy Rollins with the World Series trophy.

SUSPENDED GAME Though the Rays were having an amazing comeback season, they fell short against the Phillies, who clinched the title in Game 5, during the first suspended World Series game ever. With the game tied 2–2 in the sixth inning in Philadelphia, it started to rain, making it impossible to continue play. After a short delay, the umpires decided that they would be unable to finish the game that night. They announced that the wind and rain were so bad the game would have become "comical." Phillies second baseman Chase Utley agreed, saying that "the infield was basically underwater." The game resumed two nights later with the Phillies batting in the bottom of the sixth. They went on to win the game 4–3 and clinch the World Series title.

guess what? *After winning the NLCS (National League Championship Series) Most Valuable Player award, Phillies starting pitcher Cole Hamels went on to be named World Series MVP as well.*

Cliff Lee

2008 MLB AWARD WINNERS

MOST VALUABLE PLAYER
AMERICAN LEAGUE: Dustin Pedroia, second baseman, Boston Red Sox
NATIONAL LEAGUE: Albert Pujols, first baseman, St. Louis Cardinals

CY YOUNG AWARD (BEST PITCHER)
AMERICAN LEAGUE: Cliff Lee, Cleveland Indians
NATIONAL LEAGUE: Tim Lincecum, San Francisco Giants

ROOKIE OF THE YEAR
AMERICAN LEAGUE: Evan Longoria, third baseman, Tampa Bay Rays
NATIONAL LEAGUE: Geovany Soto, catcher, Chicago Cubs

MANAGER OF THE YEAR
AMERICAN LEAGUE: Joe Maddon, Tampa Bay Rays
NATIONAL LEAGUE: Lou Piniella, Chicago Cubs

RECORD BREAKER

Los Angeles Angels of Anaheim relief pitcher Francisco Rodriguez broke the record for most saves in a single season. A save is when a relief pitcher comes into a game (often with his team leading by three runs or less) and pitches the remainder of the game without giving up the lead. On September 13, Rodriguez recorded his 58th save of the season against the Seattle Mariners. He broke the previous record of 57 set by Bobby Thigpen in 1990. Nicknamed "K-Rod" for his ability to strike out batters, Rodriguez finished the season with 62 saves.

Francisco Rodriguez

Little League World Series

The Waipio Little League team from Waipahu, Hawaii, beat the Matamoros Little League team from Tamaulipas, Mexico, on August 24, 2008. Representing the Western Region of the U.S. teams, Waipahu beat Matamoros by a score of 12–3 at Lamade Stadium in South Williamsport, Pennsylvania. The boys from Hawaii were led by Tanner Tokunaga, who smashed two home runs in the victory. It marked the fourth straight Little League World Series Championship for the United States.

guess what?

About 28,500 fans packed the Lamade Stadium in South Williamsport to watch the 2008 Little League World Series.

Miguel Cabrera

2008 MLB LEAGUE LEADERS

BATTING

HOME RUNS

AMERICAN LEAGUE: Miguel Cabrera, third baseman, Detroit Tigers, 37
NATIONAL LEAGUE: Ryan Howard, first baseman, Philadelphia Phillies, 48

BATTING AVERAGE

AMERICAN LEAGUE: Joe Mauer, catcher, Minnesota Twins, .328
NATIONAL LEAGUE: Chipper Jones, third baseman, Atlanta Braves, .364

PITCHING

EARNED RUN AVERAGE

AMERICAN LEAGUE: Cliff Lee, Cleveland Indians, 2.54
NATIONAL LEAGUE: Johan Santana, New York Mets, 2.53

STRIKEOUTS

AMERICAN LEAGUE: A.J. Burnett, Toronto Blue Jays, 231
NATIONAL LEAGUE: Tim Lincecum, San Francisco Giants, 265

Chipper Jones

Sports

189

Basketball

Deron Williams

NBA REGULAR SEASON

TRADING PLACES The 2007–08 season was a big one for trades as many of the NBA's biggest names found themselves packing their bags and swapping uniforms. It began right before the season started, as Timberwolves star Kevin Garnett was traded to the Boston Celtics for a slew of players and draft picks. It was the largest trade in NBA history in which one team received only one player. Over the course of the season, Shaquille O'Neal, Jason Kidd, Pau Gasol, Mike Bibby and Ben Wallace were all traded as well.

Dwight Howard

2007–08 NBA LEADERS

SCORING

	NAME	TEAM	GAMES PLAYED	POINTS PER GAME
1.	LeBron James	Cleveland Cavaliers	75	30.0
2.	Kobe Bryant	Los Angeles Lakers	82	28.3
3.	Allen Iverson	Denver Nuggets	82	26.4

ASSISTS

	NAME	TEAM	GAMES PLAYED	ASSISTS PER GAME
1.	Chris Paul	New Orleans Hornets	80	11.6
2.	Steve Nash	Phoenix Suns	81	11.1
3.	Deron Williams	Utah Jazz	82	10.5

REBOUNDS

	NAME	TEAM	GAMES PLAYED	REBOUNDS PER GAME
1.	Dwight Howard	Orlando Magic	82	14.2
2.	Marcus Camby	Denver Nuggets	79	13.1
3.	Chris Kaman	Los Angeles Clippers	56	12.7

NBA FINALS

RIVALRY RENEWED The Los Angeles Lakers met the Boston Celtics in the NBA finals for the first time since 1987. The two teams had gone head to head three times in the '80s with the Lakers winning two series out of three. The Celtics turned the tables in 2008 though, beating the Lakers four games to two.

Game 4 was the key to the series. The Lakers, playing at home, led 58–40 at halftime, but the Celtics outscored the Lakers 31–15 in the third quarter to cut the lead to 73–71. With 4:07 left in the game, the Celtics took the lead for good, and won 97–91. They won the series and the championship two games later. It was the first NBA championship for Celtics stars Kevin Garnett, Paul Pierce and Ray Allen.

TOP 5 Team Sports

According to a recent national survey, more than 35 million Americans say that basketball is their favorite sport. Kids not only like watching hoops but also love to get in the game. Here are the top team sports for kids ages six through 17.

1.	Basketball	4,127,000 players
2.	Baseball	2,531,000
3.	Outdoor soccer	2,435,000
4.	Touch football	1,998,000
5.	Court volleyball	1,894,000

Source: Sporting Goods Manufacturers Association

WNBA

WNBA Finals

2008 WNBA SEASON LEADERS

SCORING

	NAME	TEAM	GAMES PLAYED	POINTS PER GAME
1.	Diana Taurasi	Phoenix Mercury	34	24.1
2.	Cappie Pondexter	Phoenix Mercury	32	21.2
3.	Seimone Augustus	Minnesota Lynx	31	19.1

ASSISTS

	NAME	TEAM	GAMES PLAYED	ASSISTS PER GAME
1.	Lindsay Whalen	Connecticut Sun	31	5.4
2.	Ticha Penicheiro	Sacramento Monarchs	32	5.2
3.	Sue Bird	Seattle Storm	33	5.1

REBOUNDS

	NAME	TEAM	GAMES PLAYED	REBOUNDS PER GAME
1.	Candace Parker	Los Angeles Sparks	33	9.5
2.	Lisa Leslie	Los Angeles Sparks	33	8.9
3.	Cheryl Ford	Detroit Shock	24	8.7

Candace Parker

College Basketball

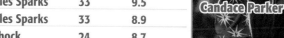

2008 NCAA MEN'S DIVISION I CHAMPIONSHIP

TEAM	1ST HALF POINTS	2ND HALF POINTS	OVERTIME POINTS	FINAL SCORE
Kansas Jayhawks	33	30	12	75
Memphis Tigers	28	35	5	68

2008 NCAA WOMEN'S DIVISION I CHAMPIONSHIP

TEAM	1ST HALF POINTS	2ND HALF POINTS	FINAL SCORE
Stanford Cardinals	29	19	48
Tennessee Volunteers	37	27	64

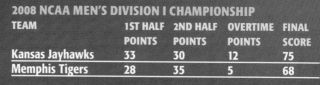

Memphis's Robert Dozier

Tennessee's Alexis Hornbuckle

Sports

Hockey

2008 STANLEY CUP

The Detroit Red Wings defeated the Pittsburgh Penguins four games to two to win the National Hockey League's Stanley Cup Championship. It was the 23rd time that the Red Wings made it to the finals. They won the sixth game 3–2 to claim their 11th Stanley Cup Championship. Left Winger Henrik Zetterberg was named Most Valuable Player.

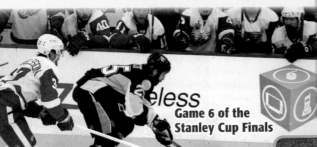

Game 6 of the Stanley Cup Finals

RECORD BREAKER

On January 1, 2008, the Buffalo Sabres hosted the Pittsburgh Penguins in the first-ever outdoor regular-season game held in the U.S. They played in Ralph Wilson Stadium (the home of the Buffalo Bills) before a record-setting crowd of 71,217 fans. The Penguins won 2–1 in a shootout.

Soccer

Soccer is the world's most popular sport, and the World Cup is the world's biggest soccer tournament. It is played every four years. The 2010 competition is slated to be held in South Africa.

EURO 2008

There was no World Cup in 2008, but there was the UEFA (Union of European Football Associations) European Football Championship, in which men's national soccer teams competed for the honor of being Europe's best team. The tournament has been going strong since 1960, occurring every four years (in the even-numbered years between the World Cup competitions).

In June 2008, Spain met Germany in the final match, held in Vienna, Austria, before a crowd of more than 51,000. Spain held off Germany 1–0 to capture its second Euro Cup title. Germany still holds the record for most Euro Cup championships. It has won three times.

guess what? Seventy-five nations have appeared in at least one World Cup tournament, but there have been only seven winning countries: Brazil, Italy, Germany, Argentina, Uruguay, France and England. Brazil leads the pack with five World Cup victories.

Tennis

Ana Ivanovic

2008 TENNIS CHAMPIONS

AUSTRALIAN OPEN
MEN'S SINGLES: Novak Djokovic
MEN'S DOUBLES: Jonathan Erlich, Andy Ram
WOMEN'S SINGLES: Maria Sharapova
WOMEN'S DOUBLES: Alyona Bondarenko, Kateryna Bondarenko

FRENCH OPEN
MEN'S SINGLES: Rafael Nadal
MEN'S DOUBLES: Pablo Cuevas, Luis Horna
WOMEN'S SINGLES: Ana Ivanovic
WOMEN'S DOUBLES: Anabel Medina Garrigues, Virginia Ruano Pascual

WIMBLEDON
MEN'S SINGLES: Rafael Nadal
MEN'S DOUBLES: Daniel Nestor, Nenad Zimonjic
WOMEN'S SINGLES: Venus Williams
WOMEN'S DOUBLES: Serena Williams, Venus Williams

DAVIS CUP (MEN'S INTERNATIONAL TEAM TENNIS)
Spain beat Argentina by three matches to one.

FED CUP (WOMEN'S INTERNATIONAL TEAM TENNIS)
Russia defeated Spain by four matches to none.

Guess what? The Australian Open and the U.S. Open are both played on a type of court similar to the ones you might find at your local tennis center. The French Open is played on clay, and Wimbledon is played on grass.

Rafael Nadal

RECORD BREAKER

Rafael Nadal's French Open win was his fourth straight at the competition. He has now tied the record set by Bjorn Borg. Nadal, who excels on clay courts, has never lost at the French Open.

Golf

Inbee Park

2008 MAJOR EVENT WINNERS

MEN
MASTERS: Trevor Immelman
U.S. OPEN: Tiger Woods
BRITISH OPEN: Padraig Harrington
PGA CHAMPIONSHIP: Padraig Harrington
U.S. AMATEUR CHAMPIONSHIP: Danny Lee

WOMEN
KRAFT NABISCO CHAMPIONSHIP: Lorena Ochoa
LPGA CHAMPIONSHIP: Yani Tseng
U.S. WOMEN'S OPEN: Inbee Park
WOMEN'S BRITISH OPEN: Ji-yai Shin
U.S. AMATEUR CHAMPIONSHIP: Amanda Blumenherst

Tiger Woods

Lingo on the Golf Course

Each hole in golf has what is called a par, which refers to the number of strokes it should take for a golfer to get the ball in the hole. If a golfer gets his or her ball in the hole in one less shot than par, it is called a birdie. If they make it in two shots under par, it's an eagle. If a golfer goes one stroke over par, he or she has shot the dreaded bogey.

Auto Racing

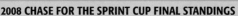

2008 CHASE FOR THE NASCAR SPRINT CUP RACE RESULTS

The Chase for the NASCAR Sprint Cup consists of the final 10 races of the NASCAR Sprint Cup Series, the top racing series of the National Association for Stock Car Auto Racing. The driver with the most points after the Chase is awarded the Sprint Cup.

RACE	TRACK	WINNER
SYLVANIA 300	New Hampshire Motor Speedway	Greg Biffle
CAMPING WORLD RV 400 PRESENTED BY AAA	Dover International Speedway	Greg Biffle
CAMPING WORLD RV 400 PRESENTED BY COLEMAN	Kansas Speedway	Jimmie Johnson
AMP ENERGY 500	Talladega Superspeedway	Tony Stewart
BANK OF AMERICA 500	Lowe's Motor Speedway	Jeff Burton
TUMS QUIKPAK 500	Martinsville Speedway	Jimmie Johnson
PEP BOYS AUTO 500	Atlanta Motor Speedway	Carl Edwards
DICKIES 500	Texas Motor Speedway	Carl Edwards
CHECKER O'REILLY AUTO PARTS 500 PRESENTED BY PENNZOIL	Phoenix International Raceway	Jimmie Johnson
FORD 400	Homestead-Miami Speedway	Carl Edwards

2008 CHASE FOR THE SPRINT CUP FINAL STANDINGS

	DRIVER	TOTAL POINTS
1.	Jimmie Johnson	6,684
2.	Carl Edwards	6,615
3.	Greg Biffle	6,467

Jimmie Johnson

Greg Biffle

Cycling

2008 TOUR DE FRANCE

In 2008 the Tour de France was held for the 95th time. Starting in Brest, France, the course spans 2,211 miles (3,559 km) before finally ending in Paris. Winner Carlos Sastre of Spain held off the other bikers and finished the grueling course in 87 hours 52 minutes 52 seconds. He finished the race 58 seconds before Australia's Cadel Evans. After the race, the 33-year-old Sastre exclaimed, "It's very moving. I've dreamt of this since I was a child!" Sastre is the third rider in a row from Spain to win the sport's biggest event.

Carlos Sastre wears the yellow jersey to show he's in the lead.

Horse Racing

2008 TRIPLE CROWN

The 2008 triple crown was one of the most exciting in history. Going into the Kentucky Derby, the favorite was Big Brown, who overcame an outside post to win thoroughbred racing's most prestigious race. He followed that up with a win in the second triple crown race, the Preakness Stakes, giving him a chance to become the first triple crown winner since Affirmed in 1978. However, 2008 was not the year that horse racing would have its next great champion. Big Brown wasn't up to it, finishing last in the Belmont Stakes, the final leg of the triple crown. Since Affirmed accomplished the feat in 1978, 11 horses have won the first two legs of the triple crown, yet failed to complete the task.

Dogsledding

IDITAROD

The Iditarod is an annual dogsledding race held in Alaska. The course covers more than 1,150 miles (1,851 km) and typically takes between 10 and 17 days to complete. Teams consist of 12 to 16 dogs and one musher, or sled driver. In the 2008 Iditarod, Alaskan native Lance Mackey defended his title, winning the race for the second year in a row with a time of 9 days 11 hours 46 minutes 48 seconds.

guess what? Teams competing in the Iditarod often have to race through blizzards and temperatures as low as −100°F (−73°C) with the wind chill. Swiss racer Martin Buser set the record for fastest time ever in 2002: 8 days 22 hours 46 minutes 2 seconds.

2008 TRIPLE CROWN RACE RESULTS

KENTUCKY DERBY
1ST: Big Brown
2ND: Eight Belles
3RD: Denis of Cork

PREAKNESS STAKES
1ST: Big Brown
2ND: Macho Again
3RD: Icabad Crane

BELMONT STAKES
1ST: Da'Tara
2ND: Denis of Cork
3RD: Anak Nakal and Ready's Echo (dead heat)

HERE IS A LIST OF HORSES THAT HAVE WON THE FIRST TWO LEGS OF THE TRIPLE CROWN BUT LOST THE THIRD.

HORSE	YEAR	PLACE AT THE BELMONT STAKES
Spectacular Bid	1979	Third
Pleasant Colony	1981	Third
Alysheba	1987	Fourth
Sunday Silence	1989	Second
Silver Charm	1997	Second
Real Quiet	1998	Second
Charismatic	1999	Third
War Emblem	2002	Eighth
Funny Cide	2003	Third
Smarty Jones	2004	Second
Big Brown	2008	Ninth

Lance Mackey shares the prize with his lead dogs, Larry and Handsome.

Summer Olympics 2008

The 2008 Summer Olympics were held in Beijing, China. Officially known as the Games of the XXIX Olympiad, the games featured 302 different events and 10,500 athletes. It was the first time China hosted the events. China is the 22nd nation to host the Olympics.

Usain Bolt

Michael Phelps

LIGHTNING BOLT

Jamaican sprinter Usain Bolt may not be faster than the speed of light, but he certainly is speedy! In Beijing, Bolt let everyone know that he is the world's fastest man. He won three gold medals in track and field, breaking world records in the 100 meter sprint, the 200 meter sprint and the 4 X 100 meter relay. He was the first man since Carl Lewis in 1984 to win gold in all three events, and the first in history to break world records in all three. His most impressive run was in the 200 meter sprint. U.S. sprinter Michael Johnson previously held the record, finishing the race in 19.32 seconds in the 1996 Olympics. Many thought that Johnson's record would not and could not be broken, but Bolt proved them wrong, finishing the race in 19.30 seconds.

BORN TO SWIM

The 2008 Olympics were full of amazing, record-breaking performances. U.S. swimmer Michael Phelps provided a number of them. After winning six gold medals in the 2004 Summer Olympics in Athens, Phelps came back to win eight more in Beijing, setting the record for most gold medals won at a single Olympic Games. The previous record of seven was set by Mark Spitz, also a U.S. swimmer, in 1972.

Phelps also set the record for most career gold medals with 14. The 23-year-old from Baltimore, Maryland, broke world records in seven of his eight events, making him one of the most successful athletes in Olympic history.

REDEEM TEAM

The U.S. men's basketball team, led by such NBA stars as Kobe Bryant, LeBron James, Dwyane Wade and Carmelo Anthony, captured the gold medal in Beijing, beating Spain 118–107 in the final game. After finishing a disappointing third in the 2004 Olympics, the pressure was on the Americans to bring the gold back home. Because of this, many called them the Redeem Team in honor of the 1992 men's gold-medal winning team, who were nicknamed the Dream Team. After the final game, Anthony remarked, "We were at America's lowest point in '04, and to have put USA basketball back at the top of the world, it couldn't feel better."

U.S. basketball team

GYMNASTICS

Americans Nastia Liukin and Shawn Johnson both took home gold medals in women's gymnastics.

China's gymnastics team

Johnson won for balance beam and Liukin won the women's individual all-around event (in which Johnson received the silver). For the women's team all-around event, China won gold, narrowly beating out the United States, which received silver.

On the men's side, it was an impressive showing for China, whose team won gold medals in every team and individual event except vault, which was won by Leszek Blanik of Poland. The U.S. men's team took home the bronze in the team all-around event, and American Jonathan Horton won the silver medal on the horizontal bar.

Shawn Johnson

FINAL MEDAL COUNT BY COUNTRY

	COUNTRY	GOLD MEDALS	SILVER MEDALS	BRONZE MEDALS	TOTAL MEDALS
1.	United States	36	38	36	110
2.	China	51	21	28	100
3.	Russia	23	21	28	72
4.	Great Britain	19	13	15	47
5.	Germany	16	10	15	41

Guess what? The modern Olympics began in 1896, but featured only summer events. The Winter Olympics did not get under way until 1924.

Switzerland's Edith Hunkeler

Paralympics

Table tennis at the Paralympics

In addition to hosting the 2008 Summer Olympics, Beijing was also the site of the 2008 Paralympic Games. The Paralympic Games are a multisport event, similar to the Olympics, for athletes with physical or visual disabilities. Like the Olympics, the Paralympic Games occur in both summer and winter and allow elite athletes to showcase their athletic abilities to the world. The first Paralympic Games were held in the summer of 1960.

The 2008 Summer Paralympics were the largest ever. More than 3,900 athletes from 147 different countries competed in the games. Five countries participated for the first time: Burundi, Gabon, Georgia, Haiti and Montenegro.

Sports

197

John Kucera

Winter Sports

CROSS-COUNTRY SKIING

The 2009 U.S. Cross Country Ski Championships took place in Anchorage, Alaska. Kikkan Randall defended her title, winning the women's sprint event for the second year in a row. Kris Freeman took home the men's sprint title.

ALPINE SKIING

The 2009 International Ski Federation Alpine World Ski Championship took place in Val d'Isere, France, from February 2–15, 2009. Here are the big winners.

DOWNHILL
MEN: John Kucera, Canada
WOMEN: Lindsey Vonn, USA
SUPER-G
MEN: Didier Cuche, Switzerland
WOMEN: Lindsey Vonn, USA
SUPER COMBINED
MEN: Aksel Lund Svindal, Norway
WOMEN: Kathrin Zettel, Austria
GIANT SLALOM
MEN: Carlo Janka, Switzerland
WOMEN: Kathrin Hölzl, Germany
SLALOM
MEN: Manfred Pranger, Austria
WOMEN: Maria Riesch, Germany

SNOWBOARDING

The 2009 International Ski Federation Snowboard World Championship took place in Gangwon, Korea, from January 14–24.

SNOWBOARDCROSS
MEN: Markus Schairer, Austria
WOMEN: Helene Olafsen, Norway
PARALLEL GIANT SLALOM
MEN: Jasey-Jay Anderson, Canada
WOMEN: Marion Kreiner, Austria
PARALLEL SLALOM
MEN: Benjamin Karl, Austria
WOMEN: Fraenzi Maegert-Kohli, Switzerland
HALFPIPE
MEN: Ryoh Aono, Japan
WOMEN: Jiayu Liu, China
BIG AIR
MEN: Markku Koski, Finland

FIGURE SKATING

The 2009 World Figure Skating Championships were held from March 22–29 at the Staples Center in Los Angeles, California.

Alissa Czisny

MEN
1. Evan Lysacek
2. Patrick Chan
3. Brian Joubert
WOMEN
1. Kim Yu-Na
2. Joannie Rochette
3. Miko Ando

The 2009 United States Figure Skating Championships were held at the Quicken Loans Arena in Cleveland, Ohio from January 18–25.

MEN
1. Jeremy Abbott
2. Brandon Mroz
3. Evan Lysacek
WOMEN
1. Alissa Czisny
2. Rachael Flatt
3. Caroline Zhang

guess what? There are six major types of jumps performed by figure skaters. Three of them are named after the men who originated them. The salchow (sal-kow) is named after Ulrich Salchow of Sweden; the lutz jump gets its name from Alois Lutz of Austria; and the axel comes from Axel Paulsen of Norway.

Ryoh Aono

X Games

The X Games are a biannual event in which athletes compete in extreme sports. The Winter X Games typically take place in January or February, and the Summer X Games take place in August. The first X Games competition was held in 1995 at venues in Rhode Island and Vermont.

2009 WINTER X GAMES WINNERS

SKIING: Tyler Walker (Mono Skier X), **Simon Dumont** (Big Air), **Stanley Hayer** (Men's Skier X), **Ophelie David** (Women's Skier X), **TJ Schiller** (Men's Slopestyle), **Anna Segal** (Women's Slopestyle), **Xavier Bertoni** (Men's SuperPipe), **Sarah Burke** (Women's SuperPipe)

SNOWBOARDING: Travis Rice (Men's Big Air), **Nate Holland** (Men's Snowboarder X), **Lindsey Jacobellis** (Women's Snowboarder X), **Shaun White** (Men's Slopestyle), **Jenny Jones** (Women's Slopestyle), **Shaun White** (Men's SuperPipe), **Torah Bright** (Women's SuperPipe)

SNOWMOBILING: Joe Parsons (Speed and Style), **Joe Parsons** (Freestyle), **Tucker Hibbert** (Snocross)

Lindsey Jacobellis

2008 SUMMER X GAMES WINNERS

SKATEBOARDING: Bob Burnquist (Big Air), **Elissa Steamer** (Women's Street), **Ryan Sheckler** (Men's Street), **Karen Jones** (Women's Vert), **Pierre-Luc Gagnon** (Men's Vert), **Rune Glifberg** (SuperPark)

MOTO X: Kyle Loza (Best Trick), **Ricky Carmichael** (Step Up), **Kevin Johnson** (Speed and Style), **Josh Hansen** (Men's Racing), **Tarah Gieger** (Women's Racing), **Jeff Ward** (SuperMoto), **Jeremy Lusk** (Freestyle)

BMX: Garrett Reynolds (Street), **Chad Kagy** (Big Air), **Daniel Dhers** (SuperPark), **Jamie Bestwick** (Vert)

RALLY CAR RACING: Travis Pastrana (Driver), **Carolyn Bosley** (Co-driver)

Kyle Loza

Surfing

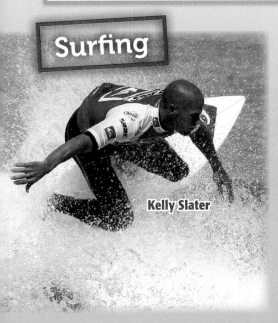

Kelly Slater

2008 WORLD SURFING CHAMPION

The World Surfing Champion is an honor given every year to the best competition surfer. The title is awarded based on points that surfers receive in competitions on the Association of Surfing Professionals (ASP) World Tour. The 2008 champ is Kelly Slater, who has been thought of as the world's best surfer for many years. His record speaks for itself. Slater has been crowned the ASP World Champion a record nine times, including five consecutive titles from 1994–98.

guess what? *Kelly Slater holds the record for youngest World Surfing Champion ever at age 20. He also holds the record for the oldest winner. Slater took the 2008 title at age 36.*

SPORTS TRIVIA QUIZ

Think you know sports lingo? Here's a chance to test your knowledge. Match each sports term to its definition to prove that you can really talk the talk. (They're tough. It's okay if you don't know them all!)

A. BULLPEN

B. MULLIGAN

C. DEAD HEAT

D. AROUND THE HORN

E. TRIPLE-DOUBLE

F. DEUCE

G. HAIL MARY

H. HAT TRICK

I. SUDDEN DEATH

J. GOOFY

1. When the score of a tennis game is tied 40–40.

2. Stance on a skateboard, surfboard, snowboard or wakeboard in which the right foot is on the front of the board.

3. Area where relief pitchers warm up before coming into a baseball game.

4. In soccer or hockey, when an individual player scores three goals.

5. In golf, when a player chooses to retake a shot.

6. In any sport, when the score is tied and the next team or player to score is automatically the winner.

7. Tradition in which infielders on a baseball team throw the ball to each other after recording an out.

8. In horse racing, when two or more horses finish a race exactly at the same time so it is declared a tie.

9. In football, a long forward pass made out of desperation that has little chance of being caught. These passes are usually thrown at the end of a game.

10. In basketball, when a player records 10 or more in three of any of these categories: points, rebounds, assists, steals or blocked shots.

ANSWERS ON PAGE 244.

Record Holders

Wilt Chamberlain

Who scored the most points in a single National Basketball Association game? Wilt Chamberlain, center for the Philadelphia Warriors, with 100 points

What athlete has the most career Major League Baseball home runs? Barry Bonds, outfielder for the Pittsburgh Pirates and San Francisco Giants, with 762 home runs

Who has the most career National Hockey League goals? Wayne Gretzky, center for the Edmonton Oilers, Los Angeles Kings, St. Louis Blues and New York Rangers with 894 goals

Who scored the most career National Football League touchdowns? Jerry Rice, wide receiver for the San Francisco 49ers, Oakland Raiders and Seattle Seahawks, with 208 touchdowns

Clue 1: I was born on January 31, 1919, in Cairo, Georgia.

Clue 2: On April 15, 1947, I played my first game for the Brooklyn Dodgers. That season I played in 151 games, leading the league in stolen bases and winning the first-ever Rookie of the Year award.

Clue 3: In 1997, my number 42 was retired by Major League Baseball, meaning that no future player on any major league team can wear it. It remains the only number to be retired by the entire league.

Who am I? _____

ANSWER ON PAGE 244.

TFK GAME

White Mountain
Named for a nearby mountain

Unalakleet
The start of a stormy stretch

ALASKA

FINISH
Nome

McGrath
First musher here wins a Spirit Mask.

Bering Sea

0   50   100
miles

Skwentna
Dogs get one of many medical checkups.

N
W   E
S

Anchorage
START

A Race Across
Alaska

The Iditarod is a grueling race through the snow. Study the trail map above and answer the questions.

1. Mushers travel in which direction from start to finish?

2. About how many miles is it from Skwentna to McGrath?

3. True or false: The weather clears in Unalakleet.

4. In what city does the race finish?

ALABAMA

CAPITAL: Montgomery

LARGEST CITY: Birmingham

POSTAL CODE: AL

LAND AREA: 50,750 square miles (131,443 sq km)

POPULATION (2008): 4,661,900

ENTERED UNION (RANK): December 14, 1819 (22)

MOTTO: *Audemus jura nostra defendere.* (We dare maintain our rights.)

TREE: southern longleaf pine

FLOWER: camellia

BIRD: yellowhammer (yellow-shafted flicker)

NICKNAMES: Yellowhammer State, Cotton State, Heart of Dixie

FAMOUS ALABAMIAN: Former Secretary of State Condoleezza Rice

 guess what? The first rocket to carry astronauts to the moon was built in Huntsville, Alabama.

Camellia

Birmingham

Montgomery

ALASKA

MOTTO: North to the future

TREE: Sitka spruce

FLOWER: forget-me-not

BIRD: willow ptarmigan

NICKNAMES: The Last Frontier, Land of the Midnight Sun

FAMOUS ALASKAN: Jewel, pop singer

CAPITAL: Juneau

LARGEST CITY: Anchorage

POSTAL CODE: AK

LAND AREA: 570,374 square miles (1,477,267 sq km)

POPULATION (2008): 686,293

ENTERED UNION (RANK): January 3, 1959 (49)

 **guess what?** The highest mountain in the United States, Mount McKinley (also called Denali), is in Alaska.

Anchorage

Juneau

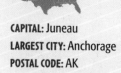

Mount McKinley

ARIZONA

CAPITAL: Phoenix

LARGEST CITY: Phoenix

POSTAL CODE: AZ

LAND AREA: 113,642 square miles (296,400 sq km)

POPULATION (2008): 6,500,180

ENTERED UNION (RANK): February 14, 1912 (48)

MOTTO: *Ditat deus.* (God enriches.)

TREE: palo verde

FLOWER: saguaro cactus blossom

BIRD: cactus wren

NICKNAME: Grand Canyon State

FAMOUS ARIZONAN: Geronimo, Native American leader

Guess what? At the Kitts Peak National Observatory in Sells, Arizona, you can find the world's largest solar telescope.

Phoenix

Cactus wren

ARKANSAS

ARKANSAS

CAPITAL: Little Rock

LARGEST CITY: Little Rock

POSTAL CODE: AR

LAND AREA: 52,075 square miles (134,874 sq km)

POPULATION (2008): 2,855,390

ENTERED UNION (RANK): June 15, 1836 (25)

MOTTO: *Regnat populus.* (The people rule.)

TREE: pine

FLOWER: apple blossom

BIRD: mockingbird

NICKNAME: Natural State

FAMOUS ARKANSAN: Bill Clinton, 42nd U.S. President

Little Rock

Guess what? The name Arkansas is a French spelling of the Sioux word arcansa, which means "downstream place."

Bill Clinton

CALIFORNIA

CALIFORNIA REPUBLIC

CAPITAL: Sacramento
LARGEST CITY: Los Angeles
POSTAL CODE: CA
LAND AREA: 155,973 square miles (403,970 sq km)
POPULATION (2008): 36,756,666
ENTERED UNION (RANK): September 9, 1850 (31)

MOTTO: *Eureka!* (I have found it!)
TREE: California redwood
FLOWER: golden poppy
BIRD: California valley quail

NICKNAME: Golden State
FAMOUS CALIFORNIAN: Sally Ride, the first American woman in space

Guess what? *California contains both the oldest and the tallest trees on Earth. The single largest tree, an ancient sequoia, has a circumference of 102 feet (31 m).*

Sally Ride

Sacramento
Los Angeles

COLORADO

CAPITAL: Denver
LARGEST CITY: Denver
POSTAL CODE: CO
LAND AREA: 103,730 square miles (268,660 sq km)
POPULATION (2008): 4,939,456
ENTERED UNION (RANK): August 1, 1876 (38)

MOTTO: *Nil sine numine* (Nothing without the Diety)
TREE: Colorado blue spruce
FLOWER: Rocky Mountain columbine
BIRD: lark bunting

NICKNAME: Centennial State
FAMOUS COLORADAN: Jack Dempsey, boxer

Guess what? *Colorado has an official state dinosaur, the Stegosaurus.*

Denver

Colorado blue spruce

CONNECTICUT

CAPITAL: Hartford

LARGEST CITY: Bridgeport

POSTAL CODE: CT

LAND AREA: 5,018 square miles (12,997 sq km)

POPULATION (2008): 3,501,252

ENTERED UNION (RANK): January 9, 1788 (5)

MOTTO: *Qui transtulit sustinet.* (He who transplanted still sustains.)

TREE: white oak

FLOWER: mountain laurel

BIRD: American robin

NICKNAME: Constitution State

FAMOUS NUTMEGGER: Harriet Beecher Stowe, novelist and abolitionist who wrote *Uncle Tom's Cabin*

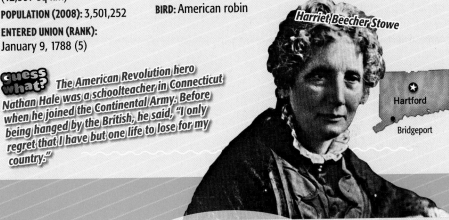

Harriet Beecher Stowe

 **Guess what?** The American Revolution hero Nathan Hale was a schoolteacher in Connecticut when he joined the Continental Army. Before being hanged by the British, he said, "I only regret that I have but one life to lose for my country."

Hartford

Bridgeport

DELAWARE

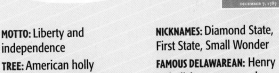

CAPITAL: Dover

LARGEST CITY: Wilmington

POSTAL CODE: DE

LAND AREA: 1,955 square miles (5,063 sq km)

POPULATION (2008): 873,092

ENTERED UNION (RANK): December 7, 1787 (1)

MOTTO: Liberty and independence

TREE: American holly

FLOWER: peach blossom

BIRD: blue hen chicken

NICKNAMES: Diamond State, First State, Small Wonder

FAMOUS DELAWAREAN: Henry Heimlich, surgeon and inventor of the Heimlich maneuver

Guess what? Delaware is the only state without a national park or national monument.

Peach blossom

Wilmington

Dover

FLORIDA

CAPITAL: Tallahassee
LARGEST CITY: Jacksonville
POSTAL CODE: FL
LAND AREA: 53,927 square miles (139,670 sq km)
POPULATION (2008): 18,328,340
ENTERED UNION (RANK): March 3, 1845 (27)

MOTTO: In God we trust.
TREE: Sabal palm
FLOWER: orange blossom
BIRD: mockingbird

NICKNAME: Sunshine State
FAMOUS FLORIDIAN: Brittany Snow, actress

John Glenn

Guess what? John Glenn, the first American to orbit Earth, was launched from Cape Canaveral in Florida.

Tallahassee Jacksonville

GEORGIA

CAPITAL: Atlanta
LARGEST CITY: Atlanta
POSTAL CODE: GA
LAND AREA: 57,919 square miles (150,010 sq km)
POPULATION (2008): 9,685,744
ENTERED UNION (RANK): January 2, 1788 (4)

MOTTO: Wisdom, justice and moderation
TREE: live oak
FLOWER: Cherokee rose
BIRD: brown thrasher

NICKNAMES: Peach State, Empire State of the South
FAMOUS GEORGIAN: Martin Luther King Jr., civil rights leader

Guess what? "Georgia on My Mind," as performed by Ray Charles, is the official state song. "Sweet Georgia Brown" and "Midnight Train to Georgia" are other famous songs with this state's name in the title.

Atlanta

Brown thrasher

PACIFIC OCEAN

HAWAII

CAPITAL: Honolulu (on Oahu)
LARGEST CITY: Honolulu
POSTAL CODE: HI
LAND AREA: 6,423 square miles (16,636 sq km)
POPULATION (2008): 1,288,198
ENTERED UNION (RANK): August 21, 1959 (50)

MOTTO: *Ua mau ke ea o ka aina i ka pono.* (The life of the land is perpetuated in righteousness.)
TREE: kuku'i (candlenut)
FLOWER: yellow hibiscus
BIRD: nene (Hawaiian goose)

NICKNAME: Aloha State
FAMOUS HAWAIIAN: Hiram L. Fong, first Asian-American senator

Honolulu

 **Guess what?** The state of Hawaii is made up of eight main islands. In the Hawaiian language, the word *aloha* means both "hello" and "goodbye."

Honolulu

IDAHO

CAPITAL: Boise
LARGEST CITY: Boise
POSTAL CODE: ID
LAND AREA: 82,751 square miles (214,325 sq km)
POPULATION (2008): 1,523,816
ENTERED UNION (RANK): July 3, 1890 (43)

MOTTO: *Esto perpetua.* (Let it be perpetual.)
TREE: western white pine
FLOWER: syringa
BIRD: mountain bluebird

NICKNAME: Gem State
FAMOUS IDAHOAN: Gutzon Borglum, Mount Rushmore sculptor

 **Guess what?** In 1805, the explorers Lewis and Clark became the first non–Native Americans to visit Idaho.

Syringa

Boise

ILLINOIS

ILLINOIS

CAPITAL: Springfield
LARGEST CITY: Chicago
POSTAL CODE: IL
LAND AREA: 55,593 square miles (143,986 sq km)
POPULATION (2008): 12,901,563
ENTERED UNION (RANK): December 3, 1818 (21)

MOTTO: State sovereignty, national union
TREE: white oak
FLOWER: purple violet
BIRD: cardinal

NICKNAMES: Prairie State, Land of Lincoln
FAMOUS ILLINOISAN: Ernest Hemingway, writer

Chicago

Springfield

guess what? A museum in Woodstock, Illinois, celebrates the comic book hero Dick Tracy and his creator, Chester Gould.

Cardinal

INDIANA

CAPITAL: Indianapolis
LARGEST CITY: Indianapolis
POSTAL CODE: IN
LAND AREA: 35,870 square miles (92,903 sq km)
POPULATION (2008): 6,376,792
ENTERED UNION (RANK): December 11, 1816 (19)

MOTTO: The crossroads of America
TREE: tulip tree, or yellow poplar
FLOWER: peony
BIRD: cardinal

NICKNAMES: Hoosier State, Crossroads of America
FAMOUS INDIANAN OR HOOSIER: Michael Jackson, pop star

Indianapolis

guess what? A 500-mile (805-km) car race, called the Indy 500, is an annual event in Indianapolis.

Indy 500

IOWA

CAPITAL: Des Moines
LARGEST CITY: Des Moines
POSTAL CODE: IA
LAND AREA: 55,875 square miles (144,716 sq km)
POPULATION (2008): 3,002,555
ENTERED UNION (RANK): December 28, 1846 (29)

MOTTO: Our liberties we prize, and our rights we will maintain.
TREE: oak
FLOWER: wild prairie rose
BIRD: eastern goldfinch (also known as the American goldfinch)

NICKNAME: Hawkeye State
FAMOUS IOWAN: William "Buffalo Bill" Cody, scout and entertainer in the Wild West

Des Moines

Guess what? Iowa has the highest literacy rate in the United States. More than 99% of its adult citizens are able to read and write.

Des Moines

KANSAS

CAPITAL: Topeka
LARGEST CITY: Wichita
POSTAL CODE: KS
LAND AREA: 81,823 square miles (211,922 sq km)
POPULATION (2008): 2,802,134
ENTERED UNION (RANK): January 29, 1861 (34)

MOTTO: *Ad astra per aspera* (To the stars through difficulties)
TREE: cottonwood
FLOWER: sunflower
BIRD: western meadowlark

NICKNAMES: Sunflower State, Jayhawk State, Wheat State
FAMOUS KANSAN: Amelia Earhart, first woman to fly solo across the Atlantic Ocean

Guess what? The geographic center of the continental United States is Lebanon, Kansas.

Cottonwood

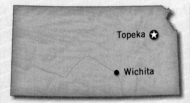
Topeka
Wichita

KENTUCKY

CAPITAL: Frankfort
LARGEST CITY: Louisville
POSTAL CODE: KY
LAND AREA: 39,732 square miles (102,906 sq km)
POPULATION (2008): 4,269,245
ENTERED UNION (RANK): June 1, 1792 (15)

MOTTO: United we stand, divided we fall.
TREE: tulip poplar
FLOWER: goldenrod
BIRD: Kentucky cardinal

NICKNAME: Bluegrass State
FAMOUS KENTUCKIAN: Muhammad Ali, boxer

Guess what? The Louisville Extreme Park, a 40,000-square-foot (3,716-sq-m) skateboarding park, is located in Louisville, Kentucky. It contains a 24-foot-long (7-m-long) full pipe.

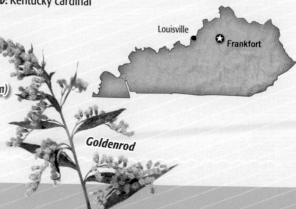

Louisville • ★ Frankfort

Goldenrod

LOUISIANA

CAPITAL: Baton Rouge
LARGEST CITY: New Orleans
POSTAL CODE: LA
LAND AREA: 43,566 square miles (112,836 sq km)
POPULATION (2008): 4,410,796
ENTERED UNION (RANK): April 30, 1812 (18)

MOTTO: Union, justice and confidence
TREE: bald cypress
FLOWER: magnolia
BIRD: eastern brown pelican

NICKNAME: Pelican State
FAMOUS LOUISIANAN: Louis Armstrong, jazz musician

Guess what? The name of the state capital of Louisiana, Baton Rouge, is a French phrase that means "red stick."

New Orleans

Baton Rouge ★

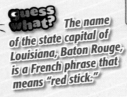

Eastern brown pelican

MAINE

CAPITAL: Augusta
LARGEST CITY: Portland
POSTAL CODE: ME
LAND AREA: 30,865 square miles (79,940 sq km)
POPULATION (2008): 1,316,456
ENTERED UNION (RANK): March 15, 1820 (23)

MOTTO: *Dirigo.* (I lead.)
TREE: white pine
FLOWER: white pine cone and tassel
BIRD: black-capped chickadee

NICKNAME: Pine Tree State
FAMOUS MAINER: Stephen King, best-selling author

Guess what? Maine is the easternmost state in the United States. Its residents are the first in the nation to see the sun rise every morning.

Chickadee

Augusta
Portland

MARYLAND

CAPITAL: Annapolis
LARGEST CITY: Baltimore
POSTAL CODE: MD
LAND AREA: 9,775 square miles (25,317 sq km)
POPULATION (2008): 5,633,597
ENTERED UNION (RANK): April 28, 1788 (7)

MOTTO: *Fatti maschii, parole femine* (Manly deeds, womanly words)
TREE: white oak
FLOWER: black-eyed Susan
BIRD: Baltimore oriole

NICKNAMES: Free State, Old Line State
FAMOUS MARYLANDER: Frederick Douglass, freed slave and abolitionist

Guess what? The first railroad station in the United States—Mount Clare Station—was completed in the 1830s in Baltimore, Maryland.

Frederick Douglass

Baltimore
Annapolis

MASSACHUSETTS

CAPITAL: Boston

LARGEST CITY: Boston

POSTAL CODE: MA

LAND AREA: 7,838 square miles (20,300 sq km)

POPULATION (2008): 6,497,967

ENTERED UNION (RANK): February 6, 1788 (6)

MOTTO: *Ense petit placidam sub libertate quietem.* (By the sword we seek peace, but peace only under liberty.)

TREE: American elm

FLOWER: mayflower

BIRD: black-capped chickadee

NICKNAMES: Bay State, Old Colony State, Baked Bean State

FAMOUS BAY STATER: Robert F. Kennedy, politician and civil rights advocate

Guess what? Harvard, America's oldest college, opened in Cambridge, Massachusetts, in 1636.

Boston ⬥

Robert F. Kennedy

MICHIGAN

CAPITAL: Lansing

LARGEST CITY: Detroit

POSTAL CODE: MI

LAND AREA: 56,809 square miles (147,135 sq km)

POPULATION (2008): 10,003,422

ENTERED UNION (RANK): January 26, 1837 (26)

MOTTO: *Si quaeris peninsulam amoenam circumspice.* (If you seek a pleasant peninsula, look about you.)

TREE: white pine

FLOWER: apple blossom

BIRD: American robin

NICKNAMES: Wolverine State, Great Lakes State

FAMOUS MICHIGANDER OR MICHIGANIAN: Henry Ford, founder of the Ford Motor Company and pioneer of the assembly line

Guess what? Michigan has 116 lighthouses spread along more than 3,000 miles (4,828 km) of coastline.

St. Joseph lighthouse

Lansing ⬥

Detroit

MINNESOTA

CAPITAL: St. Paul

LARGEST CITY: Minneapolis

POSTAL CODE: MN

LAND AREA: 79,617 square miles (206,208 sq km)

POPULATION (2008): 5,220,393

ENTERED UNION (RANK): May 11, 1858 (32)

MOTTO: *L'Étoile du nord* (Star of the north)

TREE: red (or Norway) pine

FLOWER: lady slipper

BIRD: common loon

NICKNAMES: North Star State, Gopher State, Land of 10,000 Lakes

FAMOUS MINNESOTAN: Judy Garland, actress best-known as Dorothy in *The Wizard of Oz*

Guess what? The Mall of America, the country's largest shopping mall, is in Bloomington, Minnesota. It would take 258 Statues of Liberty, laid end to end, to reach from one end of the mall to the other.

Common loon

Minneapolis

St. Paul

MISSISSIPPI

CAPITAL: Jackson

LARGEST CITY: Jackson

POSTAL CODE: MS

LAND AREA: 46,914 square miles (121,507 sq km)

POPULATION (2008): 2,938,618

ENTERED UNION (RANK): December 10, 1817 (20)

MOTTO: *Virtute et armis* (By valor and arms)

TREE: magnolia

FLOWER: magnolia

BIRD: mockingbird

NICKNAME: Magnolia State

FAMOUS MISSISSIPPIAN: Oprah Winfrey, talk show personality and philanthropist

Guess what? The 4-H Club was founded in Holmes County, Mississippi, in 1907. The organization is devoted to helping young people develop their head, hands, heart and health.

Magnolia

Jackson

MISSOURI

CAPITAL: Jefferson City
LARGEST CITY: Kansas City
POSTAL CODE: MO
LAND AREA: 68,898 square miles (178,446 sq km)
POPULATION (2008): 5,911,605
ENTERED UNION (RANK): August 10, 1821 (24)

MOTTO: *Salus populi suprema lex esto.* (The welfare of the people shall be the supreme law.)
TREE: flowering dogwood
FLOWER: hawthorn
BIRD: bluebird

NICKNAME: Show Me State
FAMOUS MISSOURIAN: Edwin Hubble, astronomer

Guess what? *Mark Twain, author of Huckleberry Finn and The Adventures of Tom Sawyer, was born in Florida, Missouri, in 1835. At age four, he and his family moved to Hannibal, Missouri, the setting of many of his stories.*

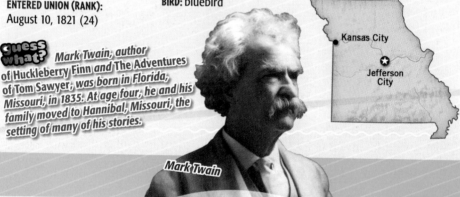

Mark Twain

Kansas City
Jefferson City

MONTANA

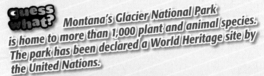

CAPITAL: Helena
LARGEST CITY: Billings
POSTAL CODE: MT
LAND AREA: 145,556 square miles (376,990 sq km)
POPULATION (2008): 967,440
ENTERED UNION (RANK): November 8, 1889 (41)

MOTTO: *Oro y plata* (Gold and silver)
TREE: ponderosa pine
FLOWER: bitterroot
BIRD: western meadowlark

NICKNAME: Treasure State
FAMOUS MONTANAN: Evel Knievel, motorcycle daredevil

Guess what? *Montana's Glacier National Park is home to more than 1,000 plant and animal species. The park has been declared a World Heritage site by the United Nations.*

Glacier National Park

Helena
Billings

NEBRASKA

CAPITAL: Lincoln
LARGEST CITY: Omaha
POSTAL CODE: NE
LAND AREA: 76,878 square miles (199,114 sq km)
POPULATION (2008): 1,783,432
ENTERED UNION (RANK): March 1, 1867 (37)

MOTTO: Equality before the law
TREE: eastern cottonwood
FLOWER: goldenrod
BIRD: western meadowlark

NICKNAMES: Cornhusker State, Beef State
FAMOUS NEBRASKAN: Malcolm X, civil rights leader

guess what? On June 22, 2003, the largest hailstone ever found in the United States fell in Aurora, Nebraska. The ice ball measured nearly 19 inches (48 cm) around–about the size of a bowling ball!

Omaha

Omaha •
Lincoln ✪

NEVADA

CAPITAL: Carson City
LARGEST CITY: Las Vegas
POSTAL CODE: NV
LAND AREA: 109,806 square miles (284,397 sq km)
POPULATION (2008): 2,600,167
ENTERED UNION (RANK): October 31, 1864 (36)

MOTTO: All for our country
TREE: single-leaf piñon pine
FLOWER: sagebrush
BIRD: mountain bluebird

NICKNAMES: Sagebrush State, Silver State, Battle Born State
FAMOUS NEVADAN: Harry Reid, U.S. Senator

guess what? Tennis star Andre Agassi founded a school in his hometown of Las Vegas, Nevada. The College Preparatory Academy opened in 2001.

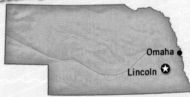

✪ Carson City

Las Vegas ——— •

Mountain bluebird

NEW HAMPSHIRE

CAPITAL: Concord
LARGEST CITY: Manchester
POSTAL CODE: NH
LAND AREA: 8,969 square miles (23,230 sq km)
POPULATION (2008): 1,315,809
ENTERED UNION (RANK): June 21, 1788 (9)

MOTTO: Live free or die.
TREE: white birch, also known as the canoe or paper birch
FLOWER: purple lilac
BIRD: purple finch

NICKNAME: Granite State
FAMOUS NEW HAMPSHIRITE: Alan Shepard, first American in space

Guess what? In 1986, Christa McAuliffe, a New Hampshire teacher who was chosen to be the first teacher in space, was killed when the Space Shuttle Challenger exploded shortly after takeoff. Today, she is honored by Concord's Christa McAuliffe Planetarium.

Christa McAuliffe

Concord

Manchester

NEW JERSEY

CAPITAL: Trenton
LARGEST CITY: Newark
POSTAL CODE: NJ
LAND AREA: 7,419 square miles (19,215 sq km)
POPULATION (2008): 8,682,661
ENTERED UNION (RANK): December 18, 1787 (3)

MOTTO: Liberty and prosperity
TREE: red oak
FLOWER: common meadow violet
BIRD: eastern (or American) goldfinch

NICKNAME: Garden State
FAMOUS NEW JERSEYITE: David Copperfield, magician

Guess what? The city of Edison, New Jersey, was named after the state's most famous inventor, Thomas Alva Edison, known for the invention of the lightbulb.

Newark

Trenton

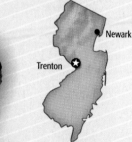

Thomas Edison

NEW MEXICO

CAPITAL: Santa Fe
LARGEST CITY: Albuquerque
POSTAL CODE: NM
LAND AREA: 121,365 square miles (314,335 sq km)
POPULATION (2008): 1,984,356
ENTERED UNION (RANK): January 6, 1912 (47)

MOTTO: *Crescit eundo.* (It grows as it goes.)
TREE: piñon pine
FLOWER: yucca
BIRD: roadrunner

NICKNAMES: Land of Enchantment, Cactus State
FAMOUS NEW MEXICAN: William Hanna, cartoonist

guess what? Roswell, New Mexico, is thought to be the landing site of a UFO crash in 1947. Since then, thousands of people have traveled there in search of proof of intelligent life on other planets.

Yucca

Santa Fe
Albuquerque

NEW YORK

CAPITAL: Albany
LARGEST CITY: New York
POSTAL CODE: NY
LAND AREA: 47,224 square miles (122,310 sq km)
POPULATION (2008): 19,490,297
ENTERED UNION (RANK): July 26, 1788 (11)

MOTTO: *Excelsior* (Ever upward)
TREE: sugar maple
FLOWER: rose
BIRD: bluebird

NICKNAME: Empire State
FAMOUS NEW YORKER: Elizabeth Cady Stanton, abolitionist and women's rights advocate

guess what? The subway system in New York City has 722 miles (1,162 km) of track.

Albany

New York

Elizabeth Cady Stanton

NORTH CAROLINA

CAPITAL: Raleigh
LARGEST CITY: Charlotte
POSTAL CODE: NC
LAND AREA: 48,708 square miles (126,154 sq km)
POPULATION (2008): 9,222,414
ENTERED UNION (RANK): November 21, 1789 (12)

MOTTO: *Esse quam videri* (To be rather than to seem)
TREE: pine
FLOWER: flowering dogwood
BIRD: cardinal

NICKNAME: Tar Heel State
FAMOUS NORTH CAROLINIAN: Fantasia Barrino, *American Idol* winner

guess what? In 1903, Orville and Wilbur Wright took their historic first airplane flight above Kitty Hawk, North Carolina.

First airplane flight

Raleigh
Charlotte

NORTH DAKOTA

CAPITAL: Bismarck
LARGEST CITY: Fargo
POSTAL CODE: ND
LAND AREA: 68,994 square miles (178,694 sq km)
POPULATION (2008): 641,481
ENTERED UNION (RANK): November 2, 1889 (39)

MOTTO: Liberty and union, now and forever, one and inseparable
TREE: American elm
FLOWER: wild prairie rose
BIRD: western meadowlark

NICKNAMES: Sioux State, Flickertail State, Peace Garden State, Rough Rider State
FAMOUS NORTH DAKOTAN: Cliff "Fido" Purpur, hockey player

guess what? Milk is North Dakota's official state beverage. To honor its dairy industry, the town of New Salem built a cow sculpture that stands 38 feet (12 m) tall and 50 feet (15 m) long. Weighing 6 tons (5 metric tons), the landmark statue is named Salem Sue.

Salem Sue cow sculpture

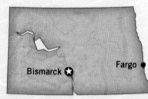

Bismarck
Fargo

OHIO

CAPITAL: Columbus
LARGEST CITY: Columbus
POSTAL CODE: OH
LAND AREA: 40,953 square miles (106,068 sq km)
POPULATION (2008): 11,485,910
ENTERED UNION (RANK): March 1, 1803 (17)

MOTTO: With God, all things are possible
TREE: buckeye
FLOWER: scarlet carnation
BIRD: cardinal

NICKNAME: Buckeye State
FAMOUS OHIOAN: Thomas Edison, inventor

Guess what? Cleveland, Ohio, is home to the Rock and Roll Hall of Fame. The 2008 inductees were John Mellencamp, Leonard Cohen, Madonna, The Dave Clark Five and The Ventures.

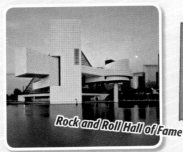

Rock and Roll Hall of Fame

Columbus

OKLAHOMA

CAPITAL: Oklahoma City
LARGEST CITY: Oklahoma City
POSTAL CODE: OK
LAND AREA: 68,679 square miles (177,879 sq km)
POPULATION (2008): 3,642,361
ENTERED UNION (RANK): November 16, 1907 (46)

MOTTO: *Labor omnia vincit.* (Labor conquers all things.)
TREE: eastern redbud
FLOWER: mistletoe
BIRD: scissor-tailed flycatcher

NICKNAME: Sooner State
FAMOUS OKLAHOMAN: Mickey Mantle, baseball player

Guess what? The Twister Museum in Wakita, Oklahoma, is dedicated to helping visitors understand how tornadoes—and the film industry—work. The museum was built to commemorate the 1996 movie Twister, which was filmed nearby.

Oklahoma City

Mistletoe

OREGON

STATE OF OREGON 1859

CAPITAL: Salem
LARGEST CITY: Portland
POSTAL CODE: OR
LAND AREA: 96,003 square miles (248,648 sq km)
POPULATION (2008): 3,790,060
ENTERED UNION (RANK): February 14, 1859 (33)

MOTTO: *Alis volat propriis.* (She flies with her own wings.)
TREE: Douglas fir
FLOWER: Oregon grape
BIRD: western meadowlark

NICKNAME: Beaver State
FAMOUS OREGONIAN: Matt Groening, creator of *The Simpsons*

 Crater Lake in Oregon is, at 1,943 feet (592 m) deep, the deepest lake in the United States.

Portland
Salem

Crater Lake

PENNSYLVANIA

CAPITAL: Harrisburg
LARGEST CITY: Philadelphia
POSTAL CODE: PA
LAND AREA: 44,820 square miles (116,084 sq km)
POPULATION (2008): 12,448,279
ENTERED UNION (RANK): December 12, 1787 (2)

MOTTO: Virtue, liberty and independence
TREE: hemlock
FLOWER: mountain laurel
BIRD: ruffed grouse

NICKNAME: Keystone State
FAMOUS PENNSYLVANIAN: Marian Anderson, singer

The Declaration of Independence and the U.S. Constitution were both signed in Philadelphia, Pennsylvania, which served as the country's capital from 1790 to 1800.

Harrisburg
Philadelphia

Marian Anderson

RHODE ISLAND

CAPITAL: Providence
LARGEST CITY: Providence
POSTAL CODE: RI
LAND AREA: 1,045 square miles (2,707 sq km)
POPULATION (2008): 1,050,788
ENTERED UNION (RANK): May 29, 1790 (13)

MOTTO: Hope
TREE: red maple
FLOWER: violet
BIRD: Rhode Island red hen

NICKNAME: Ocean State
FAMOUS RHODE ISLANDER: Robert Gray, sea captain who discovered the Columbia River

Violet

guess what? America's first Jewish house of worship, Touro Synagogue, was completed in Rhode Island in 1763.

Providence

SOUTH CAROLINA

CAPITAL: Columbia
LARGEST CITY: Columbia
POSTAL CODE: SC
LAND AREA: 30,111 square miles (77,987 sq km)
POPULATION (2008): 4,479,800
ENTERED UNION (RANK): May 23, 1788 (8)

MOTTOES: *Animis opibusque parati* (Prepared in mind and resources); *Dum spiro spero.* (While I breathe, I hope.)
TREE: palmetto
FLOWER: yellow jessamine
BIRD: Carolina wren

NICKNAME: Palmetto State
FAMOUS SOUTH CAROLINIAN: Althea Gibson, tennis player

Fort Sumter

guess what? The American Civil War began when Confederate soldiers attacked Fort Sumter in Charleston, South Carolina, on April 12, 1861.

Columbia

SOUTH DAKOTA

CAPITAL: Pierre
LARGEST CITY: Sioux Falls
POSTAL CODE: SD
LAND AREA: 75,898 square miles (196,575 sq km)
POPULATION (2008): 804,194
ENTERED UNION (RANK): November 2, 1889 (40)

MOTTO: Under God the people rule.
TREE: Black Hills spruce
FLOWER: pasqueflower
BIRD: ring-necked pheasant

NICKNAMES: Mount Rushmore State, Coyote State
FAMOUS SOUTH DAKOTAN: Crazy Horse, Sioux chief

guess what? The faces of four presidents are carved into Mount Rushmore in South Dakota. Each face measures approximately 60 feet (18 m) from hair to chin (or beard). The four Presidents depicted are George Washington, Thomas Jefferson, Teddy Roosevelt and Abraham Lincoln.

Mount Rushmore

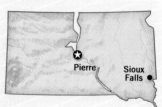

TENNESSEE

CAPITAL: Nashville
LARGEST CITY: Memphis
POSTAL CODE: TN
LAND AREA: 41,220 square miles (106,760 sq km)
POPULATION (2008): 6,214,888
ENTERED UNION (RANK): June 1, 1796 (16)

MOTTO: Agriculture and commerce
TREE: tulip poplar
FLOWER: iris
BIRD: mockingbird

NICKNAME: Volunteer State
FAMOUS TENNESSEAN: Al Gore, former Vice President and environmental activist

guess what? The Great Smoky Mountain National Park in Tennessee is home to 1,500 black bears.

Iris

TEXAS

CAPITAL: Austin
LARGEST CITY: Houston
POSTAL CODE: TX
LAND AREA: 261,914 square miles (678,357 sq km)
POPULATION (2008): 24,326,974
ENTERED UNION (RANK): December 29, 1845 (28)

MOTTO: Friendship
TREE: pecan
FLOWER: Texas bluebonnet
BIRD: mockingbird

NICKNAME: Lone Star State
FAMOUS TEXAN: Sandra Day O'Connor, first woman Supreme Court justice

 Since 1519, Texas has flown six different flags, including the Spanish, French, Mexican and U.S. flag. After Texas won its independence from Mexico, it was an independent country with its own flag. During the Civil War, the state flew the Confederate flag.

Pecan

Austin ✪ Houston ●

UTAH

CAPITAL: Salt Lake City
LARGEST CITY: Salt Lake City
POSTAL CODE: UT
LAND AREA: 82,168 square miles (212,815 sq km)
POPULATION (2008): 2,736,424
ENTERED UNION (RANK): January 4, 1896 (45)

MOTTO: Industry
TREE: blue spruce
FLOWER: sego lily
BIRD: California gull

NICKNAME: Beehive State
FAMOUS UTAHN: Philo T. Farnsworth, inventor of the television

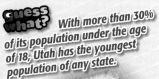 With more than 30% of its population under the age of 18, Utah has the youngest population of any state.

Salt Lake City ✪

Sego lily

VERMONT

CAPITAL: Montpelier
LARGEST CITY: Burlington
POSTAL CODE: VT
LAND AREA: 9,249 square miles (23,956 sq km)
POPULATION (2008): 621,270
ENTERED UNION (RANK): March 4, 1791 (14)

MOTTO: Vermont: freedom and unity
TREE: sugar maple
FLOWER: red clover
BIRD: hermit thrush

NICKNAME: Green Mountain State
FAMOUS VERMONTER: Joseph Smith, founder of the Mormon church

 *Burlington, Vermont, is home to Ben & Jerry's ice cream factory, founded in 1978.*

Hermit thrush

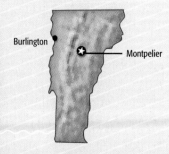
Burlington
Montpelier

VIRGINIA

Virginia flag

CAPITAL: Richmond
LARGEST CITY: Virginia Beach
POSTAL CODE: VA
LAND AREA: 39,598 square miles (102,559 sq km)
POPULATION (2008): 7,769,089
ENTERED UNION (RANK): June 25, 1788 (10)

MOTTO: *Sic semper tyrannis* (Thus always to tyrants)
TREE: flowering dogwood
FLOWER: American dogwood
BIRD: cardinal

NICKNAMES: The Old Dominion, Mother of Presidents
FAMOUS VIRGINIANS: Meriwether Lewis and William Clark, American explorers

Guess what? *More than one-third of the potato crop grown in Virginia is used to make potato chips.*

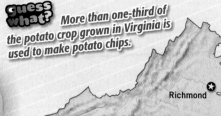
Richmond
Virginia Beach

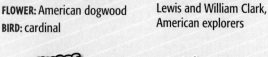
American dogwood

224

WASHINGTON

CAPITAL: Olympia

LARGEST CITY: Seattle

POSTAL CODE: WA

LAND AREA: 66,582 square miles (172,447 sq km)

POPULATION (2008): 6,549,224

ENTERED UNION (RANK): November 11, 1889 (42)

MOTTO: *Al-ki* (an Indian word meaning "into the future")

TREE: western hemlock

FLOWER: coast rhododendron

BIRD: willow goldfinch

NICKNAME: Evergreen State

FAMOUS WASHINGTONIAN: Bob Barker, game show host

 When Washington state's Mount Saint Helens volcano erupted in 1980, it blew ash that landed as far away as Maine.

Seattle

Olympia

Mount Saint Helens

WEST VIRGINIA

CAPITAL: Charleston

LARGEST CITY: Charleston

POSTAL CODE: WV

LAND AREA: 24,087 square miles (62,385 sq km)

POPULATION (2008): 1,814,468

ENTERED UNION (RANK): June 20, 1863 (35)

MOTTO: *Montani semper liberi.* (Mountaineers are always free.)

TREE: sugar maple

FLOWER: rhododendron

BIRD: cardinal

NICKNAME: Mountain State

FAMOUS WEST VIRGINIAN: Mary Lou Retton, Olympic gymnast and winner of a gold medal in 1984

The type of apple known as the Golden Delicious was first grown in Clay County, West Virginia, on the Mullin family farm. All the Golden Delicious apples in the world are descendants of a single tree from that farm.

Charleston

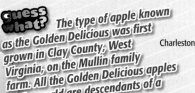

Golden Delicious apple

WISCONSIN

WISCONSIN
1848

CAPITAL: Madison

LARGEST CITY: Milwaukee

POSTAL CODE: WI

LAND AREA: 54,314 square miles (140,673 sq km)

POPULATION (2008): 5,627,967

ENTERED UNION (RANK): May 29, 1848 (30)

MOTTO: Forward

TREE: sugar maple

FLOWER: wood violet

BIRD: American robin

NICKNAMES: Badger State, Dairy State

FAMOUS WISCONSINITE: Frank Lloyd Wright, architect

 The first kindergarten in the United States was founded in Watertown, Wisconsin, in 1856, by German immigrant Margarethe Meyer Schurz.

Robin

Milwaukee

Madison

WYOMING

CAPITAL: Cheyenne

LARGEST CITY: Cheyenne

POSTAL CODE: WY

LAND AREA: 97,105 square miles (251,502 sq km)

POPULATION (2008): 532,668

ENTERED UNION (RANK): July 10, 1890 (44)

MOTTO: Equal rights

TREE: plains cottonwood

FLOWER: Indian paintbrush

BIRD: meadowlark

NICKNAMES: Big Wyoming, Equality State, Cowboy State

FAMOUS WYOMINGITE: Jackson Pollock, artist

Yellowstone National Park in Wyoming, which was dedicated in 1872, was America's first national park. There are more than 200 geysers there.

Yellowstone National Park

Cheyenne

WASHINGTON, D.C.

The District of Columbia, which covers the same area as the city of Washington, is the capital of the United States. The district's history began in 1790 when Congress took charge of organizing a new site for the country's capital. George Washington chose the spot: on the Potomac River, midway between the northern and southern states. The seat of government was transferred from Philadelphia, Pennsylvania, to Washington, D.C., on December 1, 1800, and President John Adams became the first resident of the White House.

LAND AREA: 68.25 square miles (177 sq km)

POPULATION (2008): 591,833

MOTTO: *Justitia omnibus* (Justice for all)

TREE: scarlet oak

FLOWER: American beauty rose

BIRD: wood thrush

FAMOUS WASHINGTONIAN: Duke Ellington, jazz musician

Many landmarks and memorials found in Washington, D.C., are monuments to people and events in U.S. history. Other impressive buildings are still used by government officials today. Here are a few Washington standouts.

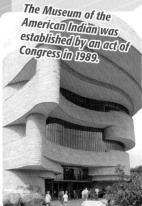

The Museum of the American Indian was established by an act of Congress in 1989.

Completed in 2004, the World War II Memorial honors the 16 million Americans who served in the Second World War.

The Capitol Building has been the meeting place for the Senate and the House of Representatives for more than two centuries.

The statue in the Lincoln Memorial is 19 feet high (6 m) and 19 feet wide (6 m) and weighs 175 tons (159 metric tons).

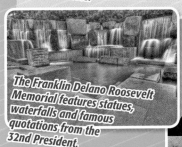

The Franklin Delano Roosevelt Memorial features statues, waterfalls and famous quotations from the 32nd President.

Located northeast of the Lincoln Memorial is the Washington Monument, built between 1848 and 1884 to honor George Washington.

Vieques

PUERTO RICO

Located in the Caribbean Sea, Puerto Rico is about 1,000 miles (1,609 km) southeast of Miami, Florida. A U.S. possession since 1898, it consists of the island of Puerto Rico plus the adjacent islets of Vieques, Culebra and Mona. Both Spanish and English are spoken there.

CAPITAL: San Juan

LARGEST CITY: San Juan

LAND AREA: 3,459 square miles (8,959 sq km)

POPULATION (2008): 3,954,037

MOTTO: *Joannes est nomen eius.* (John is his name.)

TREE: ceiba (silk-cotton)

FLOWER: maga (Puerto Rican hibiscus)

BIRD: reinita (stripe-headed tanager)

FAMOUS PUERTO RICAN: Joaquin Phoenix, actor

OTHER U.S. TERRITORIES

Here are the four other U.S. territories.

AMERICAN SAMOA, a group of islands located in the South Pacific, is located about halfway between Hawaii and New Zealand. It has a land area of 77 square miles (200 sq km) and a population of approximately 64,827.

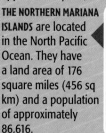

GUAM, located in the North Pacific Ocean, was ceded to the United States from Spain in 1898. It has a land area of 209 square miles (541 sq km) and a population of approximately 175,877.

U.S. VIRGIN ISLANDS, which include St. Croix, St. Thomas, St. John and many other islands, are located in the Caribbean Sea, east of Puerto Rico. Together they have a land area of 136 square miles (351 sq km) and a population of approximately 119,000.

St. Thomas

THE NORTHERN MARIANA ISLANDS are located in the North Pacific Ocean. They have a land area of 176 square miles (456 sq km) and a population of approximately 86,616.

U.S. EXTREMES

NORTHERNMOST POINT: Point Barrow, Alaska

HIGHEST MOUNTAIN: Mount McKinley (also known as Denali) in Alaska at 20,320 feet (6,194 m)

LARGEST CAVE SYSTEM IS FOUND IN: Kentucky

WINDIEST CITY: St. Paul Island, Alaska, with an average wind speed of 17.4 miles per hour (28 km per hour)

LARGEST CHINATOWN: San Francisco, California

DRIEST CITY: Las Vegas, Nevada, with 3.5 inches (8.9 cm) average annual rainfall

LONGEST RIVER: Missouri River, 2,540 miles (4,088 km), starting in Montana and flowing into Mississippi River

DEEPEST GORGE: Hells Canyon on the Snake River in Idaho is 7,900 feet deep (2,407 m), 125 miles (201 km) long

LOWEST POINT: Death Valley, California, at 282 feet (86 m) below sea level

WESTERNMOST CITY: Peaked Island, off Cape Wrangell, Attu Island, Alaska

EASTERNMOST POINT: West Quoddy Head, Maine

SNOWIEST CITY: Valdez, Alaska, with 27 feet (8 m) average annual snowfall

STATE WITH LONGEST COASTLINE: Alaska

MOST-VISITED TOURIST ATTRACTION: Times Square, New York City, with 35 million visitors per year

TOP 10 Largest Cities by Population

CITY	POPULATION
1. New York, NY	8,274,527
2. Los Angeles, CA	3,834,340
3. Chicago, IL	2,836,658
4. Houston, TX	2,208,180
5. Phoenix, AZ	1,552,259
6. Philadelphia, PA	1,449,634
7. San Antonio, TX	1,328,984
8. San Diego, CA	1,266,731
9. Dallas, TX	1,240,499
10. San Jose, CA	939,899

Source: U.S. Census Bureau

MOST VISITED NATIONAL PARK: Great Smoky Mountains National Park in Tennessee

MOST VISITED CITY: Las Vegas, Nevada, with 38.9 million visitors per year

SOUTHERNMOST POINT: Kae Le, Hawaii

United States

229

N
W E
S

PACIFIC
OCEAN

Seattle
Tacoma
Olympia
Portland
Spokane
Washington
Salem
Eugene
Oregon
Boise
Idaho
Great Falls
Montana
Helena
Billings
Bismarc
Missouri River
Yellowstone
National
Park
Wyoming
Rapid City
Pierr
Great Plains

California
Reno
Sacramento
Carson City
Santa Rosa
San Francisco
San Jose
Modesto
Fresno
Nevada
Great
Salt
Lake
Salt Lake City
Utah
Cheyenne
Denver
Colorado Springs
Colorado
Pueblo
Yosemite
National
Park
Death
Valley
Las Vegas
Grand
Canyon
Los Angeles
Flagstaff
Escondido
San Diego
Phoenix
Arizona
Tucson
Santa Fe
Albuquerque
New Mexico
El Paso
Amarillo
Lubbock
Abilen
Texas

Rocky Mountains

Kauai
Oahu
Honolulu
Hawaii
Maui
Hawaii
PACIFIC
OCEAN

ARCTIC OCEAN
RUSSIA
MEXICO
Larec
Alaska
CANADA
Anchorage
Juneau
BERING
SEA
Aleutian Islands
PACIFIC OCEAN

0 mi.   300 mi.   600 mi.
0 km   400 km   800 km

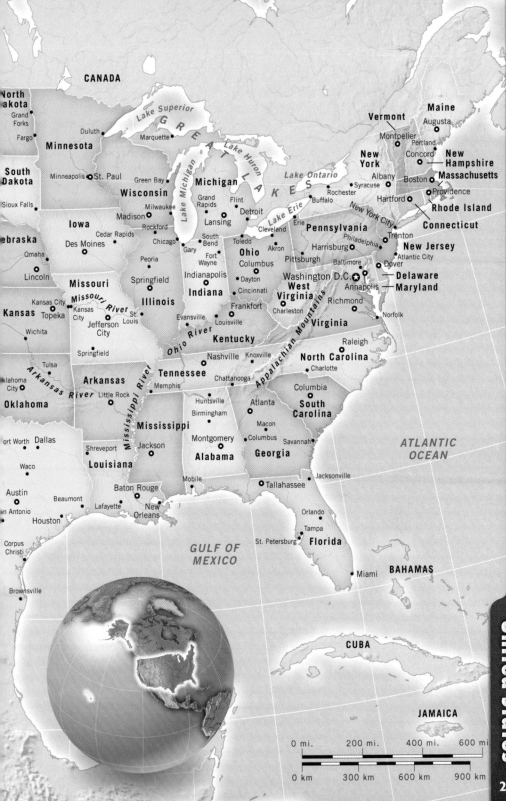

CANADA

North Dakota
Grand Forks
Fargo

Minnesota
Duluth
Marquette

Lake Superior

G R E A T

Lake Huron

Lake Ontario

Maine
Augusta
Montpelier
Portland
Concord
New Hampshire
New York
Albany
Boston
Massachusetts
Providence
Rhode Island
Hartford
Connecticut

Vermont

Syracuse
Rochester
Buffalo

New York City

South Dakota
Sioux Falls

Minneapolis
St. Paul

Green Bay

Wisconsin
Milwaukee
Madison

Michigan

Lake Michigan

Grand Rapids
Flint
Detroit

L A K E S

Lake Erie

Erie

Pennsylvania

Philadelphia

Trenton
New Jersey
Atlantic City

ebraska
Omaha
Lincoln

Iowa
Des Moines

Cedar Rapids
Rockford

Rockford

Chicago
Gary
South Bend
Fort Wayne

Lansing

Cleveland

Akron

Harrisburg

Pittsburgh

Baltimore

Dover
Delaware
Maryland

Peoria

Springfield

Indianapolis

Ohio
Columbus
Dayton
Cincinnati

Washington D.C.
Annapolis

Missouri
Missouri River

Kansas City
Kansas
Topeka
Wichita

Kansas City
Jefferson City
St. Louis

Illinois

Indiana

Frankfort

Evansville
Louisville

West Virginia
Charleston

Richmond

Virginia

Norfolk

Springfield

Ohio River

Kentucky

Nashville
Knoxville

Raleigh

North Carolina
Charlotte

Tulsa

Arkansas River

Oklahoma City

Arkansas

Mississippi River

Tennessee

Memphis

Chattanooga

Appalachian Mountains

Columbia

South Carolina

Oklahoma

Little Rock

Huntsville
Birmingham

Atlanta

Macon

ort Worth
Dallas
Waco

Mississippi

Jackson

Shreveport

Montgomery
Alabama

Columbus
Savannah

Georgia

ATLANTIC OCEAN

Austin
Beaumont
Lafayette

Louisiana
Baton Rouge
New Orleans

Mobile

Tallahassee

Jacksonville

an Antonio
Houston

Corpus Christi

GULF OF MEXICO

St. Petersburg

Orlando
Tampa

Florida

Brownsville

BAHAMAS

Miami

CUBA

JAMAICA

0 mi.   200 mi.   400 mi.   600 mi

0 km   300 km   600 km   900 km

United States

231

Volunteering

Volunteering Rocks

Whether you want to share your talents, learn more about a topic or just meet other people, you can't go wrong with volunteering. Before setting out to be a volunteer, think about the cause that you would like to help most. Here are a few causes that might interest you and some ideas for how you can work for them in your community.

1. ANIMALS If you love animals, chances are you can volunteer at your local animal shelter or for a pet rescue group. Because many shelters and rescue groups are nonprofit organizations, they rely on volunteers to help clean their facilities and take care of abandoned or abused dogs, cats and other animals. You and your family might even be able to foster a pet. Call your local animal shelter or rescue group for more information.

ATTENTION ANIMAL LOVERS
To find out more about ways you can work for animals in need, go to the ASPCA Web site for kids: **animaland.org.**

2. EDUCATION You may be able to help students from other countries speak better English. If you are good at math, you might tutor younger kids who are having trouble with the subject. If your school does not have a tutoring program, talk to your teachers about starting one. You might also offer to help the faculty decorate for special events or assist the school nurse.

3. HOMELESSNESS AND HUNGER If you live in a city, you can probably find a shelter, soup kitchen or religious group that works with people who have no place to live or who need assistance to feed their families. These and other community organizations need volunteers to make hot meals and distribute them to homeless and hungry adults and kids. They might also need people to organize canned-food or warm-clothing drives. Look online for a local shelter or soup kitchen, or call churches, mosques or synagogues to find a program in need.

4. MUSEUMS AND CULTURE
If you love art, science or history, you might be able to volunteer at a museum or cultural center. Not only will you be easing the workload of staff there, but you'll also be spending time in a place you enjoy. Talk to the staff at nearby museums or cultural institutes to see if they can use your help.

LEND A HAND!
Instead of taking a beach holiday this year, you can help Habitat for Humanity build a house for a needy family. Have your parents log on to habitat.org.

5. MUSIC Music makes people happy, and if you enjoy singing or playing an instrument, look for a choir or another group that performs for nursing homes, hospitals or community centers. The holidays are a particularly good time to contact these places—there are many people there who could use some cheering up. And who doesn't love music?

WORK TOGETHER
Psssst! Ask your parents to log on to thevolunteerfamily.org for hints on how to volunteer as a group or a family. Have them go volunteermatch.org to learn more about finding the right volunteering options for you and your family.

6. LITERACY Do you love to read or write? Why not share your passion with others? Libraries and schools might need volunteers to read stories to younger children. Another option for shyer book lovers: Libraries always need help with organizing and reshelving books.

7. ELDERLY PEOPLE If you have a grandparent nearby, you probably understand how hard it is for older people to do some things that are easy for younger folks. You might also realize that elderly people—whether they live alone or in group homes—can often feel lonely. A visit from a young person like you can go far toward comforting them or helping them accomplish small tasks. Perhaps a senior citizen in your neighborhood needs help with yard work, grocery shopping or snow shoveling. You might also call a group home to see if they need young volunteers to help out or just to hang out, play cards and share stories.

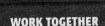

8. KIDS AND ADULTS WITH ILLNESSES

Many hospitals and clinics have opportunities for volunteers. You might sit with sick children and talk with them, play with them or read to them. You could also help serve meals, make beds and deliver gifts to patients. Call your local health care center to find out about volunteering opportunities for students your age.

GET INSPIRED
Check out these two excellent Web sites for ideas on volunteer opportunities for kids: Idealist.org and Dosomething.org.

9. SPORTS If you like running, swimming or even just walking, consider participating in a race for a cause such as cancer, AIDS or multiple sclerosis, among others. If you don't want to race, you can distribute water and cheer on others. Special Olympics International, a program that provides sports training and competition for adults and children with disabilities, relies on volunteers for everything from training and coaching to administrative tasks. Log on to the Special Olympics Web site for more information (specialolympics.org).

10. THE ENVIRONMENT Because there are a lot of different ways you can help the environment, you should let your imagination run wild. Organize a recycling drive, have a contest to see which street in your town can recycle the most trash, or start a gardening club at school. Volunteer at a nearby state or national park or organize a tree-planting day at your school every year—maybe on Arbor Day or Earth Day (see page 39). Become part of the Green Squad (visit nrdc.org/greensquad) and learn how to make your school a healthier and greener place.

Volunteering

Kids Make a Difference

Free The Children

When Craig Kielburger, of Toronto, Canada, was 12 years old, he came across an article in his local newspaper about another boy his age. This 12-year-old was a Pakistani boy who had probably been murdered for speaking out against child labor in his country. Craig was so moved by the heart-wrenching story that he decided to do something. What he started in 1995 as a small group of friends collecting signatures and giving speeches in schools about child labor has since grown into a massive international organization. Its aim is to free children from poverty, especially through education. Free The Children has built more than 500 schools in Asia, Africa and Latin America. Craig also cofounded Me to We, which encourages children to be socially responsible. **Freethechildren.org**

Kids for a Clean Environment (F.A.C.E.)

Melissa Poe started Kids F.A.C.E. after she watched a television show that made her realize what terrible shape Earth would be in if people didn't stop polluting it. Seeing how upset 9-year-old Melissa was, her mother suggested that she take action. So Melissa began writing letters to the President, asking him to help the environment. Then she called companies and asked them to donate advertising space to raise awareness about the damage being inflicted on the planet. Now, with more than 2,000 chapters in 22 countries, Kids F.A.C.E. is one of the world's largest youth environmental organizations. It educates children about environmental issues and holds leadership workshops for kids. Since 1989, Kids F.A.C.E. has also planted more than 1 million trees. **Kidsface.org**

Ryan's Well Foundation

Ryan Hreljac of Canada was in first grade when his teacher told the class about the number of people in the world dying from a lack of clean drinking water. Ryan wanted to help these people. It took him four months to raise $70, but he continued until he raised $2,000, which he donated to help build a well in the African country of Uganda. The Ryan's Well Foundation has since built more than 484 wells in 16 countries and has given more than 611,512 people access to clean water. **Ryanswell.ca**

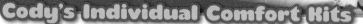

Cody's Individual Comfort Kits

After 8-year-old Cody Clark visited the emergency room in Kemptville District Hospital in Ontario, Canada, he decided that he wanted to do something to help make hospitalized children feel more comfortable, less alone and less afraid. He held a fund-raising drive, then put together some kits, which included books, toys, blankets, videos, teddy bears and a personal letter from Cody. These kits were delivered to sick infants, toddlers and children as old as 18 in the Kemptville District Hospital. The program has grown very popular, and it continues to have strong support in Cody's community. He even expanded it to include "Grandma and Grandpa kits" for elderly patients. **Codyscomfortkits.com**

Raising Money for Donations

Often the best way you can help people or charitable organizations is by sending much-needed money. Here are some ways to raise funds for good causes. Just make sure to tell everyone involved which cause you've chosen to support.

ARRANGE A WALK-A-THON, READ-A-THON, DANCE-A-THON OR JUMP-ROPE-A-THON. Collect pledges from friends, family and others for each mile you walk, book you read, hour you dance or minute you jump rope!

PLAN A CAR WASH. Gather your friends (during the warmer weather, of course) and hold a weekend car wash. Design colorful flyers and hang them up in local stores and restaurants, making sure that everybody knows that the money will go to a worthy cause.

HAVE AN AUCTION. Ask people in your community or school to donate items or services to be auctioned off. A local store might give a $50 gift certificate, a restaurant might contribute a nice meal, an artist or musician may offer to give lessons and babysitters may donate hours of their time. Then invite your parents' friends and coworkers, your friends' families and other adults from your community to the auction.

HOST A BAKE SALE. Bake sales are a tried-and-true method used by schools and communities to raise money. There's a simple reason why bake sales work—almost everybody loves treats! Make sure you get a lot of volunteers to bake and work the tables. Label all of the treats carefully and make sure to offer a variety of foods.

PUT ON A SHOW. Prove that America really does have talent! Hold a student talent show and charge admission to attend. Create posters to get the word out and ask your parents to help you call your local newspaper to advertise the event.

TICKET 33818

A Little Sure Can Help a Lot

You may think that you need to make a large contribution to a charity to accomplish something significant, but that's not the case. Here are some examples of what some small donations can purchase.

ORGANIZATION	DONATION AMOUNT	WHAT IT CAN BUY
Just a Drop	about $2	a 10-year supply of safe drinking water for a child
Heifer International	$10	tree seedlings
Heifer International	$10	1/12 share of a goat, sheep or pig
Oxfam America	$18	children's books
Oxfam America	$18	mosquito nets
Oxfam America	$20	irrigation for a farmer's land for two months
Heifer International	$20	a flock of geese, ducks or chicks
Just a Drop	about $20	a lifetime supply of safe drinking water for one person
Oxfam America	$25	school supplies
Heifer International	$30	honeybees

Weather
WILD WEATHER

Good weather is a balance between cold and hot, wet and dry, and calm and wild. When the weather hits extremes in temperature, precipitation or wind speeds, land is damaged and people suffer. Some extreme weather conditions, like droughts, occur slowly. Others, like tornadoes, form rapidly without much warning and generally last just a few minutes or hours.

DROUGHTS

Droughts can lead to dry, cracked earth.

A drought is an unusually long period of insufficient rain or snowfall. Droughts can last for years, though most last only a few weeks or months. Warm-weather droughts affect agriculture immediately and can lead to large crop losses. Cold-weather droughts, however, cause trouble the following spring, when rivers, streams and the ground fail to fill with water from melting snow and ice.

ANCIENT DROUGHT From 1202 B.C. to 1200 B.C. in Egypt, rainfall did not fill the Nile River. The Nile usually flooded every year, leaving rich soil behind. The people then planted their crops as the floodwaters receded. But when the floods failed to arrive, the land could not sustain agriculture. As a result of this ancient drought, huge numbers of people died from starvation and disease.

WORST DROUGHT IN U.S In the 1930s, vast areas of the Great Plains, from Texas to Canada, suffered from drought, creating huge "dust bowls" of swirling, dry dirt. Thousands of farmers abandoned their homes and headed to other parts of the country, looking for new lands to settle. Many emigrated to California, leading to a huge growth in population in that state.

HURRICANES, CYCLONES AND TYPHOONS

Wreckage caused by Hurricane Katrina

These are tropical storms with winds stronger than 75 miles per hour (120 km/h). They're called **hurricanes** when they form in the northern Atlantic Ocean and the northeastern or southern Pacific Ocean, **typhoons** when they form over the northwestern Pacific and **cyclones** when they form over the Indian Ocean. No matter what they're called, they can cause serious harm.

HOW DO HURRICANES FORM? Hurricanes form when tropical winds gather moisture as they pass over water that is at least 80°F (27°C). The winds of a hurricane rotate around an eye, or center, of the storm. Within the eye of the storm, the weather is calm. It can even be sunny. Outside the eye, however, the warm ocean waters give energy to the storm, causing swirling wind and pounding rain. Hurricanes are strongest when they're over water, but they can remain fierce after reaching land, which is where they do the most damage. They are measured in categories, ranging from a Category 1, which have winds from 74 to 95 mph (119 to 153 km/h) to Category 5, which have winds greater than 155 mph (250 km/h).

The eye of a hurricane

How Do Hurricanes Get Their Names?

Before 1953, most hurricanes were named for the location where the storm hit land. In the 1940s, some meteorologists (at the time, the job was held primarily by men) at the National Hurricane Center began naming the storms informally after their girlfriends, wives and mothers. This practice became the formal naming strategy in 1953, when the center began giving women's names to storms that formed over the Atlantic.

In 1979, a new system was put in place that alternated men's and women's names in alphabetical order. Six lists of names were created, which covered six years of storms. The names are repeated in cycles. However, if a storm is particularly noteworthy, such as Katrina in 2005, the name is retired forever. In 2011, when Katrina would have come up again in the cycle, the name Katia will be used instead.

NAMES CHOSEN FOR 2010 TROPICAL STORMS				
Alex	Earl	Igor	Matthew	Richard
Bonnie	Fiona	Julia	Nicole	Shary
Colin	Gaston	Karl	Otto	Tomas
Danielle	Hermine	Lisa	Paula	Virginie
				Walter

TORNADOES

Tornadoes often knock down trees.

Tornadoes are funnel-shaped clouds made of fast-spinning winds that can reach 300 mph (483 km/h). They generally form out of giant storms that occur when warm, moist air on the ground rushes upward and smacks into cooler, drier air. This colder air causes the warm air to cool down. As the warm air cools, the moisture in it condenses and forms huge thunderclouds. The thunderclouds pull up warm air from the ground, which causes air to swirl around. It is this process that creates the distinct funnel shape of a tornado.

Some tornadoes measure only a few feet in diameter. Others are much wider—up to a mile in diameter. Some build up quickly and disappear. Others move across the land at 30 to 70 mph (48 to 113 km/h) sometimes for hundreds of miles. The winds that make up a tornado can be strong enough to pick up homes, cars, trees and anything else in their path. While wind causes most of a tornado's destruction, hail formed in the thunderclouds can also do a lot of damage.

Most large tornadoes form in the central and southern United States, an area known as tornado alley. Though tornadoes do occur in other countries, by far the most occur in the United States— roughly 1,000 a year.

FLOODS

Flood damage

Floods are usually caused by rivers or lakes overflowing their banks or by surges of ocean water during tropical storms. The **Galveston Flood of 1900** in Texas was caused by a hurricane surge and took the lives of more than 5,000 people.

However, some floods, like the **Johnstown Flood of 1889**, are caused by failures of engineering. An earthen dam 14 miles (23 km) from Johnstown, Pennsylvania, collapsed, unleashing 20 million tons of water. The dam had been constructed by a fishing and hunting club, whose members included some of the richest, most influential men of the time. They had built the dam to create a fishing lake, but ignored pleas from Johnstown's civic leaders to strengthen its walls. After days of heavy rains, the managers of the club knew that the dam might not hold and tried to warn the citizens. But because there had been warnings before, most residents ignored the alert. The water crashed down the valley, sweeping up everything—houses, trains, horses, people—in its path. In the end, more than 2,200 people died.

MEASURING TEMPERATURE

Thermometers measure temperature. The most common thermometers may contain a column of alcohol or mercury that expands in the presence of heat, or they may be digital and use liquid crystals or electricity.

When it comes to weather, **air temperature** is important. The air temperature of a location is affected by:

- the heat that is given off by the ground and rises into the air.
- how close the area is to a body of water.
- the effect of air masses as they pass through the area.

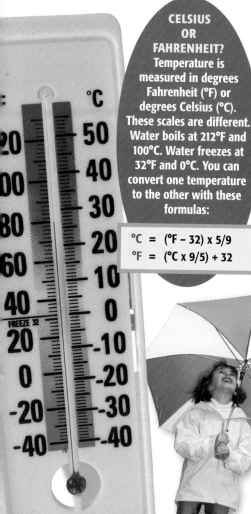

CELSIUS OR FAHRENHEIT? Temperature is measured in degrees Fahrenheit (°F) or degrees Celsius (°C). These scales are different. Water boils at 212°F and 100°C. Water freezes at 32°F and 0°C. You can convert one temperature to the other with these formulas:

$$°C = (°F - 32) \times 5/9$$
$$°F = (°C \times 9/5) + 32$$

WINDS AND AIR PRESSURE

Winds are caused by the sun's heat falling on different parts of Earth at different times of the day and year. The temperatures over water and land change at different rates during the day and night. In addition, warm air rises and cool air sinks. These fluctuations cause the movement of air in different patterns, called winds. Two kinds of winds, **global** and **local**, affect the weather of a place.

GLOBAL WINDS are caused by the spinning of Earth on its axis. In the regions just above and below the equator, global winds move from east to west. In the regions just below the North Pole and above the South Pole, global winds appear to move from west to east. Major weather patterns move in the direction of the global winds.

LOCAL WINDS depend on the temperature, humidity and air pressure of an area at a particular time. **Air pressure** is the force exerted on you by the weight of air molecules, which are tiny, invisible particles in the air. It is also called barometric pressure because it is measured with a device called a barometer. Clear weather is caused by high pressure; storms are caused by low pressure. Air pressure tends to decrease the higher you go.

TOP 5 Rainiest U.S. Cities

As the saying goes, April showers bring May flowers, but some places get soaked every season. Here are the U.S. cities that get the most rain each year.

1. Yakutat, Alaska	160 inches annually
2. Hilo, Hawaii	126 inches
3. Mount Washington, New Hampshire	102 inches
4. Quillayute, Washington	102 inches
5. Annette, Alaska	101 inches

Source: National Climatic Data Center

TYPES OF CLOUDS

Clouds are classified first by their distance from the ground and then by their shapes.

- Low clouds (below 6,000 feet/1,829 m above ground) are called stratus.
- Middle-altitude clouds (6,000–20,000 feet/1,829–6,096 m above ground) are altostratus.
- High clouds (above 20,000 feet/6,096 m) are cirrus.
- Clouds that span a large range of heights (from as low as a few hundred feet to about 6,000 feet/1,829 m) are cumulus.

Particular cloud formations get their names based on their height and their shapes.

STRATUS clouds are gray and look like fog. They often seem to cover the entire sky. They may hold enough moisture to cause a drizzle, but they do not hold heavy rains.

STRATOCUMULUS clouds are low and fluffy.

ALTOCUMULUS clouds appear as gray, puffy masses and are often seen against a backdrop of clear blue sky.

CIRRUS clouds are thin and wispy and look like they've been blown across the sky. They can often be seen on sunny days.

CUMULONIMBUS clouds look like marshmallows. They are relatively flat along the bottom and puff up at their highest elevations. Thunderstorms form in cumulonimbus clouds.

TFK GAME

A SNOWY DAY

Look closely at the picture. Answer the questions below.

1. How many people are cleaning up after the snowstorm? _____

2. How many people are playing snow sports? _____

3. Look for things that do not make sense. Circle all the silly things.

ANSWERS ON PAGE 244.

What's Next
AMAZING SCIENCE

UP, UP AND AWAY!

When others want to go to the beach during their summer break, do you dream of going to, say, Saturn? The possibility of taking off in a rocket for your vacation may be closer than you think. "Space tourism" is looking like an up-and-coming blast for the jet set. Virgin Galactic is already preparing a list of passengers to bring as tourists into space on a six-person rocket called *SpaceShipTwo,* in 2010. These lucky few have to go through preparations on Earth—like real astronauts—to get them used to the difficulties of space travel. Once they go up, the travelers will get to unbuckle and float around in zero gravity while the windows show a view of Earth far below.

NOW YOU SEE ME! NOW YOU DON'T!

Believe it or not, researchers at the University of California at Berkeley say they are very close to inventing a "cloak of invisibility," not so far off from the one Harry Potter wore at Hogwarts. They've designed two new substances called **metamaterials.** One is composed of small wires, and the other has a fishnet of tiny metal layers. Both materials exhibit something called **negative refraction.** In other words, the materials don't absorb or reflect light waves. If you were to wear them, light would bend around you, and—voila!—you'd be invisible!

BREAKING THE PETAFLOP BARRIER

Peta-what? Peta-who? A petaflop is 1 quadrillion calculations per second, which is the speed of operations the latest generation of supercomputers are capable of performing. In June 2008, an IBM supercomputer named Roadrunner broke the petaflop barrier. By November, a computer called Jaguar did too. Jaguar features more than 180,000 processing cores with 2 gigabytes of memory each—that's like 180,000 average laptop computers all rolled into one! These superspeedy machines will transform the way scientific research is conducted. For example, climatologists might use them to more accurately forecast weather and predict earthquakes.

In February of 2009, the U.S. government hired IBM to build Sequoia, an even more powerful computer that will, among other things, simulate the behavior of nuclear weapons. By doing so, scientists hope that they can learn valuable information about the country's nuclear arsenal without having to test explosions.

Jaguar can handle 1.64 quadrillion mathematical calculations per second.

IT'S ALL IN YOUR HEAD

If you think the Wii—with its motion-sensitive controllers—is cool, imagine this: controlling a game with your thoughts. The EPOC headset by Emotiv is designed to do just that. Wear it on your head, and it detects the electrical activity in your brain. It can identify patterns in brain activity and translate them to emotions, expressions or even actions in a game. This is just the beginning for this kind of technology. In the future, a similar device could be used to control your computer, or help you to—scary as it might seem—communicate with other people without speaking.

The EPOC headset uses 16 brain-wave sensors to "read" a person's thoughts.

FLYING TO WORK?

A plane introduced recently might make many more people able to fly their own aircrafts. The A5, created by a company named Icon, is a lightweight two-seater seaplane that is so compact that owners can store it in their yards or even their garages! The streamlined, cool-looking plane, which has wings that fold up, can launch from both land and water. It uses GPS navigation, has a 100-horsepower engine and relies on unleaded gas—that means that it can be easily refueled. The A5 will be available for purchase in the next year or two for about $139,000. As planes get smaller and lighter, and possibly cheaper, perhaps one day soon your mom or dad will fly you to school!

FIGHTING HUNGER WITH HARDIER RICE

Rice is a food that many Americans eat only occasionally, but it is a staple food for about half of Earth's population. If rice crops fail due to flooding or other natural disasters, it can mean that many people will starve. As world weather patterns grow more erratic because of climate change, people have become concerned about the potential loss of millions of tons of rice crops.

Scientists at the University of California at Davis and at the Philippines-based International Rice Research Institute have spent about 10 years testing and trying to generate a hardier type of rice that can withstand flooding. Their hard work paid off: They came up with a solution that will go far in helping to feed people whose diets contain a lot of rice. The scientists used a water-resistant type of grain from India, then genetically combined it with other kinds of rice to create a delicious rice grain that is able to live longer under water. As this grain is planted around the world, it should lead to a decline in the starvation and devastation caused by flooding in countries like Bangladesh.

University of California at Davis professor Pamela Ronald, one of the scientists who worked on the project, says, "Farmers have asked us, 'Can you develop varieties that are drought tolerant, salt tolerant? Can you develop varieties that are insect resistant?' There are always more things to work on." Perhaps in the near future, she and her colleagues will work to develop more crops that can withstand the ups and downs of nature.

Icon's A5 plane

What's Next
ENERGY OUTLOOK

Flying wind turbines

SELF-SUFFICIENT SKYSCRAPERS

Buildings that create their own electricity? Some bold architects are already working on this idea by using wind and solar power. The World Trade Center building in Bahrain (an island nation in the Persian Gulf) is the first skyscraper in the world to use wind power as part of its design. Three 95-foot-wide (29-m) turbines, hundreds of feet up, connect the two towers. The 787-foot-tall (240-m) building was positioned and shaped to aim the wind into the turbines, which can produce about 15% of the electrical needs for all 50 floors.

One company has plans for a building in Chicago that will use dozens of wind turbines along with a solar shell on the top of the building. Calling it the Clean Technology Tower, the planners hope the building will create all of the electricity it needs.

The World Trade Center in Bahrain

REALLY HIGH TECH

When we capture the power of the wind and turn it into electricity, we're being smart and helping the environment. The more we rely on the power of nature to create energy, the less we rely on the dwindling supply of fossil fuels on the planet. Plus, wind turbines don't release fumes that pollute our air. The question is, how can we get the most power from the wind? The faster the wind is, the more power we get, and to find strong, constant winds, we have to go high in the sky.

In the future, instead of building super-tall wind turbines, we may use flying turbines to harness the wind way up in the jet stream. Companies like Sky Windpower are testing prototypes of flying windmills that are tied to the ground yet work between 15,000 and 45,000 feet (4,600 and 11,000 m) up in the sky! The same motors that fly these turbines into the sky are then used to generate power with the wind. Some day much of our electricity might be coming to us from the sky.

CREATING FUEL WITH ALGAE

There are a lot of good reasons to avoid using petroleum products, like oil and gasoline, but what do we do with all the cars and machines that now use these fuels? Scientists at Arizona State University are working on a solution for the future by growing algae that can be made into a replacement fuel. Calling it green crude, a name that refers to the crude oil found underground, the algae actually uses carbon dioxide to grow, which balances out the carbon dioxide released into the air when it is used as fuel. Also, unlike other biofuels, green crude does not require corn or grains that are otherwise part of our food supply.

BIG NEWS IN MEDICINE

THE GENOME REVOLUTION ARRIVES

Scientists spent many years working to decode the human genome, and in 2003, they succeeded. The human genome is like a blueprint that shows all of the things that make up a person. Every cell in your body contains a copy of your genome. By studying your genome, scientists can tell a great deal about how your body works. They hope to use this information to prevent and combat disease.

After scientists figured out how to sequence the human genome, some companies began offering the service to anyone who could afford it. At the time, the total cost was about $200,000. With a price like that, only wealthy people could take advantage of the service. Recent technological developments have made it possible to purchase your genetic readout at a much more affordable rate. A company called 23andMe sells a $399 saliva test that can reveal your predisposition for nearly 107 traits and conditions. That's pretty cheap compared to $200,000!

The test might estimate the likelihood that you will get Parkinson's disease or go bald. While many people view this as an exciting development and an important scientific milestone, health and government authorities worry about how it will affect our privacy. Former President George W. Bush signed a bill in May 2008 making it illegal for companies to discriminate against individuals on the basis of their genetic makeup.

The easy availability of these types of tests raise other questions. For example, what will people do if they find out they have a high risk of a certain condition?

INDIVIDUALIZED TREATMENT

For the first time, doctors sequenced the entire genome of a cancer patient, which allowed them to figure out the exact mutations in her genes that caused her illness. Not only does this information help doctors better understand the disease, but it also makes it easier for them to tailor their treatment to address the patient's specific needs.

NEXT UP IN THEATERS

Keep an eye out for awesome new characters and the return of some of your favorites! Here are just a few of the movies that will hit the silver screen soon.

Get ready for two more installments of the Harry Potter series.

- Alice in Wonderland
- Cars 2
- The Chronicles of Narnia: The Voyage of the Dawn Treader
- The Hobbit
- Harry Potter and the Deathly Hallows, Part I
- Harry Potter and the Deathly Hallows, Part II
- How to Train Your Dragon
- Iron Man 2
- Old Dogs
- Prince of Persia: Sands of Time
- The Princess and the Frog
- Puss in Boots
- Rapunzel
- Shrek Goes Fourth
- Spider-Man 4
- Toy Story 3

What's Next

Answers

Page 23:
Sleepy Season:
1. C
2. D
3. A
4. B

Page 33:
Mystery Person: Gwendolyn Brooks

Page 47:
Mystery Person: Michael Dell

Page 99:
Puzzles
1. Tricycle
2. Man overboard
3. Once in a blue moon
4. Ring Around the Rosie

Picture Puzzle:

Page 102:
Mystery Person: Vitus Bering

Page 125:
Mystery Person: Hattie Caraway

Page 135:
Digging Up the Past:
1.

2. B1
3. C2

Page 139:
Mystery Person: George Ferris

Page 143:
Feeling the Words: Reach for the Stars

Mystery Person: Annie Sullivan

Page 155:
Mystery Person: Philo T. Farnsworth

Page 159:
Mystery Person: Ella Fitzgerald

Page 200:
Sports Trivia Quiz:
1. F
2. J
3. A
4. H
5. B
6. I
7. D
8. C
9. G
10. E

Page 201:
Mystery Person: Jackie Robinson

A Race Across Alaska:
1. Northwest
2. About 150 miles
3. False
4. Nome, Alaska

Page 239:
A Snowy Day:
1. 2
2. 8
3.

Index

Photo Credits